ROOTS OF OUR RENEWAL

Roots of Our Renewal

. . . .

Ethnobotany and Cherokee Environmental Governance

Clint Carroll

University of Minnesota Press

Minneapolis | London

FIRST PEOPLES
New Directions in Indigenous Studies

Publication of this book was made possible, in part,
with a grant from the Andrew W. Mellon Foundation.

Published by the University of Minnesota Press
111 Third Avenue South, Suite 290
Minneapolis, MN 55401-2520
http://www.upress.umn.edu

Library of Congress Cataloging-in-Publication Data

Carroll, Clint.
Roots of our renewal : ethnobotany and Cherokee
environmental governance / Clint Carroll.
(First peoples : new directions in indigenous studies)
Includes bibliographical references and index.
ISBN 978-0-8166-9089-3 (hc)—ISBN 978-0-8166-9090-9 (pb)
1. Cherokee Indians—Ethnobotany. 2. Cherokee Indians—Medicine. 3. Political
ecology—Cherokee Nation. 4. Environmental policy—Cherokee Nation. 5. Land
use—Cherokee Nation. 6. Cherokee Indians—Politics and government. I. Title.
E99.C5C226 2015
975.004'97557—dc23   2014028048

Printed in the United States of America on acid-free paper

The University of Minnesota is an equal-opportunity educator and employer.

21 20 19 18 17 16 15   10 9 8 7 6 5 4 3 2 1

For C. J.

Contents

Note to the Reader

THROUGHOUT THE TEXT, I use the terms *Native, American Indian,* and *Native American* to refer to the descendants of the original inhabitants of North America in what is now known as the United States. I use the term *tribe* interchangeably with *nation* to describe North American indigenous nations, reflecting the common usage of the term throughout North American indigenous contexts (although many would agree that *nation* is a more accurate term that also avoids the negative connotations associated with the word *tribe*). I also use *tribal* as an adjective in the context of common phrases like *tribal government* and *tribal environmental policy.* In certain contexts, I use *indigenous* to refer to indigenous peoples worldwide; more often, I refer to those indigenous nations that have been subsumed by settler states (e.g., the United States, Canada, New Zealand, and Australia) but who nevertheless continue to maintain their own nationhood and political relationships with the settler state.

I generally use the term *nonhuman* to discuss collectively plants, animals, spirits, and other beings with whom many Native peoples maintain relationships, although this choice is mostly a matter of brevity rather than preference. The term *other-than-human,* which I prefer and use sparingly, more accurately conveys the view inherent in many Native philosophies that humans are not the measuring stick to which all other life is held. Lastly, while I am aware that the term *tradition* comes with much intellectual baggage, I proceed to use it with the practical realization that—especially in Indian Country—we all know what it is, even if we can never quite pin it down. It is a shorthand and accessible (if imperfect) way to communicate concepts, behaviors, practices, ethics, and values that are grounded in the cultural forms and identities of a people. Its use also comes with the risk of temporalizing indigenous practice, as in its common juxtaposition with modernity, but herein I take for granted their coexistence (see Lyons 2010, 10–13, for a useful discussion).

In my ethnographic anecdotes, I use real names when individuals have given me their consent. Some have consented to use only their Cherokee name. In other cases where I have not received consent, I protect the anonymity of my consultants by using pseudonyms or omitting names altogether. However, I always use real names when discussing public figures outside of ethnographic contexts. All ethnographic material is taken from interviews (both taped and hand recorded) and field notes recorded during my twenty-one cumulative months of fieldwork in the Cherokee Nation between June 2004 and October 2013. This has entailed fieldwork during the summers of 2004–6, ten continuous months from April 2008 to January 2009, and an additional two months from follow-up trips during 2009–13.

Preface

THIS WORK IS BORN out of an equal passion for scholarly inquiry and community commitment, which is to say that its personal significance cannot be separated from the professional endeavor that it has become. I am an enrolled Cherokee Nation tribal citizen, although I grew up in Dallas, Texas, away from the Cherokee Nation land base in northeastern Oklahoma. My Cherokee ancestors, who bore the surnames Sevier, Ore, and Boggs, originally came from present-day eastern Tennessee, in the Old Cherokee Nation. After the western relocation, they inhabited the Canadian district of the Cherokee Nation, Indian Territory—at the westernmost edge of the Ozark foothills. The vicinity would soon become known as Hogshooter's Place, after my great-great-great-grandfather Reverend John "Hogshooter" Sevier, although today the area is called Brewer's Bend. The Seviers (and later the Carrolls—of Scots-Irish descent) eventually inhabited the nearby towns of McLain and Warner, and now most of my Cherokee relatives who still live in Oklahoma reside in the town of Muskogee, at the very perimeter of the Cherokee Nation border.

My research has been a cherished opportunity to reconnect with family and to forge important ties with Cherokee communities and individuals. While living in Tahlequah, a small but bustling town and the capital of the Cherokee Nation, I was able to spend time with relatives, study the Cherokee language, learn from tribal elders, and establish connections to place. My work with the Cherokee Nation Office of Environmental Programs and later the Natural Resources Department enabled me to get out on the land and better understand the ecology and geography of northeast Oklahoma. Working for the Cherokee Nation also exposed me to numerous cultural revitalization initiatives taking place at the time, including adult immersion Cherokee-language classes. During my fieldwork, I volunteered for the Cherokee Nation Self-Help Housing Program, and as a result, I spent time pouring concrete foundations with a crew of four other Cherokee men. Out of this experience came new friendships, two of which led to me playing lead guitar in their band, Joshua Street—a Christian rock ensemble associated with Calvary Southern Baptist Church in Stilwell, Oklahoma. And through the gracious invitations of friends, I also spent time at Cherokee stomp grounds, participating in and learning about older forms of Cherokee worship. All these experiences contributed greatly to my education both as a Cherokee and as an ethnographer, and I am grateful for such an opportunity.

Writing about one's own community (and its politics) can be daunting, and doing ethnography as a Native researcher, while a positive statement of change in the relationship between anthropology and American Indians, poses difficult questions (see Medicine 2001). For instance, how do you enter into a dialogue about the nature and form of tribal government without appearing overly critical? How do you discuss political debate while not letting simplistic notions of "factionalism" define the community or structure your analysis? How do you make sense of being an actor in the processes you claim to be studying? These questions speak to issues of accountability. Shawn Wilson (2008, 97–125; Cree) argues that Native researchers are held to higher levels of accountability, something he terms "relational accountability" to describe the ongoing familial and relational commitments many Native researchers must maintain during and after the research process. Furthermore, the work is expected to benefit the community in practical and tangible ways. In other words, the research must be accountable in terms of its applicability to community needs.

Such accountability to the research "subjects" has historically been disputed by those who claim that this dynamic compromises the "objectivity" of the data (for a discussion, see Ranco 2006). Yet, recently, a critical response has flowed from indigenous researchers and academics who claim that this assertion only serves to reinforce imperial/colonial perspectives that have characterized many social science research practices. Maori scholar Linda Tuhiwai Smith's *Decolonizing Methodologies* (1999) is a breakthrough work for understanding the role of research both for and by indigenous peoples. Her work involves critically understanding the "assumptions, motivations and values which inform research practices" (20), and she asserts that while not totally rejecting all theory or research founded in Western knowledge, "decolonizing methodologies" is about "centering our [indigenous] concerns and world views and then coming to know and understand theory and research from our own perspectives and for our own purposes" (39). Smith maintains that indigenous research "should set out to make a positive difference for the researched" (191).

As such, I aim to promote healthy dialogue about tribal governance and environmental policy in the Cherokee Nation while maintaining my relational accountability to the people and to the integrity of the nation. This is a fine line, but one that I think is possible in light of Robert Warrior's commentary on Native research. I believe one can maintain relational accountability without compromising "a critical discourse that is willing and able to stand against the tide, calling into question the moral and ethical basis of the assumed authority of every and any claim to power" (Warrior 2005, 216; see also Russell 2010). Most would agree that healthy dialogue that engages with the tough issues of indigenous governance in a productive way is essential to the well-being of indigenous nations. Ultimately, the work is invested in helping to build a strong Cherokee Nation, as I am invested in positively contributing to it as a tribal citizen.

I view this contribution in terms of both applied work and theory production. On an applied level, my work engages tribal environmental policy and cultural revitalization through an ongoing ethnobotanical project that I helped to initiate as a Cherokee Nation employee in 2004. This is a lifetime endeavor that contributes to enduring initiatives to recover and reclaim Cherokee traditional ecological knowledge and practices. I also think there is value to generating theory and that such theory, as Cherokee scholar Eva Garroutte (2003) asserts, can employ indigenous theoretical traditions while drawing on other critical theory to produce something new. I do this by engaging with political ecology, a field that brings fresh perspectives to the study of American Indian environmental issues. Linking these two fields helps frame the balance of what I identify as the "resource-based" approach and the "relationship-based" approach to environmental governance in Indian Country. I argue that both approaches are necessary within our current settler-colonial framework. In speaking the language of "resources," indigenous nations are able to assert some form of sovereignty over them. As flawed as this discourse may be, commensurate within it are indigenous assertions of territory and resource control. Yet this approach noticeably does not account for traditional indigenous views. While romanticized stereotypes abound, a prevalent indigenous view toward the nonhuman world is one of respect and reciprocity. This view is often encompassed by unique traditions that strive to maintain relationships with the land and the various nonhuman entities that dwell on it. Conceptualizing the resource- and relationship-based approaches in the context of linked theoretical perspectives from political ecology and American Indian studies helps clarify both the hurdles and goals of indigenous environmental governance.

I feel strongly that ethnography is essential to understanding contemporary indigenous governance. Hearing and making sense of utterances, seeing the interpersonal dynamics of governance play out before one's eyes, and witnessing the fluidity of seemingly predefined roles (state/local actors, resource users/managers) are invaluable experiences in understanding and appreciating the nuances that make up these very unique structures and their ongoing processes of formation. Equally essential, of course, is the self-reflexivity that comes with indigenous ethnography and, perhaps more important, the "refusal" of ethnography and research when it interferes with community responsibilities and expectations (Simpson 2007; see also TallBear 2013, 14–22). I share Mohawk scholar Audra Simpson's (2007, 70, 77–78) perspective that research must always be tempered by a "staking of limits" telling us when "enough is enough" and that indigenous ethnography must ultimately commit itself to furthering self-determination and community empowerment.

I also find Gillian Hart's (2006) concept of "critical ethnography" valuable, as it acknowledges linkages to, and influence from, external forces. Instead of an ethnography of "what is there" (taking for granted established social forms and relations), following Hart I will focus on how social institutions are being formed (looking at processes) and what they have the potential to become. As Hart emphasizes, this method allows us to envision alternatives—"new understandings of the possibilities for social change" (996). I also focus on the process of alliance-building and the resulting articulations that are produced out of these coalitions. Studying institutional change as the product of coalitions allows us to visualize what Hart calls "relational comparison," whereby "instead of comparing pre-existing objects, events, places, or identities, the focus is on how they are constituted in relation to one another through power laden practices in the multiple, interconnected arenas of everyday life" (ibid.). Thus, for example, the constructions of tribal government and community, tribal complex and rural area, scientific and traditional knowledge, and so on, get broken down to a practical level where, rather than their distance from each other, one can focus more on the connections between them and the potential to mobilize these connections to solve problems. I augment this poststructural perspective of networks and relational forms of power with a healthy attention to structural aspects (e.g., the workings of tribal bureaucracy). In the course of my analysis, it became clear that consideration of both the structure of Cherokee government and the process by which government actors fulfill their duties in relation to ordinary tribal citizens is necessary for understanding Cherokee ideologies of organization and governance.

Narratives and critiques of "ecological nobility" have plagued the study of indigenous environmental issues (e.g., Krech 1999). While important work has intervened to show the complexity of why Native people either engage or refute this trope (e.g., Ishiyama 2003; Nadasdy 2005; Ranco 2007), I reject the debate as a starting point for thinking about environmental issues in Indian Country. As Anna Willow (2009) contends, discourses on the ecological Indian often mask the politics of what is at stake in indigenous environmental activism, which entails counteracting histories of dispossession by reasserting sovereign claims to land. This book centers such political struggles while not losing sight of the ultimate goal of indigenous environmental action: to present the world with alternatives to status quo assumptions of how we ought to interact with one another and with the beings and spirits that collectively constitute "the environment."

Keepers of Knowledge

Indigenous Environmental Governance

ᎾᏉᏘ. *Nvwoti*. Medicine. As someone with a working knowledge of the Cherokee language, this is the word I clung to on that mild October day, listening to two old Cherokee men speak about the plants growing on the hillside in front of us. They spoke to one another in fluent Cherokee, and I stood politely among them trying to pick up as much meaning as I could, based on my ongoing study of the language. Although I attempted to follow the conversation, I was quickly lost. Yet this word continued to surface, and eventually I was content in knowing only the basic idea of what they were saying. After all, the topic of plant medicine was a large part of what we were gathered there to discuss. The midmorning air was crisp in this secluded hollow nestled in the hill country and lush deciduous forests of northeastern Oklahoma. The leaves had only just begun to change colors, and there were still plenty of green ferns and other perennials on the forest floor.

• • •

Working as a researcher for the Cherokee Nation Natural Resources Department (NRD), I had called together a small group of elders and knowledge-keepers[1] to meet about the state of Cherokee ethnobotanical knowledge. The place we were gathered was the headquarters for a Cherokee community nonprofit organization. The two leaders of this organization had been cooking all morning in preparation for the meeting, and for the sake of their hard work and all the food available, I hoped that the rest of the folks I had invited would actually show up. The topic of the meeting itself presented a potential disincentive. Throughout the course of my work on a tribal ethnobotany project, I had learned that when asking people about their knowledge of wild plants, they will first assume

Figure 1. The headquarters of Blue Sky Water Society, Inc., a nonprofit organization near Marble City, Cherokee Nation (Oklahoma). Photograph by author.

you want to talk about medicine—a topic that most Cherokees will not discuss openly without first getting to know you and your intentions. For Cherokees, medicine is at once a revered and feared topic. It encompasses stories of miraculous healing as well as tales of malevolent conjuring. This latter element is enough to make it somewhat of a taboo topic, but add to that a history of its ridicule and exploitation, and you end up with something that is seldom discussed with anyone, let alone with outsiders.[2]

I had been working on the ethnobotany project for three consecutive summers—first through the Cherokee Nation's Office of Environmental Programs and later through the NRD—with the goal of developing a database that would inform Cherokee Nation policy makers about what plant species and habitats were of cultural significance and should be targeted for conservation. Despite the Cherokee Nation's sophisticated environmental programs that had been functioning under tribal control since the 1990s, this cultural element remained a gap to be filled, and I had hoped that the project could do just that. Yet, in my interviews with elders and knowledge-keepers, while everyone agreed that Cherokee plant knowledge was fading through lack of transmission and that the goals of the project were valuable, most were still reluctant to talk freely about their knowledge. Even though many had come to know me—an enrolled Cherokee citizen (although one who was raised away from the tribal community)—and they did not doubt my good intentions, the stakes still seemed just too high. My association with the tribal government, as opposed to inquiring just out of personal curiosity, added a level of skepticism—there was always the possibility that the knowledge could be taken out of my hands and used in ways that were not intended by my informants.

The purpose of the gathering that day was to provide a forum for keepers of this knowledge to discuss this issue with NRD staff. Pat Gwin, the natural resources supervisor, initially proposed the idea, having sensed that while some were very supportive of the project, they needed more than just their own opinion to move forward. I assembled the group based on the individuals I had been interviewing during my previous summer work since 2004 and my then seven months of continuous residency in Tahlequah (the tribal capital) for my dissertation fieldwork. In addition to me, Pat, and one other NRD staff member,[3] the group comprised ten women and men over the age of fifty, the majority of whom were fluent Cherokee speakers. We thought that if the elders came together and were able to voice their concerns in such a forum, we might develop more confidence and trust in the NRD ethnobotany project. We chose the location of the meeting based on the existing relationship between the NRD and the nonprofit organization—the NRD had helped to establish the boundaries of the nonprofit's five-acre tract of land. Furthermore, the organization was founded on the goals of cultural revitalization and environmental stewardship. Thus, as a place that could also accommodate the group and provide a relaxed atmosphere, it seemed a perfect choice.

So far, things were going smoothly. More people began to show up and gather around the fire that had been lit earlier that morning. There was plenty of coffee available (one could argue this is a staple of Cherokee meetings), and everyone was glad to see one another. Newcomers chimed in on the conversation in Cherokee, sometimes drifting into English out of politeness for the handful of nonspeakers present (mostly NRD staff). They all knew the topic to be discussed and were making small talk on the subject already. Soon the meeting began. I gave each guest a small bundle of "old tobacco" (*Tsola agayvli*, or *Nicotiana rustica*) that had been grown by NRD staff that summer as an effort to revitalize traditional heirloom crops. Meanwhile, Pat opened by briefly stating the purpose of the meeting. He then asked what the group thought about the state of Cherokee plant knowledge and how the NRD could best contribute to its perpetuation.

Charlie Soap, one of the older men there, assumed a speaker role and started the discussion. An esteemed leader both among the communities and at the tribal complex, Charlie commands respect by nature of his experience and stature. He is a tall man with long, black and gray, tied-back hair, and he is often seen in typical Oklahoma Cherokee garb— blue jeans, boots, wide-brimmed cowboy hat, and bolo tie. He is equally seen donning work boots and gloves due to his close work with Cherokee community development projects. He has dedicated most of his life to this work, and at the time of the meeting, he was serving as the Director of Cherokee Nation Community Services. He is also well known as the husband of the late Principal Chief Wilma Mankiller. Charlie began his comments by noting the style and setting of the meeting itself. Bringing folks away from an office setting to a rural area near a Cherokee community was really appropriate and important for a topic of this sort. Most important, he praised the NRD and nonprofit organization staff for building a fire. He remarked how the old timers always said to build a fire when a meeting was to be held. The presence of that divine element brings people together and focuses their thoughts on important issues. He also thought that many officials from the tribal complex don't often come out to the communities to hear what people think, so what we were doing here was good.[4] For these reasons, he said the project was "on the right track."

As others joined in, the discussion gravitated toward the topic of traditional medicine. Many emphasized the need not only for perpetuating the knowledge of wild plants but for the protection and stewardship of the plants themselves, along with the animals, water, and land. From a Cherokee perspective, plants must be used in order to ensure their continued availability to the people, although the proper prayers and respectful harvesting practices must accompany this practice. To not use them is to neglect gifts from the Creator. Animals have their own medicine to offer, and they also teach humans about other medicines through both their spiritual and material forms. Clean and pure spring water is required for making medicine, and the availability of this resource is just as important as the plant materials. Finally, the land itself on which everything lives and grows is essential. Thus the emphasis on maintaining these relationships with the nonhuman world was vital to a project of this sort.

The tone of the meeting so far was positive; however, soon more troubling issues were raised. Charlie returned to Pat's question: "How do we preserve this knowledge? Do we tell everything we know now, or what? How do we get this knowledge to the kids?" He said that Cherokees are apprehensive about documenting and putting the knowledge in a book because there is no guarantee of its respectful treatment. For example, many Cherokees fear that someone will copyright the information and proceed to "make money off of us." He said this is one of the main reasons why people do not talk about medicine and the spiritual realm.

Someone else brought up the issue of tribal citizens overharvesting certain plants, likely due to the lack of education about how to do this respectfully and sustainably. How would a group of people propose to regulate the use of plants on tribal lands in order to prevent this? Who would act as gatekeepers to the privilege of harvesting, and under what authority? How could the proper way to harvest plants be taught more widely to mitigate such overharvesting? Furthermore, a few members of the group that day who use traditional sustainable harvesting methods have been stopped and questioned by Cherokee Nation marshals when gathering plants on tribal land. Could the NRD issue gathering permits so as to prevent such unnecessary confrontation? And what about the scarceness and checkerboarded nature of tribal trust land? Many plots of tribal land are landlocked by non-Indian private property, making access to certain plants difficult at best. In this regard, many proposed the reacquisition of tracts of land as a necessary measure in order to carry out the goal of "managing" such things and revitalizing Cherokee environmental knowledge.

There was also much talk of "the elders" and how hearing what *they* thought was important before moving on with this project. The irony of this was that many of them *were* elders. This point was brought up before long, when one of the group members, Hastings Shade—a former Cherokee Nation deputy chief and a Cherokee National Treasure—realized that he *was* an elder in his community of Lost City. Many had passed recently, leaving his generation to take up the reigns. This sparked several nods of accord among the group.

Shortly thereafter, another car approached the meeting area. Not recognizing it at first, I left the group to greet the new arrivals. As they stepped out of the vehicle, I realized it was the elderly couple I had been visiting lately in order to discuss the ethnobotany project, in addition to lending a hand with various chores around their homestead. They had gotten lost due to the hard-to-find entrance to the nonprofit's headquarters. By that time, I had assumed they weren't coming, so when it dawned on me who they were, I knew that it was a special moment. The husband, Crosslin Smith, is a highly respected Cherokee medicine man, then in his late seventies. Crosslin comes from a line of influential Cherokee leaders, the most notable being Redbird Smith (Crosslin's grandfather), who led a political and spiritual movement during the turn of the twentieth century that both resisted the federal allotment policy and revived traditional Cherokee religious dances and practices. Crosslin himself has been a leader in this regard, having served as a community liaison during the latest revitalization of the Cherokee Nation government in the late 1960s and early 1970s. Furthermore, he is a skilled healer known throughout Indian Country. His wife Glenna, although she is Navajo, is a well-known advocate of Cherokee cultural revitalization.

The social atmosphere was transformed upon their arrival. While others in the group had been raised with plant knowledge and felt conversant in traditional plant medicines, here was a renowned practicing medicine man (and an elder to everyone there) who had come to show his support for the initiative. As Crosslin and Glenna approached the fire and started to greet folks, many in the group made amazed comments or gave each other expressive looks. Crosslin's attendance imparted a completely different level of endorsement and credibility to the initiative. Charlie's tone changed instantly, as he was impressed and humbled by Crosslin's presence. Aside from all his compliments earlier about the setting and style of the meeting, he exclaimed, "Man, I *really* like this meeting now!"

Later when Charlie again expressed reservations about moving forward with the project without getting approval from elders throughout the communities, Crosslin spoke out and said, "If we try to go around doing that, there will be those who inevitably have something bad to say or an objection of some sort. There are a lot of people out there who use medicine for bad reasons, but we need to dismiss such manipulation and negativity." In this way, Crosslin was saying that despite the taboos associated with the subject, now is the time to start talking about this knowledge in order to ensure its perpetuation. With that, Charlie asked Crosslin directly if he thought the project should proceed, and Crosslin gave a resounding "yes." He said, "I'll support you. I may not be able to be there all the time, but you have my support." Charlie took this very seriously and counted that as fulfilling his requisite elder support.

Clearly, Crosslin's backing had made a difference, and according to Hastings in a phone call the following day, the meeting "needed to happen" in order to continue with the NRD ethnobotany project. Meetings with this group have continued to the present, and they have resulted in the support and recognition of the NRD initiative to catalog Cherokee environmental knowledge for revitalization and preservation purposes. They have also led to the formation of a focus group on Cherokee cultural-environmental issues, composed of most of the original group members plus a few others who have joined since then. In May 2012, four years after the first meeting, the group elected a seven-member board of directors. The following month, during its tenth meeting, the group formally incorporated with the adoption of a declaration and bylaws. The group now serves as a cultural advisory council to the Cherokee Nation Office of Administration Support[5] and is in the process of acquiring nonprofit status to fund its cultural revitalization projects. Its long-term goals include the creation of tribal conservation areas, traditional medicine education programs for Cherokee youth, and an environmental education center.

The story of this group and the circumstances that led to its formation provide a glimpse into Cherokee environmental governance—the process by which Cherokees make decisions with regard to the human relationship to the nonhuman world. The meeting illuminated the social weight that environmental (specifically medicinal) knowledge carries in Cherokee society and the significance of overcoming the fear of its disclosure in the face of its loss. The meeting also illuminated Cherokee perspectives toward the nonhuman world and political-ecological concerns that ranged from external restrictions on resource access to internal conundrums about tribal resource control. Further, the success of the uncharacteristic setting of the meeting revealed how not all forms of Cherokee environmental governance are the same.

As with most American Indian nations, Cherokee environmental governance is multifaceted. In North America, indigenous environmental governance operates within a continuum of *resource-based* and *relationship-based* practices. The term *environmental governance*, when used outside Indian Country, implies governance over the human use of "the environment," a category that is primarily seen as devoid of humans but over which humans have control. Thus water, animals, trees, and land are treated as resources, and the human use of them is governed according to certain protocols and laws. Similarly, *natural resource management* is the process of allocating and administering the resources themselves to achieve mostly economic goals. Indian Country is no stranger to this resource-based approach, and many American Indian nations have developed natural resource management programs (as with the Cherokee Nation's NRD) in order to oversee their own affairs that were previously directed by the U.S. Department of the Interior. Within the current context of settler colonialism, in which its "specific, irreducible element" is settler state *territoriality* and the "elimination of the native" (Wolfe 2006, 388), the resource-based approach is necessary in order for American Indian nations to take control over tribal resources that have been severely mismanaged despite the "trust" relationship with the federal government.

Yet accounting for indigenous worldviews complicates *environmental governance* in its typical usage. As shown in the preceding discussion by the group, Cherokees believe that they have a responsibility to maintain certain relationships with nonhuman beings in ways that acknowledge the separate agency of those beings. Vine Deloria Jr. (Standing Rock Sioux) has articulated this perspective in terms of recognizing nonhuman nations or peoples. He writes, "Other living things are not regarded [by American Indians] as insensitive species. Rather, they are 'people' in the same manner that various tribes of human beings are people. . . . For some tribes the idea extends to plants, rocks, and natural features that Westerners consider inanimate" (Deloria 2003 [1973], 88–89). From this perspective, there is no artificial separation of human beings from the rest of creation.[6] It follows that indigenous environmental governance—at least in its relationship-based approach—must account for this agency of nonhuman beings and the maintenance of relationships with them. Additionally, the prevalence of noncoercive ideals of governance among indigenous peoples challenges the assumption that humans alone can or should govern such nonhuman beings.

Until recently, this relationship-based approach has been notably absent in Cherokee Nation policy. Because most of the environmental work done by the Cherokee Nation since the early 1990s has entailed the development of bureaucratic departments based on U.S. federal models, Cherokee Nation policy has tended to assume the dominant resource-based approach to environmental governance. Reasons for this stem from the continued bureaucratic oversight of the Bureau of Indian Affairs (BIA), which encourages resource management activities that generate a profit. Such activities include monocrop forestry programs and cattle leases on tribal lands. There is also the need for tribal land managers to attend to more immediate needs, such as securing land acquisitions for low-income tribal housing. In many cases, it is seen as impractical (or at least not a priority) to focus on a relationship-based approach at the expense of these other activities. Yet another reason is that the relationship-based approach does not fit nicely within the heavily bureaucratized Cherokee Nation polity. For one, similar to what anthropologist Paul Nadasdy (2003) has shown in his work with the Kluane First Nation in Canada, integrating this approach into state environmental agencies can be counterproductive when traditional environmental knowledge is taken out of its social context. Moreover, as expressed in the introductory story, getting folks to shed their skepticism of bureaucracy requires the establishment of trust, which is a slow and unpredictable process.

The process of consultation demonstrated by this meeting was a step toward addressing the absence of the relationship-based approach. By providing a forum for dialogue about environmental issues between a tribal department and a small group of elders, the resource- and the relationship-based approaches converged. While the elders articulated their obligation to maintain proper relationships with the nonhuman world, they also discussed their desire to both gain and restrict access to certain resources—thereby indicating the need for balancing both approaches. Thus, through this convergence and the deliberation that it requires, the ethnobotany project and the focus group that has emerged from it represent the beginnings of a new chapter in Cherokee environmental governance.

Roots of Our Renewal analyzes the historical roots of this transformation, examines how Cherokees are currently dealing with its related obstacles, and discusses the implications for Indian Country and beyond. In doing so, I hope to accomplish three goals. First, I tell the story of how Cherokees in Oklahoma have developed material, spiritual, and political relationships with new lands. The forced march of the Cherokees from their homelands in the southeast to lands west of the Mississippi (then known as the Indian Territory) in 1838–39 had devastating effects on Cherokee society. But this history is equally characterized by the resilience of the Cherokee people and the rebirth of a nation. Thus Cherokees who live in what is now northeastern Oklahoma view their environmental knowledge as both an ancient cultural heritage (with regard to those elements that were transferred from the homelands) and a relatively recent legacy of survival and renewal in a new land. Through various environmental practices, these new lands have been inscribed with a Cherokee identity, and conversely, the new lands have inscribed themselves on Cherokees in profound ways. Additionally, the lands have meant *territory* to a nation whose history has been punctuated by its immense loss. Telling the story of the development of these relationships will provide deep context for a discussion of contemporary Cherokee environmental governance.

Second, I examine Cherokee negotiations of the *resource* versus *relationship* approach in the context of indigenous governance more broadly speaking. Viewed in this light, the interface between resource- and relationship-based approaches mirrors larger questions regarding the interface between people and polity, or citizens and the state. As expressed before, while the establishment of tribal environmental programs has been an important contribution to the assertion of tribal sovereignty, it has been accompanied by the need to maintain complex bureaucracies that are often impediments to the representation of local environmental knowledge, values, and practices within tribal environmental policy. For the Cherokee Nation, the task of representing such knowledge, values, and practices has become more than merely fulfilling an institutional requirement to incorporate "tradition" into tribal policy. Rather, it is part of a larger effort to restructure relationships and reform institutional processes with regard to the communities and individuals that possess and live such traditions and who in the past have been marginalized by the tribal governmental apparatus. Put another way, reconciling the resource- and relationship-based approaches has meant coming to terms with the development of an indigenous state.

Drawing from theories of the state and state formation, I ask this question: How has the development of contemporary indigenous states affected indigenous lands and influenced environmental politics, both without and within indigenous societies? In addressing this question, I take into account the historical development of bureaucratic Cherokee governance structures and their actions toward (and presumed authority over) the environment. More important, I look at how traditional authority intersects that narrative, thus focusing on nonbureaucratic forms of governance and their impact on local environmental politics. I then explore how these disparate forms inform and influence each other through the dialectics of what I call indigenous state transformation.

My third goal is to bring together two multidisciplinary areas of study: critical American Indian studies and political ecology. Although each field eludes a hard and fast definition, the former could be characterized by its analysis of the history, arts, literature, and politics of American Indian nations and individuals as they relate to both shared experiences of settler colonialism and tribally specific traditions, languages, religions, and homelands (Champagne and Stauss 2002; Kidwell and Velie 2005).[7] My emphasis within this field concerns indigenous relationships to land/environment in the context of histories of dispossession and the subsequent imperative of claiming territory as both a reaction to this dispossession and a need to carve out space to enable the perpetuation of land-based practices and beliefs. Political ecology is largely concerned with the use, access, management, allocation, and control of natural resources and how cultural, socioeconomic, political, and ecological factors shape these practices (Robbins 2004; Agrawal 2005, 210).[8] State-building has long been a primary topic for the field of political ecology precisely because of the territorial and jurisdictional claims that state architects wield and the impact of those claims on local human populations and their environments. It follows that this intellectual merger complicates my analysis of two terms that have often been juxtaposed rather than combined: *indigenous* and *state*. Yet, despite this complication, I propose that the pursuit yields valuable new theoretical and pragmatic approaches to environmental issues in Indian Country. In all, I argue that indigenous employments and adaptations of modern state forms can articulate alternatives to the way humans interact with and "govern" the environment. What follows is an in-depth discussion of my latter two goals.

The Political Is Environmental

Political ecology's critical focus on environmental governance has illuminated the connections between nature, state, territory, and knowledge, and therefore how that which is *environmental* is inherently *political* (e.g., Fairhead and Leach 1996; Neumann 2004; Agrawal 2005). The field's main contribution to environmental studies lies in its distinction from what Paul Robbins (2004, 5) has called "apolitical ecology." Robbins writes that this contrast is "the difference between identifying broader systems rather than blaming proximate and local forces; between viewing ecological systems as power-laden rather than politically inert; and between taking an explicitly normative approach rather than one that claims the objectivity of disinterest." Political ecology emerged from the need to counteract explanations of environmental issues that neglected the influence of political economy and tended to view local peasants as the source of environmental degradation (see Blaikie 1985; Blaikie and Brookfield 1987). The interdisciplinary work of political ecologists offers alternative explanations to environmental problems by asserting that "the environment" is a political thing.

In American Indian studies, I find it more effective to invert the phrase: The *political* is inherently *environmental*. In common with other indigenous peoples throughout the globe, American Indian political struggles always come back to the issue of land and the degree of our connection to it. The many ills that disproportionately plague American Indian communities in the United States, such as psychological distress (e.g., high suicide rates), alcohol and substance abuse, domestic violence, cancer, diabetes, poverty, and language loss are all political problems when viewed within the context of settler colonialism, which Patrick Wolfe (1999, 2) has aptly identified as "a structure, not an event." Each could be addressed through renewing connections to the land, revitalizing traditional diets, supplementing meager income with natural foods and products, and reducing environmental pollutants and risks. Yet these activities are often constrained by the degree to which American Indian nations can reacquire land, manage their own resources on their own terms, formulate and enforce tribal environmental policy within and beyond tribal land bases, and protect and perpetuate traditional ecological knowledge and practices. The root causes of these problems are all found in the political economy of settler colonialism, which is inextricably linked to the exploitation of indigenous lands (see Wolfe 2011).

Political ecology and American Indian studies stand to gain from each other new contexts and meanings for the relationship between "the political" and "the environmental." On the one hand, American Indian studies benefits from political ecology by gaining new theoretical tools to address the challenges of contemporary indigenous environmental governance. With the growing prevalence and sophistication of American Indian resource management programs and their increasing ability to control and distribute access to tribal lands (Royster and Fausett 1989; Tsosie 1996; Clow and Sutton 2001; Nettheim, Meyers, and Craig 2002; Fleder and Ranco 2004; Wilkinson 2005), American Indian communities face difficult questions about the nature of these institutions. To what extent are tribal natural resource managers assuming the role of state authorities in their ability to restrict citizen access to tribal lands? How do tribal conservation areas differ from state-sanctioned enclosures throughout the globe that often disenfranchise customary use by local peoples? Political ecology provides a framework for understanding the issues that arise around resource access when "management" becomes a dominant policy paradigm.

Arun Agrawal's (2005, 226) work on the formation of environmental subjects—what he calls "environmentality"—has highlighted how "knowledges, politics, institutions, and subjectivities . . . come to be linked together with the emergence of the environment as a domain that requires regulation and protection." Similarly, Nancy Peluso and Christian Lund (2011, 668) offer important insights on the topic of land control, or "practices that fix or consolidate forms of access, claiming, and exclusion." They write that territoriality "produces and maintains power relations among governed environmental subjects and between subjects and authorities." These power relations create unequal opportunities and benefit flows for different groups and can eliminate the rights and decision-making authority of earlier resource users. Peluso and Lund's analysis of territorialization and enclosure as components of land control points to the cautions tribes must take when assuming state forms and "claiming the power to govern territorially" (673).

Political ecology has also broken down the perceived distance between state and local actors. K. Sivaramakrishnan (1999), Michael Dove (1999), and Paul Robbins (2000) have all argued against the presumption that state agencies are represented solely by nonlocal "experts" who marginalize or displace local peoples and their respective environmental practices and knowledges. Their work shows that state actors in some cases can be resource users themselves or in other cases can form "knowledge communities" (Robbins 2000, 127) with local producers that defy assumptions of top-down decision-making processes. This analysis is useful for understanding the dynamics of tribal resource management, where scale and proximity are important to keep in mind when thinking in terms of "authorities" and "subjects." Drawing from such studies, my work seeks to figure out how indigenous states operate on the ground and what this can tell us about their potential as well as their limitations.

On the other hand, political ecology benefits from American Indian studies through an analysis of the unique political histories of American Indian nations and their relationships to the U.S. settler state. Indigenous nations within settler states exist among a nested set of geographical scales, and in the United States, these scales consist of the federal, tribal, and state (Silvern 1999). American Indians maintain nation-to-nation relationships with the federal government based on treaties that articulate indigenous sovereignties—sovereignties that predate the formation of the United States (see Wilkins and Stark 2011). However, as Lumbee scholar David Wilkins (1993, 391) has noted, the peculiar nature of this relationship lies in the fact that American Indian nations are "recognized sovereigns with rights that can be systematically quashed." The ability of American Indian nations to practice their sovereignty has been eroded through acts of Congress, treaty cessions, and the numerous cases that make up federal Indian law today (Wilkins and Lomawaima 2001). But despite this erosion, the political relationship that American Indian nations uphold with the U.S. settler state has afforded them a unique semisovereign status that distinguishes them from many other indigenous peoples throughout the globe.

While scholars have emphasized the need for First World political ecology (McCarthy 2002; Robbins 2002; Walker 2003),[9] few have engaged explicitly with indigenous nations within this context. Many of those that do nonetheless have not fully addressed the theoretical implications for the field (see Braun 2002; Wainwright and Robertson 2003; Natcher, Hickey, and Davis 2004). Despite a call for land and property questions to embark on a "long intellectual journey home [to North America]" (Fortmann 1996, 545), political ecology has largely passed over Indian Country, which arguably makes up the very foundation of land and property questions in settler-colonial societies like Canada and the United States.[10]

Beth Rose Middleton has initiated this important conversation, stemming from her work with the Mountain Maidu in Northern California (Middleton 2010). She focuses on how regaining access to traditional territories and resources contributes to North American indigenous community health and how this fundamentally decolonial project has addressed cases of intergenerational trauma among the Mountain Maidu community. Middleton thus works toward a "political ecology of healing" that centers decolonization and indigenous self-determination. I build on her valuable work and argue that key concepts within American Indian studies have further theoretical implications for First World political-ecological inquiry.

For peoples whose history has been punctuated by immense losses of land by way of colonial and capitalist forces, it is not surprising that the field of study dedicated to the historical and contemporary condition of American Indian nations has centered *land* and *sovereignty* as analytical categories. Of course, the concepts of land and sovereignty in American Indian studies do more than merely describe territories and methods of resource control. As analytical categories, they enable strategies for maintaining relationships to place and nonhumans and for perpetuating land-based knowledges and practices as critical components of Native peoplehood (Holm, Pearson, and Chavis 2003). Fully accounting for pervasive settler-colonial structures—Middleton (2010, 2) frames this in terms of enduring "coloniality"—and the ongoing occupation of indigenous lands would more closely align First World political ecology with the field's roots in social justice. And while the ways in which American Indian political leaders wield sovereignty are not exempt from critique, I assert that supporting the underlying goals of indigenous self-determination (often achieved via sovereignty claims) is a process that benefits everyone.

Bruce Braun (1997) and Kay Anderson (2000) have addressed how indigenous peoples complicate and upset settler narratives of nation and settler sovereignty itself, but as I have gathered, such works have not addressed what this means for political-ecological analyses of territoriality, the state, and environmental governance—in other words, how the analytical categories of land and sovereignty in American Indian studies inform the approaches of political ecology. As I contend in this book, political ecology offers critical lenses for assessing indigenous formations of environmental governance; conversely, such formations (like indigenous states) offer new ways of looking at the common approaches of political ecology. Placing key concepts from American Indian studies within First World political ecology maintains analytical perspectives on methods of land control while acknowledging the imperatives of land and sovereignty to Native nations.

American Indian studies thus expands political-ecological approaches to territoriality, as it occurs under very different circumstances. The concept of American Indian sovereignty, along with the existence of tribal governments that represent such sovereignty and the dynamic land-based practices and traditions that American Indians maintain, position American Indian territorial claims to space—often invoked in terms of *homelands* or *land bases*—as cornerstones of American Indian political and cultural continuance (Wilkinson 1987; see Deloria 2007 [1970]). Additionally, American Indians are both authorities with regard to their tribal lands and citizens (however limited that authority may be) and subjects of the settler state at the same time. This stands in contrast to the standard focus of Third World political ecology, wherein singular states make up the operational governmental authority to which their subjects must react.

Indeed, much work in political ecology has focused on state schemes for controlling resources and the livelihoods attached to those resources—and for good reasons. Peasants, disenfranchised ethnic groups, and indigenous peoples have often been the victims of state programs that have turned once commonly held resources into national property, resulting in the criminalization of subsistence lifestyles.[11] Nevertheless, identifying and labeling the political extensions of many American Indian nations as *states* (in line with political scientist Walker Connor's [1978] definition of a state) allows for new ways of thinking about states and state space because of how indigenous states have the potential to operate from entirely different perspectives toward the nonhuman world. Thus the approach I take in this book both draws from and stands in contrast to works that analyze large-scale, high-modern states and their territorial claims (e.g., Kuehls 1996; Scott 1998; Storey 2012). By doing so, I acknowledge the important contributions of these studies while I pursue alternative narratives and analyses of state formation.

To be sure, scholars in American Indian and indigenous studies continue to debate whether nationalism—in the sense of mimicking dominant forms of political organization and governance—is an appropriate goal for indigenous peoples, and so admittedly I am stepping into controversial terrain. This important work within the field has highlighted the dangers of uncritically adopting forms that originated in ideologies of hierarchy, coercive power, and heteropatriarchy (see Alfred 1999, 2005; Denetdale 2006; Coulthard 2007; Ramirez 2007; Huhndorf 2009a; Goeman 2009).[12] At the same time, however, Yup'ik scholar Shari Huhndorf (2009b, 367) suggests that alternative visions need not replace nationalism altogether but that they can coexist "in relationships that are simultaneously complementary and contradictory, one strategy illuminating the possibilities and limits of the other, as both expand the range and subversive possibilities of indigenous politics." And while some have questioned the extent to which American Indian expressions of nationalism and sovereignty must lead to statehood (Simpson 2000; Biolsi 2005), I question the extent to which statehood has a singular meaning and shape in light of recent works that seek to describe this phenomenon throughout Indian Country (Nesper 2007; Carroll 2012).

The question I aim to address, then, is not *should* indigenous nations make use of state structures, but rather, *how* are they forming them? One might relate the former question with the influential work of Taiaiake Alfred (1999, 56; Mohawk), who argues that indigenous leaders, in accepting sovereignty and statist institutions as political aspirations, inevitably legitimate a colonial framework and the subordinating relations that this framework demands. By contrast, the latter question points toward indigenous appropriations of state forms in order to counteract ongoing injustices. Approaches to this question demand close, locally specific studies—ethnographies of indigenous states—that illuminate how indigenous nations have been able to envision the state form for themselves and which attributes of this form have been addressed to account for various indigenous situations and values.[13] And while not all indigenous nations employ this form of political organization, in the case of many American Indian nations, what are these bureaucratic political structures if not states? Scholars must be willing to call a spade a spade, as the expression goes, albeit with expanded and complex theories of "the state" in indigenous contexts. Building on an established body of literature devoted to particular understandings of state formation (Corrigan and Sayer 1985; Abrams 1988; Corrigan 1990; Joseph and Nugent 1994a), I propose a line of study devoted to indigenous state *transformation*, which focuses on the use and modification of state structures by indigenous nations.

Central to this area of study are questions concerning the social and political processes of indigenous state transformation both "externally" (in relations with settler states) and "internally" (regarding intratribal dynamics). For example, how are indigenous state actors and their constituent citizens and communities engaging with each other as state forms expand in order to maintain the legitimacy of these forms while protecting tribal sovereignty? In this book, I describe how indigenous (more specifically, Cherokee) state transformation entails a complex interplay between state structures and ideologies on the one hand and community-based institutions and ways of operating on the other. I describe this process using the term *dialectics*. Following anthropologist David Graeber (2001, 52), I invoke *dialectics* in a Heraclitian sense—"one that sees objects as processes, as defined by their potentials." I propose studying the Cherokee state not as something fixed in a "certain abstract moment, outside time, but . . . by what [it] has the potential to become" (254). Such an approach allows for an analysis of Cherokee institutions as transformative structures and as sites of transculturation and resistance.[14]

Furthermore, the study of indigenous state transformation seeks to understand how indigenous states represent what political theorist Kevin Bruyneel (2007, 6) calls a "third space of sovereignty" in both settler-state and global politics and, in doing so, enable indigenous nations to "gain the fullest possible expression of political identity, agency, and autonomy." Bruyneel describes how spatial and temporal boundaries created by American political discourse present American Indian nations with false choices constructed by imperial binaries—"assimilation or secession, inside or outside, modern or traditional" (217). Employing postcolonial theories, Bruyneel outlines how the refusal by American Indian nations to choose between these dualisms is an assertion of a political "third space" (Bhabha 1994; see also Johnson 2008).[15] Thus a third space of sovereignty allows for "promising contradictions" (Tsing 2007, 33) in indigenous relations with settler states: claiming difference and autonomy without implying secession, and holding the settler state to its responsibilities toward indigenous nations without accepting its paternalism.[16]

This view of sovereignty correlates with other approaches that see sovereignty as more than a territorial claim and assertion of autonomy. Jessica Cattelino (2008, 129, 200) writes, "Indigenous sovereignty unsettles the singularity of sovereignty as it was developed in Europe and its colonies. . . . [It] is constituted by relations of interdependency that take material form in people's bodies, houses, and lands." Likewise, Seneca scholar and activist John Mohawk envisioned sovereignty "not as a fait accompli, but as a dynamic process in need of constant regeneration and recovery" (Barreiro 2010, xxi). Such insights highlight the intricacies of the concept of sovereignty in American Indian studies and show how American Indian nations both understand sovereignty and make use of its discursive power.

While political ecology and related fields like radical ecology are skeptical of sovereignty because of the consequences it holds for marginalized populations (including nonhuman ones), for American Indians, sovereignty—and the political structures that uphold it—continues to act as a vehicle for self-determination and justice in the face of ongoing settler colonialism. Recent calls from radical ecologists to do away with "ecological sovereignty" (Smith 2011), although they purport to speak for the voiceless nonhuman beings and ecosystems that are often the victims of human actions, do not adequately address the many contexts in which sovereignty is being employed and thus the many different forms and meanings that it assumes for different peoples (see Barker 2005). As legal scholar Sarah Krakoff (2002, 178) writes, "Tribal sovereignty is sacrosanct yet entirely vulnerable. Its vulnerability calls for vigilant defense." I view indigenous states as instruments for the defense of tribal sovereignty.

The merger of American Indian studies and political ecology reinforces how "the environment" cannot be separated from the practices and politics of people. Whereas American Indian studies centers relational and spiritual approaches to land and nonhuman beings, political ecology emphasizes the deeply political process of land and resource allocation and control. And whereas political ecology is wary of claims to sovereignty, American Indian studies cannot afford to dismiss the concept because of how it is inseparably tied to the maintenance of Native peoplehood. The two approaches augment each other and show how the study of indigenous states—in their potential to protect indigenous homelands and territories, nurture tribal knowledges and perspectives, and create new approaches to conservation—is a fundamentally environmental endeavor.

Indigenous State Transformation and Environmental Governance

Discussions of "the state" often invoke images of militaries, violent coercion, and what Max Weber (1946b, 78) described as "the monopoly of the legitimate use of physical force within a given territory." While Weber's identification of *legitimacy* and *territory* as key features of state practice informs my overall analysis, my approach to the study of indigenous states differs in many ways from the view of the state as a monolithic and coherent structure. Following the work of Phillip Abrams (1988), Timothy Mitchell (1991), Philip Corrigan and Derek Sayer (1985), and others, I am more interested in state *formation* as "a cultural process with manifest consequences in the material world" (Joseph and Nugent 1994b, 13). Corrigan and Sayer (1985, 1–2) describe state formation as "cultural revolution," where *culture* refers to everyday practices and *revolution* explains the process of reconfiguring "the way the world [is] made sense of."

Here I must distinguish *culture* in the state formation sense from *Culture* in the anthropological sense, which has tended to dominate discussions in American Indian studies. Gilbert M. Joseph and Daniel Nugent (1994b, 15–18) make this distinction in terms of *popular* culture as "the symbols and meanings embedded in the quotidian practices of subaltern groups" and *folkloristic* culture as a particular people's traditions, mores, values, legends, and so on. Although the two are in dialogue and inform each other, I am primarily concerned with culture *as practice* and how altering the ways in which people interact with one another, with the land and nonhuman beings, and with government constitutes the "cultural revolution" of which Corrigan and Sayer speak.

The Cherokee Nation is a fitting case for this analysis because of its long history of engagement with the state form. Early Cherokee state-building in the mid-nineteenth century entailed this type of cultural revolution: In the face of colonial encroachment, confederated Cherokee "towns" were required to give up some of their former autonomy in exchange for centralized political unification. Arguably, this altered the way Cherokees made sense of the world in that they looked to a new central entity to represent them politically. State-building also directly impacted Cherokee relationships to the environment and nonhuman beings. Decentering the clan system in political life disconnected decision making from the plants, animals, landforms, and elements that were represented in each of the seven matrilineal clans. Through time, this process produced other transformations—from the establishment of environmental laws that regulated citizens' use and treatment of the land according to formalistic and abstract mechanisms (e.g., calendar dates and legal categories) to the replication of colonial systems of natural resource management and exploitation (e.g., monocrop economic forestry programs).

Nevertheless, these transformations have been mediated through a dialectical relationship between Cherokee central government and semi-autonomous Cherokee communities. Although the structure of the Cherokee Nation's centralized form of government has changed significantly since its inception due to the repeated intervention of the U.S. federal government, there has been a consistent pattern of Cherokee resistance to total central-ization and bureaucratization. This dialectical relationship is embodied in historical and contemporary Cherokee social movements. In moments when the tribal government has seemed to direct its priorities away from the traditional base of the nation, an equal and opposite force has been exerted by communities (or collective groups that represent community interests) in order to bring government practice back to a more balanced position.

This is not to say that such dialectics are unique to indigenous state transformation. Joseph and Nugent (1994b, 20) describe this dynamic as the "relational constitution" between the state and its subjects. But although indigenous state transformation displays this common relational dynamic of reaction and counterreaction, the process among indigenous nations appears progressively to be a more one-sided enterprise. Whereas early Cherokee state-building required speaking the language of state-hood, more and more Cherokee communities are demanding that their state speak their own language. In other words, while the legitimacy of Cherokee state structures was once predicated on the critical and time-ly resistance to colonial force, recently it appears to move more in the opposite direction: In being compelled to address the relationship-based approach to environmental governance, the state (i.e., Cherokee Nation land management programs and actors) is being asked to perform its own revolution in the way it makes sense of the world. This dynamic—which I explore throughout the book—exemplifies what I mean by indigenous state *trans*formation.

The circumstances that led to the ethnobotany project and elders' meeting presented previously are indicative of this process. While the Cherokee Nation government has focused on the development of envi-ronmental bureaucracies, "traditional" forms of environmental knowledge and stewardship have not been represented in these structures. This lack of representation has led to the desire by tribal officials to "incorporate" traditional knowledge into such programs (the ethnobotany project), which in turn has created a forum (the elders' meeting) in which to raise larger issues of tribal environmental governance and policy. In this case, the process is by no means complete, but the scenario serves as a contem-porary example of what it can entail.

In light of recent works that call attention to the decline of state influ-ence in environmental governance (see Agrawal and Lemos 2007), the diminished solidity of states due in part to neoliberal economics and other forces of globalization (Rose 1996, 1999; Dean 1999), and the ability of the global indigenous movement to transcend international boundaries and challenge state governance (Niezen 2003; Tsing 2007), one might question my focus on indigenous states and their transformation. But for many American Indian nations, these institutions continue to serve as vital political barriers between indigenous communities and settler-state governments. And although the Cherokee state—as it serves to both protect and govern access to tribal lands—is being met with difficult questions, of which tribal communities are ever watchful and critical, the reality is that Cherokee state actors and land managers are in the position to defy common "statist" tendencies by adopting relationship-based approaches and thereby acknowledging alternative perceptions and uses of "the environment." Indigenous state transformation provides a theoretical framework for making sense of how indigenous states have formed and how they continue to do so. Implicit in this project is understanding how indigenous individuals and communities engage with these structures and the transformative potential of this process.

Furthermore, the decline of state influence has not led to the demise of states or their irrelevance to local and global politics but rather new understandings of state forms and how they work (see Hempel 1996, 150–78). Localizing and historicizing the study of state forms, Thomas Hansen and Finn Stepputat (2001) claim, advances these new understandings. They write, "Instead of talking about the state as an entity that always/already consists of certain features, functions, and forms of governance, let us approach each actual state as a historically specific configuration of a range of languages of stateness, some practical, others symbolic and performative, that have been disseminated, translated, interpreted, and combined in widely differing ways and sequences across the globe" (7). This ethnography of the state views it neither as a monolith nor as a particular closed group of individuals but as an ideological configuration, albeit with material presence and effects. Hansen and Stepputat's ethnography is an inquiry into how each unique formation is produced and reproduced, imagined and reimagined by and through its subjects. Their claim illuminates that *not all states are the same* and, further, that not all state projects are necessarily "bad." They elaborate, "Whereas certain forms of state intervention may be loathed and resisted, other and more egalitarian forms of governance, or more benign forms of authority, may at the

same time be intensely desired and asked for" (9). Thus, while some forms
of state power have disastrous potential, there is also variation between
states and differing degrees of coercion among state projects: There are
many paths to "stateness." Viewing states and state formation as such offers
some conceptual space within which to discuss indigenous state transformation as a creative process through which indigenous nations can
articulate unique expressions of stateness (drawing from Clifford 2001).
Such expressions, as the elders' group shows, can embody nonhierarchi-
cal, relational approaches to governance.

It bears saying that the Cherokee state is not immune—both historically and at present—to the dismal effects of state forms that Corrigan and
Sayer (1985, 4) identify as the power to regulate human social capacities
by "suppressing, marginalizing, eroding, [and] undermining... [certain]
ways in which social life could be lived." Circe Sturm (2002) has shown
how Cherokee mimicry of dominant narratives of race and national
identity has served over time to privilege some Cherokee citizens while
disenfranchising others. Tiya Miles (2005, 120–28) has elucidated the
drastic implications that the fledgling Cherokee state's conceptions of
race (as founded on the elite practice of slavery) had for early marriage
laws, which prohibited the intermarriage of Cherokees and blacks. And
Lenape scholar Joanne Barker (2011, 198–205) illuminates the Cherokee
Nation's contemporary codification of laws to regulate human social
activities through her discussion of the prohibition of same-sex marriage in 2004. Additionally, Barker's (2011, 41–78) discussion of the
adversarial political relationship between the Cherokee Nation and the
Delaware (Lenape) Tribe—who in 1866 were removed to the Cherokee Nation and were problematically but nonetheless "incorporated"
into the tribal body politic—shows what Corrigan and Sayer (1985, 10)
describe as the monopolizing tendency of the state to "stand alone in its
authority claims to be the only legitimate agency equally for this or that
form of knowledge, provision, regulation or—that wonderfully neutral
word—'administration.'"

I do not intend to make excuses for these repressive acts. Rather, I
hope to add to their critique by emphasizing transformational capacities
as pathways for achieving something better. I underscore the necessity
of interfacing with the U.S. state while not justifying the structures of
oppression—slavery, racism, heteropatriarchy, and hierarchy—that have
enabled this and that continue to plague the Cherokee state today. In line

with this goal is not losing sight of the multiscalar, settler-colonial context in which these sanctions of unethical ideologies take place. It is the restriction of the Cherokee state's regulatory power enacted by the U.S. settler state through its own institutions of law (e.g., the "plenary power" of Congress—see Wolfe [2012]) that renders conventional analyses of state formation (Corrigan and Sayer 1985) and governmentality (Dean 1999; Agrawal 2005) inadequate. However, as the Cherokee state works to increase this regulatory authority, these analyses provide important reference for understanding the cost at which we engage on this ideological terrain (Corrigan and Sayer 1985, 206). They also point to the liberatory potential of this engagement. As Timothy Mitchell (1991, 94) claims, the "metaphysical" nature of the state—in which such divisions as "society" and "state" are taken for granted—lies in its ability to present an appearance of coherence out of the collective actions of individuals. Indigenous nations, through their transformation of state structures that remain indisputably *theirs,* have the potential to redefine the state in ways that align with their conceptions of social identities, moral orders, and processes of relating to one another and to the nonhuman world.[17]

While the Cherokee state displays some negative qualities of the state form, the primary function of this structure is, as Cherokee scholar Daniel Justice (2006, 8) writes, "to preserve a sociopolitical boundary by which the sacred is protected." "The sacred" that is guarded by this sociopolitical boundary refers to the spiritual elements of indigenous nationhood, which Justice claims set indigenous nations apart as unique collectivities. He writes, "Indigenous nationhood is more than simple political independence or the exercise of a distinctive cultural identity; it is also an understanding of a common social interdependence within the community, the tribal web of kinship rights and responsibilities that link the People, the land, and the cosmos together in an ongoing and dynamic system of mutually affecting relationships. At its best, it extends beyond the human to encompass other peoples, from the plants and animals to the sun, moon, thunder and other elemental forces" (24). Juxtaposing Justice's notion of indigenous nationalism with the work of K. Sivaramakrishnan and Gunnel Cederlöf (2006, 6–10) allows for the possibility of an "ecological nationalism" that is indigenist at its core—relationally and spiritually attached to place and the nonhuman world—but one that also employs indigenized state structures in order to converse with and contest those of the settler state.[18]

While insular nationalism has proven necessary in order to defend tribal homelands against outside resource exploitation, indigenous nations
also have the opportunity to teach the world valuable lessons about environmental governance. Indigenous state transformation presents the
global state community with alternative forms of governance that both
recognize the persistence of the state system and foster within it norms
of deliberative democracy, hybridized economies that value subsistence
practices, and relational approaches to environmental management and
sustainability. Indigenous redefinitions of the state create new epistemic
communities (e.g., the Cherokee elders' group) that contest neoliberal
ideologies through their communal and land-based foundations and upset
the logic of settler colonialism through their persistence as political entities.[19] These epistemic communities can provide forums for meaningful
dialogue between nonindigenous progressive leaders and indigenous
nations, much like the role of NGO think tanks in global climate-change
discussions (Lemos and Agrawal 2006, 316).

In this light, American Indian nations—through their transformation
of political structures that connect indigenous land ethics with resource
management—have a central role to play in the global ecological crisis.
This role is not based on a presumed innate indigenous ecological wisdom.[20] While I do contend that American Indian communities possess
deep and intimate knowledge of their lands, this knowledge alone is not
the basis on which I make this claim. Rather, I propose that potential
indigenous contributions lie in systems of governance that can translate
the foundational values of these knowledge systems and demonstrate
what these ethics look like in practice (see also Richardson 2009).[21]

Rebecca Tsosie (1996, 324; Yaqui) notes that for American Indian
nations, balancing traditional norms and the need to be stakeholders in
global policy is crucial. And while the global state system is plagued with
unequal power relations—as evinced in the structure of the United Nations
(Carroll 2012)—indigenous nations have begun to create their own international forums and to reinvigorate treaty making among themselves. The
formation of the United League of Indigenous Nations on August 1, 2007,
as a result of treaty negotiations between eleven indigenous nations from
the United States, Canada, Australia, and Aotearoa (New Zealand) exemplifies this transnational approach to affecting change, and this entity has
become an active voice in global climate-change issues (Parker and Grossman 2012). This shows how the ability to make contributions that reach

a global audience, and in turn affect the localities of indigenous communities, rests in what Scott Richard Lyons (2010, 136; Ojibwe/Dakota) describes as a "willing[ness] to speak the language of nations."[22]

Scholars of environmental governance have grappled with the ineffectiveness of states in addressing environmental concerns (see Hempel 1996; Agrawal and Lemos 2007). One obvious shortcoming of the state system is that both ecological processes and environmental pollutants do not act in accordance to state borders or laws. Other limitations have to do with the way certain conceptions of sovereignty and territory constrain social relations. Thom Kuehls and Steven Silvern have highlighted the pitfalls of sovereignty and territoriality in the contexts of indigenous struggles over resource control and regulation (Silvern 2002b; Kuehls 2003). For Silvern, the "rigid spatiality of state centrism" inhibits pathways for cooperation between states (e.g., Montana) and indigenous nations due to its "obsessive concern with sovereignty" rather than a "positive view of power sharing" (134). For Kuehls, "the environmental circumstances of sovereignty," or the notion that "sovereignty is bound up with a particular orientation to environment . . . that requires the land to be used in particular ways," restricts indigenous efforts to reclaim ancestral homelands (181).

Silvern's cooperative approach is commendable in its intent for social harmony, but it nevertheless deemphasizes unequal power relations between state and tribal governments that render cooperation a precarious enterprise. Further, it lends legitimacy to state territoriality itself (i.e., the fact that many states have been illegally superimposed on nonconsenting indigenous nations). Cooperation between tribes and state governments is sometimes preferable to costly litigation and the continuance of adversarial relations, but predicating those relations on good faith and "power sharing" is asking tribes to accept a watered-down version of sovereignty that in the long run normalizes state claims rather than rightfully challenging them. And Kuehls's critique of sovereignty, while an informative look at its European philosophical baggage, still makes the assumption that sovereignty is the same for everyone and can only be articulated one way.

My perspective on indigenous state transformation and its potential contributions to global environmental governance joins recent scholarship that has sought—against the tide of state critics (including radical political ecologists)—to "reinstate the state" and thus to illustrate possibilities for "state-based ecological renewal" (Barry and Eckersley 2005, x).

John Barry and Robyn Eckersley, along with their cocontributors, seek to question the "political resignation to the idea of a weakened and ineffectual state, and to the idea that ecological degradation is inevitable" (ibid.). Thus, with regard to American Indian nations, discrediting or circumventing indigenous state structures because they do not mirror "traditional" models may not necessarily result in more freedom for indigenous nations. In fact, doing so may work to sidestep protective barriers and ultimately extend neoliberal markets into indigenous communities, as Andrew Curley and Roxanne Dunbar-Ortiz (2012) have argued. Returning to Kuehls's critique, then, when we acknowledge multiple sovereignties and articulations of state forms—ones that have different goals than the European-specific definition—we can begin to decenter structures founded on imperialism and settler colonialism while upholding our own structures that are designed to keep them at bay.[23]

Physical and Sociopolitical Landscapes of the Cherokee Nation

The Cherokee Nation is the largest in population of three federally recognized Cherokee political entities, including the Eastern Band of Cherokee Indians in North Carolina and the United Keetoowah Band of Cherokee Indians also headquartered in Tahlequah.[24] Comprising most of fourteen counties in northeastern Oklahoma, the historical Cherokee Nation boundary is now commonly known as the Cherokee Nation Tribal Jurisdictional Service Area (TJSA).[25] Because Cherokee Nation lands were deeded in fee simple by the U.S. government as a result of the forced relocation of the nation in the late 1830s and subsequently annexed by the federal government during the Allotment Era of the late nineteenth century, the Cherokee Nation TJSA is neither a reservation nor a contiguous land base. In fact, current tribal trust lands are scattered parcels in mostly Adair and Delaware counties (Figure 2).[26] These tracts were put in trust as a result of a series of laws in the 1930s and 1940s, including the Oklahoma Indian Welfare Act, which aided in the revitalization of the Cherokee Nation government and the reestablishment of its land base. At that time, the owners of these parcels received full real estate value for these lands, which were deemed "prime" agricultural lands but were actually the tops of mountains and infertile valleys.

Of the original 4.42 million acres (roughly 7,000 square miles) that were owned in fee simple by the Cherokee Nation, only about 55,000 acres

Cherokee Nation
Lands

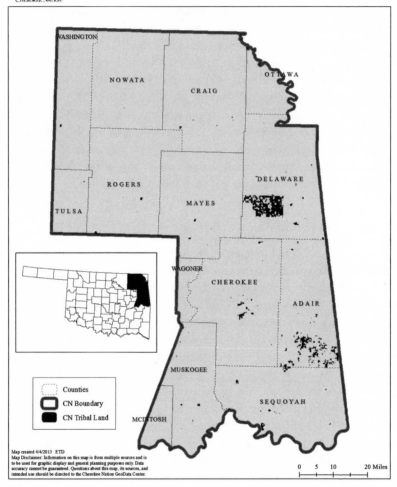

Figure 2. Current extent of tribal trust land in the Cherokee Nation. Whereas once the entire area was owned in fee simple by the nation, now the only significant reserves of tribal land are located in Adair and Delaware counties (and even these areas are severely "checkerboarded"). Courtesy of Cherokee Nation Geodata Center.

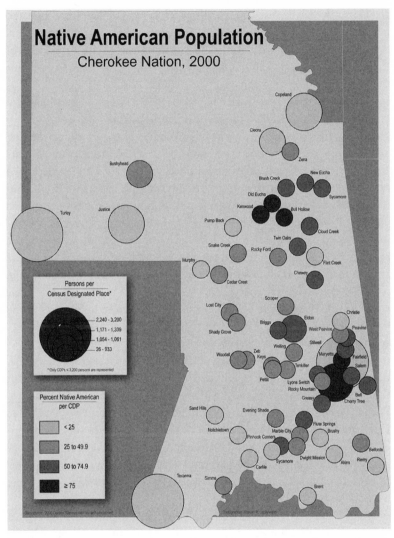

Figure 3. Cherokee communities represented by U.S. Census data, 2000. Courtesy of Dr. Justin Nolan, Department of Anthropology, University of Arkansas–Fayetteville.

are currently tribal trust lands, with another 45,000 that are designated as individual restricted lands.[27] Therefore, only about 100,000 acres total are considered Cherokee Nation land. Furthermore, about 10,000 acres of these tribal trust lands are completely landlocked and away from major thoroughfares, which means access to them is severely impeded. The remaining pattern of land ownership within the TJSA is a checkerboard of federal, state, and private (Cherokee and non-Cherokee) land.

Within the five-county area of Cherokee, Sequoyah, Adair, Delaware, and Mayes exists a network of rural, tight-knit Cherokee settlements that have maintained degrees of historical and cultural continuity since arrival in the area after Removal (see Figure 3; Wahrhaftig 1968). It is in these settlements—now mostly referred to as communities—where the cultural, linguistic, and religious aspects of Oklahoma Cherokee peoplehood are lived and grounded. Although outnumbered by whites in the area, Cherokees make up the largest minority in these counties. Economic conditions are generally poor for all demographic groups throughout the region; nevertheless, Cherokee incomes often fall below those of their white neighbors.[28] While Cherokee communities exist in all areas of the Cherokee Nation, my research primarily focuses on those within the five-county region.

The landscape of the Cherokee Nation TJSA is characterized by lush deciduous forests and rolling hills to the east (coinciding more or less with the five-county area mentioned earlier) and prairie flatlands in the west. Lakes, rivers, streams, and springs abound throughout the area, giving the Cherokee Nation and northeastern Oklahoma an edge in the recreational tourism market. The Illinois River that intersects Cherokee County is known for its meandering pace and scenic vistas, and the numerous resorts and raft rental businesses alongside the adjacent Highway 10 make it a popular summer destination.

The Cherokee Nation tribal government operates under the 1999 Cherokee Nation Constitution, which maintains a tripartite body consisting of executive, legislative, and judicial branches. The executive branch consists of a principal chief, a deputy principal chief, three cabinet positions (secretary of state, treasurer, and secretary of natural resources), an office of attorney general, and an office of marshal. The legislative branch consists of a tribal council of seventeen elected members—fifteen of whom represent the citizens who live within districts of the Cherokee Nation TJSA, as well as two at-large council members who represent citizens that live outside of the nation's boundaries. The judicial branch maintains two primary tribal courts: a Supreme Court and a District Court. The District Court deals with criminal, civil, and juvenile matters within the fourteen-county area, while the Supreme Court attends to cases of appeals and other cases as conferred by statute.

The historic Cherokee Nation courthouse building in downtown Tahlequah still houses the Cherokee Nation judicial offices; however, the rest of the Cherokee Nation governmental and service offices are headquartered just south of town in the W. W. Keeler Tribal Complex. Established in 1979, and named after the Cherokee Nation's first popularly elected principal chief since Oklahoma statehood in 1907, the tribal complex has been described by Sturm (2002, 84) as "a low-slung, angular, brown-brick giant that seems to sprawl across the ground with limbs akimbo. . . . The place is clean, modern, and has an institutional feel, with buzzing fluorescent lights and the click of heeled shoes across linoleum." Sturm's depiction aptly describes the drab architecture and bureaucratic atmosphere of the building.

Cherokee Nation roles outside of government consist of numerous services and management responsibilities, including community services, career services, health (the Cherokee Nation now maintains the W. W. Hastings Memorial Hospital in Tahlequah, formerly operated by the Indian Health Service), education, natural resources, finance, legal, and so on. In all, the Cherokee Nation employs around three thousand individuals, not including those employed by Cherokee Nation enterprises and Cherokee Nation businesses. With such an infrastructure and employee base, the Cherokee Nation's political influence is significant. Its contribution to the state economy through jobs, tribal casino revenues, roads, and other elements of county infrastructure within the TJSA has firmly established its presence in northeastern Oklahoma and has earned it a leading role in local, tribal, and statewide affairs.

Producing Sovereign Landscapes

On a truck ride through a field in rural Adair County, a Cherokee man in his fifties from a nearby community is talking to me about the internal conflicts he often faces as a field worker for the NRD. His job sometimes requires him to administer herbicides to tracts of tribal land that have been leased out for cattle grazing so as to ensure the viability of Bermuda and fescue grasses that are seeded on native prairies to achieve "improved" pastures. Because of this management activity, he has been noticing a decline in many plants that he was raised to value as medicine. We have been driving around looking for one such plant—milkweed (*Asclepias* L.)—for a while now, and as we approach a promising specimen, he points out its discoloration and shriveled shape. Indeed it is the plant we have been looking for, but it has been sprayed and is unfit for medicine. He has been giving this much thought, and he proposes that in lieu of spraying, brush-hogging could accomplish the same goal of clearing fields but without harmful chemicals that render plants unusable. Additionally, certain areas could be left alone to promote the growth of prairie plant medicines. Later I find out that his idea has taken hold and the NRD has begun to phase out its use of herbicides.

On another truck ride through rural Oklahoma, the NRD supervisor and I are discussing the value of the "cultural work" being done within Cherokee Nation departments. In his opinion, the work on ethnobotany is especially important because even though much has been lost or otherwise fallen out of practice, environmental knowledge is an essential aspect of Cherokee identity. He cites the natural cycles that continue to govern the traditional stomp dances, most notably the harvests throughout the year. I ask him about his thoughts on the ethnobotany project in light of his other job responsibilities that consume the majority of his time. He says it's a shame that it's not the other way around; he'd be much happier doing work on ethnobiology than surveying land. "Unfortunately," he says, with a play on words that references the NRD's grazing-lease activities, "[the cultural work] doesn't feed the bull." In other words, the ethnobotany project, although it seeks to contribute to the heart of traditional Cherokee lifeways, is expendable when it comes to meeting the requirements of tribal natural resource management. Nevertheless, throughout my fieldwork I notice that he successfully incorporates "cultural work" (such as regenerating culturally significant plants) into his otherwise "noncultural" field outings, even if it means using personal funds and his own private land.

While the backgrounds of these two Cherokee men are disparate— one a fluent Cherokee speaker raised in a small rural community, the other a non-Cherokee speaker from a suburb of Tulsa—both sense something askew with the way their job requires them to approach the nonhuman world. At first glance, it might appear that resource-based approaches are incommensurable with relationship-based ones—that Cherokees are faced with an unresolvable "Weberian dilemma" (Niezen 2003, 140–41), wherein nature spirituality must be traded in for state bureaucracy. Yet, at closer inspection, we see that rather than a zero-sum game, their approach to this situation is more a balancing act. My companion in Adair County ponders ways to mitigate his conflicting duties and values without invalidating either one. The NRD director pursues his work on Cherokee ethnobotany even if it is lacking in his formal job description. These types of approaches lead to the production of sovereign landscapes—spaces where environmental governance and management take place on indigenous terms and in indigenous ways, however complex and multifaceted they may be. Producing sovereign landscapes involves fashioning modes of environmental governance that are more in line with indigenous traditional values and perspectives toward the nonhuman world while upholding the political structures that support and enable this process.

Environmental production (as opposed to narratives of environmental destruction or construction) concerns the dialectical relationships between conflicting human groups and between those groups and the nonhuman world—relationships that *produce* landscapes. Paul Robbins (2004, 209) writes, "As political ecologists continually emphasize, the environment is not a malleable thing outside of human beings, or a tablet on which to write history, but instead a produced set of relationships that include people, who, more radically, are themselves produced." In other words, "the environment" is formed by a multitude of actors, including humans, soils, weather, institutions, plants, policies, and so on. The key to understanding this process lies in looking at the interplay between them. This entails detailed analyses of bureaucracy and "the state" as much as ecosystems and traditional communities. It also entails breaking down hierarchical chains of explanation in favor of heterarchical networks of relation between actors (Crumley 2003; Robbins 2004, 210–12).[29] As such, this book is a story of environmental production; it is the story of how the Cherokee Nation—as a place, a people, a government, and a large sophisticated bureaucracy—has found itself in a new era of environmental governance, one wherein tribal leaders (both in the government and in the communities) are continually modifying state practices in order to balance resource- and relationship-based ways of operating.

Overview of the Book

The first part of the book lays some necessary groundwork in order to place Cherokee political development and relationships to environment in relevant historical context. In chapter 1, "Before Removal," I explore pre-Removal Cherokee state-building in the late eighteenth century. I highlight how this anticolonial project simultaneously maintained key elements of Cherokee governance ideals and entailed significant trade-offs that impacted Cherokee relationships with nonhumans and with each other.

Chapter 2, "Shaping New Homelands," explains the transference and development of Cherokee environmental knowledge and practices upon forced relocation to lands west of the Mississippi River and thus how Cherokees came to call them home. Through written and oral histories, I sketch the early environment of the Indian Territory as a *human-produced* environment that Cherokees not only inherited from previous indigenous peoples but also sustained by continuing management activities like controlled burning. I also discuss how politics shaped the Cherokee Nation environment, including internal debates over land use, the invasion of the railroad companies in the 1860s, and the devastating Allotment Era of the late nineteenth and early twentieth centuries.

In chapter 3, "The 'Greening' of Oklahoma," I discuss how more recent politics have shaped the Cherokee Nation environment, including fire suppression policies in the 1930s and the development of Oklahoma state tourism. I look in depth at the legacy of the federal allotment policy in relation to the ability of Cherokees to access resources. In this context, I also describe the resurgence of the Cherokee Nation as a political entity and its subsequent development of sophisticated environmental departments. Starting here in the second half of the book, I move into my ethnographic assessment of the challenges of contemporary tribal natural resource management in settler-colonial contexts, including the NRD's negotiation of BIA paternalism and the trials of regulating tribal resource access. I then trace the recent emergence of "cultural forestry" programs in the NRD— including the ethnobotany project that led to the formation of the elders' group—as steps toward implementing relationship-based approaches to Cherokee environmental governance.

Chapter 4, "Indigenous Ethnobotany," describes the significance of ethnobotanical knowledge in Cherokee culture in the present day and the traits of this knowledge in the context of Cherokee medicine. I discuss the significance of ethnobotany as a tribal project and how it represents both a tool for cultural revitalization and an object of critique in the context of settler colonialism and the cultural politics of knowledge. Here the "politics of plants" come to light, and I describe a recent controversy surrounding the distribution of a small informational booklet produced in collaboration with the elders' group in order to illuminate the stakes of knowledge revitalization in the Cherokee Nation.

In chapter 5, "The Spirit of This Land," I discuss current attempts by the Cherokee Nation government to deal with the paradoxes of Cherokee state-building. I describe how Principal Chief Chad Smith's administration made significant attempts to bridge the gap between the central government and Cherokee communities, and the obstacles that arose in the process. Such obstacles were manifested both in the structure of the current Cherokee Nation government and in the process by which the tribal administration sought to carry out its goals. As such, I propose key areas for reform based on past iterations of the Cherokee Nation government, as well as new approaches to *process* based on my experience with the elders' advisory group. Here I emphasize how the relationship-based approach to environmental governance not only entails attentiveness to relationships with the nonhuman world but also entails a focus on interpersonal relationships. Through a discussion of the main themes from the elders' group meetings, I highlight the transformation of certain NRD practices from bureaucratic to community based and the recognition by tribal officials of alternative, traditional sources of knowledge and protocol. I argue that this dialectical process encapsulates a key facet of indigenous state transformation—the opening up of channels of communication that connect community concerns and knowledge to tribal governmental policy.

In the conclusion, I explore the wider implications of this study for global environmental governance and return to a discussion of how political ecology and indigenous studies might be articulated. Throughout the book, I highlight various countermovements that exemplify the dialectics of Cherokee state transformation, or the complex interplay of modes of establishing and maintaining legitimacy. For the Cherokee Nation, state-building has always been a contested process, but it is precisely the engagement of Cherokee communities and community groups that has made the state form successful. Today this engagement is most prominently manifested in the balancing of the resource- and relationship-based approaches to environmental governance. Cherokees have much work ahead of them in this regard due to colonial acts that disrupted Cherokee relationships to the land and led to significant environmental changes. Nonetheless, I hope to demonstrate that in the Cherokee Nation, state structures help create and maintain the political, physical, social, and ideological space for the protection and stewardship of our lands on our own terms and that we all have something to learn by looking closely at this process.

· CHAPTER 1 ·

Before Removal

The Political Ecology of the Early Cherokee State

AN ENDURING CHEROKEE STORY tells of when the animals called councils among themselves to discuss their grievances against the human beings and to determine their methods of retaliation.[1] The people had grown increasingly disrespectful in their wanton killing of nonhumans, from the smallest insect to the swift deer who provided vital sustenance and clothing. The animal councils presented numerous proposals, including an outright war against humans, but found the most effective means of retaliation in the creation of disease. The deer introduced rheumatism into the human experience, crippling hunters who failed to pay respect to the spirits of those they killed. The fish and reptiles released numerous ailments that caused vomiting, loss of appetite, fevers, and ultimately death. As the animal councils devised and inflicted their diseases on the people, the plants took pity and came to the humans' aid. The trees, shrubs, forbs, and grasses offered themselves as medicine to counteract the diseases created by the vengeful animals. In addition to learning the cures, the humans learned to respect the power of the animal world. In order to avoid disease from a vengeful animal spirit, they learned to leave offerings and recite the proper prayers as thanks for the animal giving its life in order for the people to survive. Such is the origin of disease and medicine. To this day, elders say that each plant, no matter how small, has sixteen cures associated with it, even if many of these uses have been forgotten.

Another Cherokee story recounts an ancient priestly society whose unchecked authoritarian rule of the people ultimately cost them their lives. They were known as *Anikutani*.[2] The legend describes how the Cherokees once held in awe this hereditary society of men due to their heightened spiritual abilities. The awe people felt toward the *Anikutani* eventually gave way to fear, and the priests exploited this situation by formulating moral codes in order to maintain social control. However, as time went on, the moral example of the *Anikutani* began to diverge drastically from their teachings. They became arrogant, disrespectful, domineering, and licentious to the degree that their behavior was no longer tolerable by the people. A young warrior who had been wronged by a member of the *Anikutani* led an uprising, and the resulting massacre decimated the entire priesthood (Fogelson 1984).

These two stories provide ethical lessons on proper behavior toward fellow humans and nonhumans alike. Both also offer perspectives on the many realms of governance in Cherokee philosophy. The origin of disease and medicine reminds Cherokees of their responsibility of respect toward nonhumans as *peoples* in their own right, with governing councils that can influence human life in very real—and sometimes dire—ways. The legend of the *Anikutani* is a cautionary tale about the disastrous results of authoritarian rule. The story also teaches by contrasting the form of governance and the behavior of the *Anikutani* with foundational Cherokee ideals of egalitarianism, respect for others, the maintenance of social harmony, and the importance of individual autonomy (see Thomas 1958; Wahrhaftig 1975a, 1979; Fogelson 1984; Cooter and Thomas 1998). As Raymond D. Fogelson (1984, 260) writes, the story of the *Anikutani* highlights "the conflicting tension between tendencies toward hierarchy and movements toward egalitarianism." As we will see, the relational tensions represented in the stories of the *Anikutani* and the origin of disease and medicine surface at key moments throughout history and illuminate the struggle within Cherokee society to codify proper relationships with one another and with the nonhuman world amid profound social, cultural, and environmental change.

In their study of English state formation, Philip Corrigan and Derek Sayer (1985, 1–2) write that the process entailed reconfiguring "the way the world was made sense of." The period of 1790–1830 certainly entailed a similar experience for the Cherokees, but obvious differences exist that set this history apart and demand new approaches to the study of state formation. For one, in their efforts at state-building, Cherokees were resisting colonialism. The primary purpose of Cherokee state-building was to protect Cherokee people, lands, and sovereignty in direct response to the violent birth of the United States. This act in itself produced a unique Cherokee articulation of the state form, and thus, from its very origin, I speak of Cherokee state *transformation*. In other words, I argue that from its inception as an anticolonial political instrument, the Cherokee state has been a transformative project. I do so while attempting not to overshadow how key elements of Cherokee governance were decentered as a result of this project. Cherokee relationships to land and nonhumans were central to traditional understandings of their place in the world. Thus, in looking at the extent to which state-building reconfigured the way Cherokees made sense of the world, we must ask, how did this process alter people's relationships with land and nonhumans, as well as with each other? Similarly, how did environmental changes influence their development of state forms?

As such, this chapter discusses early Cherokee state transformation with a focus on both social and environmental change. Amid the backdrop of colonial forces—encroachment, war, disease, and new markets—I suggest that Cherokee state transformation and changes in relationships to the environment coconstituted each other. But even while the Cherokee way of life was in extreme flux, the voices and actions of Cherokee people in response show how this process was mediated and influenced in profound ways. Movements of resistance, led by individuals who feared the repercussions of radical change and advocated for traditionalist perspectives, created spaces of dialogue about state transformation and thus set in motion a dialectic between state-building and traditional ideals of governance. This illuminates how indigenous state transformation has been a journey rather than a destination, constantly in flux and undergoing modification.

Political Disunity and Early Attempts at Centralization

The original extent of the Cherokee homelands spans five ecoregions in the southeast, including the mountainous Central and Southwestern Appalachians, Blue Ridge, and Ridge and Valley regions, as well as the hilly Piedmont region. The regions include three ecosystem provinces: the Eastern Broadleaf Forest (Oceanic) Province, the Central Appalachian Broadleaf Forest / Coniferous Forest / Meadow Province, and the Southeastern Mixed Forest Province. This wide-ranging area—encompassing large parts of what are now the states of Kentucky, West Virginia, Virginia, North Carolina, South Carolina, Georgia, Alabama, and Tennessee—is characterized by mixed oak/pine woodlands in the lower elevations; hardwood forests of birch, beech, maple, elm, red oak, and basswood (with some hemlock and white pine) in the middle elevations; and spruce/fir forests and meadows found on the highest peaks (up to 6,684 feet) of the Allegheny and Great Smoky Mountains. Precipitation is abundant, averaging 40–60 inches per year, and the climate is temperate, with four distinct seasons. Overall, the Cherokee homelands are lush, with plentiful over- and understory plant species and a variety of typical North American fauna (Bailey 1995).

During the early eighteenth century, roughly sixty confederated villages made up Cherokee society, each having a population between 350 and 600 people (Gearing 1962, 3). Villages consisted of a central council house surrounded by clustered homesteads and were almost always oriented around prominent waterways that supported physical and spiritual sustenance. Village-based communal fields of corn and smaller gardens of corn, beans, and squash provided the staples of the village diet, while the surrounding lands supported hunting and gathering of wild game, berries, nuts, fruits, medicines, and other materials.[3]

The political structure of each autonomous village was a dual system made up of a "White" organization and a "Red" organization. Functioning independently of one another, but not simultaneously, these two "structural poses" defined the political organization of a Cherokee village "at a particular moment for a particular purpose" (Gearing 1962, 15).[4] The White political organization was the most common structural pose and governed domestic affairs in times of peace. The structure consisted of a hierarchy of peace officials and a council of town elders (including "beloved" men and women) who made decisions through consensus and embodied "quiet diplomacy" (Fogelson 1971, 328). The Red political organization, made up of younger warriors (mostly men), was given decision-making authority in times of war and mainly dealt with affairs outside the village, such as hunting and commerce with other villages, tribes, or Europeans. Red officials led through more assertive means, using inspiration and charisma to gain followings. Operating throughout the village political structure was the matrilineal clan system. The seven clans played a major part in village governance to the extent that it was "necessary to have local representatives of all clans in each village in order to conduct major civic and religious activities" (ibid.).[5] Thus Cherokee society at this time consisted of a network of autonomous villages with decentralized local governments connected to each other through a shared sacred history and ceremonial cycle, a common language (although there were four major dialects), a corporate territory, and clan/marriage relationships.

Toward the mid-eighteenth century, the increasing encroachment of European settlers disrupted the village-organized system. Whereas before each of the four major regions of Cherokee towns (the Overhill, Valley, Middle, and Lower settlements) dealt with external affairs on the level of a single village or a small alliance of villages, colonial governments operating with an entirely different political structure began holding Cherokee villages responsible for the corporate whole of the "Cherokee tribe." As Fred O. Gearing (1961, 131) states, with reference to the new Colony of South Carolina,

If a [European] trader were killed in Echota, the cornfields of Tugalo might be burnt.[6] More hurtful still, trade to all the village might be cut off leaving Cherokee without ammunition and vulnerable to enemy tribes on the south, west, and north. By the early 1750's Cherokee had recurrently experienced such reprisals, and with increasing frequency. Their first moves toward statehood were explicitly in response to this new fact: Persons in any village had no control over the behavior of other villages, and yet could be made to suffer because of that behavior.

The tendency of colonial governments to assign corporate responsibility to individual Cherokee villages was based on the authoritarian rule and state structure of European countries. Prominent male leaders in single Cherokee villages were often perceived as "chiefs" who spoke for all Cherokees. As the cessation of lands by these "chiefs" became an increasingly common act, Cherokees across villages began to debate the prospect of political centralization. As Gearing (1962, 109) states, "Cherokee villages began their career toward statehood under conditions of external duress; the recognized choice was statehood or pain."[7]

The process of centralization was not without complications. Creating a singular government that represented nearly sixty formerly autonomous towns proved to be a delicate procedure. The first approach to this situation by the Cherokees was to "elevate their least coercive and most sensitive persons into the positions of greatest influence" (132). Thus former "White" officials assumed positions of leadership as a central council and occupied the village of Echota—the first capital of the young Cherokee state (89). Yet despite the intent to govern through quiet diplomacy, the reality was that this form of governance did not possess the necessary coercive sanctions in order to maintain a unified stance against colonial forces. Cherokee/Osage scholar Rennard Strickland (1975, 5) notes, "The central problem faced by the Cherokee people during this period was resistance to white advancement through merging into a national state from highly individualized Indian towns under separate and often extremely jealous village leaders." Further, the most immediate need for centralization was to control the widespread raids on settlers by young Cherokee men. These raids were escalating, as was the retaliation by settlers without discriminating between "friendly" and "hostile" Cherokee villages. The response was to turn to the former "Red" leaders for a solution. In the 1760s, such leaders moved into positions of power and enforced tribal policy through coercive force. Gearing (1961, 133) notes the birth of jails in the Cherokee Nation during this time.

The Red leaders did not offer many solutions to internal conflicts among the Cherokees. Although fiercely nationalistic, the young warriors had "thrown the political structure away," and Cherokee governance had slipped into "virtual anarchy" (Gearing 1962, 104). A tribal schism was created in 1775 by the sale of Cherokee lands that make up the present-day state of Kentucky. The White chiefs had approved this sale, yet the Red chiefs vehemently opposed it. The White chiefs reacted by once again regaining control over Cherokee affairs; however, because of a severe lack of organization, the attempt soon failed, and the Cherokee "priest state" was never realized again. The schism between the young warriors and the elder priests became solidified in the breaking off of Chief Dragging Canoe's band of warriors called the Chickamauga Cherokees. The Chickamaugas continued to inhabit the Kentucky territory and to make raids against encroaching whites. The retaliation from colonial forces resulted in catastrophic destruction of Cherokee villages throughout Cherokee territory. Thus the 1760s to the 1780s were characterized by chaos and disorder (102–4). Cherokee historical demographer Russell Thornton (1990, 30) notes that the Cherokee population decreased significantly during this time. Struck hard by disease and brutal warfare, including the French and Indian War (1760–61) and multiple smallpox epidemics, Cherokees numbered eight to twelve thousand—the lowest population on record.

Cherokee political relations with a newborn American state added to the chaos and disorder during this time. The Chickamaugas had fought alongside British Loyalists during the Revolutionary War, and there were, once again, major ramifications for all Cherokees. The backlash from colonial frontiersmen consisted of continued raids on Cherokee villages as well as forced land cessions in 1783–84 (Gearing 1962, 21). To prevent further atrocities and establish order, the federal Continental Congress managed to convince the new states that it should have the sole authority to deal with Indian affairs. In 1785, Cherokee representatives signed the Treaty of Hopewell, marking the first national treaty between the Cherokees and the United States. In this document, the Cherokees made considerable concessions with the hopes of obtaining peace. For one, they recognized that they were, according to the treaty, "under the protection of the United States." They also acknowledged the role of the federal government to regulate trade and manage such affairs with Indian nations as it saw fit. However, the treaty is significant in that it established Cherokee territorial boundaries and gave Cherokees permission to expel whites settled within those boundaries. Thus, to the Cherokees, the establishment of territorial sovereignty was worth a cession of some political sovereignty. Unfortunately, the states saw this treaty in a very different light—they considered it to eliminate Cherokee sovereignty altogether. Further, the Cherokees had not realized how weak the federal government was at this time in its ability to prohibit the encroachment of white settlers (Gearing 1962, 22). Regardless, although encroachment and fighting continued, the treaty had established Cherokee borders, recognized Cherokee self-government and nationhood, and, for all intents and purposes, "agreed to protect what was left of Cherokee territory" (21).

In 1792, the Chickamauga resistance was weakened with the death of Chief Dragging Canoe. Shortly after, in 1794, Colonel James Ore of the new state of Tennessee defeated the Chickamauga Band. Around this time, many of Dragging Canoe's followers, along with an ultraconservative faction that no longer wished to live in proximity to whites, began to move west of the Mississippi River into Arkansas territory (McLoughlin 1986, 163, n. 37).

Changing Landscapes and the Move toward Statehood

By the early 1780s, Cherokees were experiencing intense changes to their way of life. New markets, such as the lucrative deerskin trade, combined with warfare, disease, and encroachment, had severely compromised Cherokee land ethics. The breakdown of community checks and balances that had once governed hunting practices led to the drastic depletion of deer in the southeast; the warnings of the old stories gave way to the political economy of settler-colonial turmoil. The act of hunting itself was changing, as the prevalence of guns made hunting less of a communal endeavor than before (Goodwin 1977, 142). Increasingly, due to the depletion of game, settler encroachment on the hunting grounds, and "civilizing" programs that stressed nuclear families and domestic production, Cherokees began to move into a lifestyle of subsistence farming and animal husbandry (McLoughlin 1986, 25–30). This shift from hunting and communal agriculture to a more sedentary agrarian lifestyle, in turn, affected the Cherokee village structure. Although Cherokees still associated themselves with "towns" that in many ways preserved the continuity of old village sites, individual, dispersed homesteads and farms replaced the clustered and communal formations. Cherokee dwellings also changed during this time from bark-sided huts to log cabins (Goodwin 1977, 114).

The change in village organization and communal agricultural production gravely impacted Cherokee ceremonial life. The ceremonial cycle that previously defined and divided village life into six distinct periods throughout the year was reduced to an annual Green Corn Festival. As this social reorganization decentered the earth-based spirituality that had overtly governed Cherokee life, it also dispersed the medicine people who retained this knowledge (Fogelson 1984, 260; McLoughlin 1986, 15–18). Further, the practice of Cherokee medicine had suffered some loss of esteem after 1740 due to the ineffectiveness of healers when confronted with smallpox epidemics. Although Cherokee healers continued to practice traditional medicine, Gearing (1961, 104) notes that the informants of the nineteenth century anthropologist James Mooney "pointed to [the 1780s] as the time when the last great medicine men (read: priests) died."

The Cherokee landscape was also changing significantly during this time. The reduction of seasonal controlled burns, in addition to increased land clearings to enable plantation-style farms and roads, led to changes in soil and plant composition (Goodwin 1977, 150). By about 1760, the large animals of the southeast were decreasing in numbers or disappearing altogether, including deer, wolf, bison, elk, panther, and bear (132). Of these large animals, the deer, wolf, panther, and bear served as clan totems, which connected Cherokees to them as animal teachers and relatives. Thus it is not surprising that as these animals decreased in numbers, and as village structure underwent radical change, the influence of the clan system waned as an overt component of governance. Cherokees gradually adopted new large animal species: the horse, pig, and cow—all of which accompanied their shift to agrarian ways of life.

In tandem with a changing environment and changing social relations instigated by settler colonialism, Cherokees began their development of state structures. At the turn of the nineteenth century, Cherokees again attempted centralization, this time experimenting with U.S. models of government. A loose group of village headmen had evolved into a deliberative central council with a principal chief and a second principal chief (Strickland 1975, 56–57). Although still strongly representing a system of village autonomy, this council was charged with the task of creating and enforcing national laws to control disputes among all Cherokees. A council meeting was held in 1797, and national laws were declared against horse thievery (a major source of disputes between young Cherokee males and settlers) and retaliation against accidental murders (which prohibited the blood law, wherein a member of the murderer's clan was killed for the offense). At the same meeting, the council established an ad hoc law enforcement agency (McLoughlin 1986, 56).

In 1808, this council became the formalized Chiefs and Warriors in National Council Assembled. At this time, the first written law of the Cherokee Nation was enacted, which permanently established a national police force (dubbed the Lighthorse Patrol) and completely abolished the blood law (Strickland 1975, 58). During the following council meeting in 1809, the National Council created the National Committee—a mechanism to relieve the overburdened council (McLoughlin 1986, 157). The National Committee comprised thirteen members to be elected by the chiefs of council. Responsibilities of the committee members included more bureaucratic tasks, such as managing the national treasury, dealing with the local Indian agency daily, and settling minor disputes and business matters. More important, the committee served as "a permanent, representative authority responsible and available at all times to oversee the general welfare." The committee met throughout the year, whereas the council had only one annual meeting. Its tasks also included setting the agenda for council meetings by condensing the issues for discussion, as well as setting policies and priorities. All the actions of the committee were subject to annual ratification by the council (ibid.).

The emergence of the National Committee sparked a change in Cherokee political ideology. As an organized and central governmental entity, the committee was able to effectively stave off further land

cessions that had been the result of disorganized and easily influenced regional chiefs. The emphasis among both the council and the
committee on retaining tribal lands, along with the creation of a successful centralized system of government, resulted in a stronger sense
of national unity. Cherokees displayed solidarity in the face of ongoing attempts by Indian agents and the federal government to divide and
conquer. One of these attempts, instigated by the Indian agent Return
J. Meigs, was to convince more Cherokees to leave the homelands and
settle west of the Mississippi in exchange for monetary compensation.
The majority of Cherokees held their ground, believing that survival
meant remaining as a nation on the land of their ancestors. Only a small
amount of Cherokees took this offer, and the council responded by
declaring them "expatriates" whose citizenship in the Cherokee Nation
was no longer recognized. Thus the Cherokee Nation "was not simply
a people; it was a place" (McLoughlin 1986, 163). The Cherokee "peoplehood" that consisted of a shared sacred history, ceremonial cycle,
language, and territory (Holm et al. 2003) was becoming secondary to
Cherokee "nationhood," which focused on citizenship, loyalty to the
National Council, and residence within defined borders. Cherokees saw
nationhood as a necessary measure for political survival.

During this time, it is notable that a small group of "mixed bloods" were
becoming heavily involved in Cherokee politics. Children of European
and Cherokee heritage had more access to formal European-style education and were encouraged by their families to pursue this goal. Yet, instead
of producing individuals completely assimilated to Euro-American ways,
this process produced fiercely patriotic Cherokee nationalists like John
Ross, John Ridge, and Elias Boudinot. Armed with an acute knowledge
of the Euro-American legal and political process, individuals like them
played a major role in the resurgence of the Cherokee Nation. In 1817,
John Ross, the son of a white trader and a Cherokee mother, became the
president of the National Committee. The National Council meeting that
year brought forth some major changes in the Cherokee political structure, codified in a political reform act. For one, the National Committee
was redefined as the "upper" house of the Cherokee government, which
maintained its bureaucratic duties but was also given the ability to draft
resolutions and acts (although the council reserved final veto power).
Significantly, the council meeting had also produced an unwritten understanding that the committee would comprise mainly educated persons of

mixed ancestry who could read and write English. The council, however, would remain representative of the "full-blood" majority of the nation (McLoughlin 1986, 224–25).

Other significant facets of the political reform act of 1817 were the formal affirmation of Cherokee emigrants to Arkansas as expatriates and the reassertion of traditional matrilineal property rights. The former was in response to the Treaty of 1817, signed by yet another group of Cherokees (this time numbering four thousand and known as the "Old Settlers") who ceded land in Tennessee and moved west to Arkansas. The latter secured the rights of women to land in the case that their husbands moved west and the U.S. government claimed that property in return for Arkansas lands. In this provision, husbands could not "dispose of" their wives' property (McLoughlin 1986, 225). The reform act was a strong step forward in institutionalizing Cherokee nationhood, and it represented another move toward secular governance. Whereas the old religion and the roles of the medicine people (i.e., priests) were not obsolete, it was clear that the religious laws had taken a backseat to the new national political order. McLoughlin aptly notes that this move freed the religious institutions from the responsibility of dealing with the new political and economic problems facing the Cherokee people (226).

In 1820, a resolution passed by the National Committee and Council established a judicial branch of the Cherokee government. According to Strickland (1975, 63), the National Committee had been serving as the executive, legislative, and judicial body since 1817, and the resolution sought to relieve some of these responsibilities. This resolution modeled the judiciary branch after the Euro-American version. It consisted of four circuit courts and eight district courts, with additional positions created for marshals, light-horsemen, and rangers (64). A supreme court of the Cherokee Nation was established in 1823, and in 1827, a full Cherokee constitution was adopted, which created three branches of government (executive, legislative, judicial), with a bicameral legislature (the National Committee and Council). Although much of the language was modeled on the U.S. version, its most significant divergence was that it declared all lands within Cherokee Nation common property of the nation. This statement not only defined the territorial aspect of Cherokee sovereignty but also reinforced the idea that land belonged to the nation as a whole, and no individual could sell or cede any portion of it. The Cherokee Nation now had its constitution and government, and this presented a considerable obstacle to neighboring state governments, who were reluctant to recognize any form of Cherokee sovereignty.

Over the next ten years, the Cherokee Nation used its sophisticated political apparatus to fight antagonistic and encroaching states and their citizens in the U.S. courts. The state of Georgia proved to be the most hostile in its pursuit of Cherokee lands, and the legal battle between it and the Cherokee Nation is well documented in the Supreme Court cases *Cherokee Nation v. Georgia* (1831) and *Worcester v. Georgia* (1832). Initially, the Cherokee Nation was successful in its appeal to the U.S. courts, and Chief Justice Marshall declared legal victory for the Cherokees in *Worcester v. Georgia*: "The Cherokee Nation . . . is a distinct community, occupying its own territory, with boundaries accurately described, in which the laws of Georgia can have no force, and which the citizens of Georgia have no right to enter, but with the assent of the Cherokees themselves, or in conformity with treaties, and with the acts of Congress" (31 U.S. [6 Pet.] 515).

However, it is often recounted that President Andrew Jackson, a strong supporter of states' rights and Indian removal, purportedly said, "Marshall has made his decision, now let him enforce it."[8] Further, another schism had run throughout Cherokee politics during this time regarding removal. Many individuals who had participated in the Cherokee renaissance, such as John Ridge, his father Major Ridge, and Elias Boudinot, made up what came to be known as the Treaty Party. This faction was in favor of voluntary removal to the Indian Territory on account of the hardships that many Cherokees had been suffering due to encroaching whites. They viewed removal as an inevitable outcome and wished to negotiate its terms with the federal government. The opposing faction, who represented by far the majority opinion of the nation, came to be known as the Ross Party—spearheaded by John Ross, who had been principal chief since 1828. This faction adamantly opposed removal from the ancestral homelands, insisting on the moral and legal obligations of the federal government to honor its agreements and respect Cherokee Nation sovereignty. Yet, contrary to the original purpose of centralization, the Treaty Party, consisting of only a small group of men, fraudulently claimed to represent the Cherokee Nation by signing the Treaty of New Echota in 1835—a capital offense for which they would later pay their lives. With Andrew Jackson as president and the Treaty of New Echota ratified, the Cherokee Nation had little recourse. The Cherokee political structures that had been developed to mimic and stave off colonizers on their own terms ultimately could not win over colonial force and legislative fiat. The result was the infamous Trail of Tears in the winter of 1838, which decimated the tribal population to one-third of its original size.

Dialectics of Early Cherokee State Transformation

The purposes of Cherokee centralization and state transformation, although the specifics varied over time, were couched in the resistance to colonialism. National unification, the retention of the tribal land base, and an institutional memory of treaties and agreements with the colonizers were all reasons for the development of a Cherokee nation-state. As McLoughlin (1986, 278) states, Cherokees needed to "confront power with power." To be sure, there were limits to the success of this process. Although in many cases centralization had been accomplished by melding Euro-American models with Cherokee ones, the tendency of Cherokee leaders to replicate the Euro-American models grew in light of increasing colonial pressures. As Cherokee political structures began to differ progressively from traditional forms, internal social conflicts surfaced. McLoughlin notes, "Some began to ask how the [Cherokee] country was being preserved when it was daily changed to conform to white patterns. . . . [I]n order to survive as red men, they were told to become more and more like white men" (289). He highlights the difficulty of reconciling two competing systems of thought:

> The laws were Cherokee versions of white political structures. They created a professional bureaucracy for administration and record keeping. The General Council tried hard to reconcile old communal patterns and nomenclature (chiefs, council, speaker) with new structures. Behind the restructured system lay a new individualistic, competitive, acquisitive system of values that was almost impossible to reconcile with the tradition of harmony and cooperation. The Cherokees wished to demonstrate that they could govern themselves in an orderly, democratic, efficient manner while providing civil liberty for the individual. In the new market economy that generated the nation's prosperity, the political structure was designed to protect property and contractual rights with which the older generation and town councils were not familiar and could not deal adequately. (287)

Further, by 1825, agrarian capitalism had begun to exacerbate class divisions among Cherokees (301). A wealthy class of plantation owners had developed among the nation, many of whom owned slaves. Not surprisingly, federal actors both encouraged and condemned this development—yet another attempt at divide and conquer. When the wealthy plantation class had reached a point of prosperity that rivaled their white counterparts, federal agents began to launch criticisms that aimed to position the wealthy class as exploiting the poor "full bloods," who were the "real Indians" (402). Even though economic success was not solely determined on racial composition (Major Ridge, an individual of high blood "quantum" and a fluent Cherokee speaker, was a successful plantation farmer and slave owner), many outsiders were quick to make rash connections between skin color and social differentiation. Missionaries, who had become prevalent in the Cherokee Nation by this time, helped create this interracial ill will (363).

While class formation and the pressures of capitalist incorporation posed significant challenges to Cherokee society—including the elite practice of slavery and the push toward patriarchy—traditionalist countermovements throughout this period show how the less well-to-do population (still very much the majority) continued to nurture foundational Cherokee values and traditions and thus exerted significant influence on Cherokee state-building. Cherokee women were especially vulnerable to the development of state structures, which supported patriarchal systems like agrarian capitalism. Yet, although the Cherokee state signaled the ascendancy of patriarchy (most notably in that women were prohibited from voting and holding political office), Theda Perdue (1998) has shown that Cherokee women were not necessarily rendered powerless as a result. She writes, "The growing involvement of men in the world beyond may, in fact, have enhanced the power of women within Cherokee society" (10). This was no accident, as Cherokee women performed numerous acts of resistance in the course of state transformation. During 1811–13, Cherokee women spearheaded a cultural revitalization movement that called for the return to traditional agricultural practices.[9] The women invoked *Selu*, the Corn Mother of the Cherokee knowledge-belief system, dubbing her the "Mother of the Nation" and declaring that she "'was calling them back to a simpler form of agricultural life' when women engaged in communal farming and the production of most of the subsistence needs of families" (Dunaway 1997, 174). Wilma Dunaway discusses how this movement restored the annual Green Corn Ceremony that had fallen out of observance and called for the revitalization of traditional plant-based healing practices (175). Women also employed everyday acts of resistance that entailed the continued assertion of control over institutions and practices they had traditionally overseen, such as the matrilineal clan system, land stewardship, and household agricultural production.

A subsequent women's resistance movement between 1820 and 1828 was in response to increasing missionary activity that directly undermined women's status and power in Cherokee society. Christian missionaries had begun to influence greatly the National Council, and as a result, many of the new written laws further diminished the already weakening traditional authority of matrilineal clans. Missionaries were also adamantly opposed to plant-based and ritualistic healing (referred to as "conjuring"), which had significantly become a realm of women: Midwives and medicine women made up more than half of Cherokee traditional healers by the 1820s (177). Cherokee women responded to these affronts by reinvigorating the grassroots power of Cherokee "towns" (read: community organizing) and by nonviolent demonstrations and protests to shame and/or heckle missionaries in their attempts to condemn traditional practices (177–79). The momentum gained by this extended antimissionary women's movement led to what became known as White Path's rebellion in 1827–28.

Missionary presence and dogma was compounded by the rise to prominence of many Cherokee Christians in tribal politics, which had directly informed the resistances of the 1820s by many Cherokee women and their traditionalist allies. One such case was that of White Path, an old respected chief who was expelled from the National Council in 1825 for allegedly opposing too strenuously the rapid changes in Cherokee politics. Elijah Hicks, a Christian, replaced him. With the support of prominent medicine women and other traditionalists, White Path reacted by leading a rebellion against the Cherokee constitutional convention for the sake of bolstering the old Cherokee way of life. The movement was nonviolent and was carried out by employing the traditional Cherokee method of withdrawal to express disagreement and protestation. White Path was mainly concerned with the limits of acculturation—how far was too far? Many Cherokees, including both traditionalists and sympathetic Christians, "mixed bloods" and "full bloods," got behind White Path in order to raise important questions concerning the future of the Cherokee Nation (McLoughlin 1986, 388–402).

The rebellion took form in extralegal councils and speeches held at the town of Ellijay, close to White Path's home settlement. To White Path, the Cherokee Nation was on the cusp of abandoning all forms of traditional governance in favor of top-down aristocratic rule. Moreover, the aristocracy that had developed not only seemed to foster the adoption of Euro-American values and customs but also seemed indifferent and even ashamed of Cherokee traditions (390). The balance that had characterized Cherokee political and cultural change in the recent past was being upset. The Cherokee legal government heard this message, and shortly thereafter, both parties agreed to a meeting. Free from federal intervention (both parties desired to keep outsiders unaware of this matter), the factions hashed out their differences and ultimately agreed to promote harmony between themselves in the interest of national unity. In a written agreement, White Path's party consented to seek reform within the Cherokee Nation legal system (395).

Because there are no minutes of this meeting, many unknowns remain. What is apparent is that not all the dissenters were on board with this agreement. Notably, White Path himself did not sign the written document. What is known is that the Cherokee Nation was under extreme pressure to move from the homelands, and the majority of White Path's contingency were opposed to this idea. One could deduce from this situation that some frank conversations were had with the rebels with regard to projecting an appearance of national unity so as to fight removal by any means necessary. It is also significant that after these deliberations the constitution was drastically modified from its original Christianity-laden form to include more suitable language that respected Cherokee traditions and religion (396).

Regardless, the end of White Path's rebellion signified neither the full compliance of traditionalists with the state of Cherokee politics nor the cooptation of traditionalist leaders by the legal government. The continued influence and power of such leaders was evident in their majority in the council and in the national population (363, 404, 441). The reality was a matter of this population making concessions for the sake of outward appearance—an appearance of unity and "civilization." Most Cherokees accepted the new constitution as one such outward projection: It was an "ideological statement to head off the vigorous efforts to remove them or take their land" (401). Whereas to some it may have conveyed another step toward acculturation, in effect it did not significantly alter established practice. In fact, traditionalists had begun to get behind their regular system of government as a tool to prevent further divisions (406). When John Ross was elected principal chief in 1828, it marked the first time a "learned" person had occupied this position. Previously, the Cherokee Nation had been represented in this manner by non-English-speaking traditionalists. As the new "face" of the Cherokee Nation, Ross would soon lead the Cherokee resistance to removal, with the backing of "virtually all of the elected chiefs and local headmen [i.e., traditionalists and elders]" (437).

Conclusion

Settler-colonial forces of encroachment, disease, warfare, and agrarian capitalism led to profound social and environmental changes for the Cherokees. These changes prompted adaptations, such as political centralization and the reorganization of village structure and governance, which combined to facilitate Cherokee state transformation. This political innovation created a protective barrier for the Cherokee Nation and served as a formidable vehicle for resistance against settler colonialism. But the process was incredibly nuanced and multidimensional—it was internally contested and deliberated, and this entailed debate and compromise. As such, the result was not perfect. There were trade-offs.

To many historians, this period marks the end of traditionalism in Cherokee politics. The Cherokee ceremonial cycle that emphasized the continual maintenance of relationships to land, nonhumans, and each other ceased its overt influence on Cherokee governance. Gearing (1962, 103) reports that after the 1780s, councils no longer opened their meetings with prayer, thus secularizing what had once been an inherently spiritual aspect of Cherokee life. In her discussion of the impact that the abolishment of the blood law had on Cherokee society, Perdue (1998, 142–43) writes, "The Cherokee government, rather than a Cherokee's family, now assumed responsibility for punishing murder and, by implication, for protecting a person's life. . . . [A] most sacred duty had passed from the matrilineal clan, an extended kin group that included women and conveyed membership through women, to the exclusively male council." Cherokee state-building had effectively decentered the relationships that had once made up the foundation of Cherokee governance.

But while this may be true, and while we should consider this a huge blow to how Cherokees made sense of the world, the Cherokee state had, in the words of Patrick Wolfe (2011, 23, 40), "staked a claim on the future," and by doing so, it had directly confronted settler colonialism's "logic of elimination." No doubt, this constituted an "x-mark," in Scott Richard Lyons's (2010, 20) sense. Furthermore, through asserting dialectical tension on state-building, Cherokee revitalization and resistance movements maintained key elements of traditional ideals in Cherokee governance. The structure allowed for the persistence of cultural forms like town autonomy, the role of elders in governance, and the authority of women and the matrilineal clan system in local domestic affairs.

Under the pressure of removal, Cherokee leaders had, to a degree, solidified their roles in the Cherokee Nation government. Traditionalists mainly served in the National Council, overseeing internal community affairs and advising the committee from this grounded perspective. Formally educated individuals were needed in the National Committee to oversee bureaucratic affairs and to guide the nation's policy with colonial powers. While the National Committee tended to be made up of a Christian-oriented elite minority, they served the entire Cherokee people, the majority of whom were represented in the National Council. It was a system developed under colonial pressures in order to deal with two very different views of the world. Nevertheless, it was a system that saw the value in synthesizing these views in certain areas in order to play the colonizer's game while contesting its terms. In the case that leaders (both in the council and in the committee) moved too far away from a foundational body of beliefs and ethics, there were community sanctions (e.g., community organizing and rebellion by withdrawal) that created dialogue and led to reconciliation. The development of Euro-American-style political structures was a dialectical process that involved engaging with these forms while always viewing them against the backdrop of culture and tradition.[10]

William Cronon (1983, 164), writing of indigenous peoples' responses to changing social and physical landscapes during early colonial times in New England, states, "By ceasing to live as their ancestors had done, they did not cease to be Indians, but became Indians with very different relationships to the ecosystems in which they lived." The same holds true for Cherokees. New perspectives on the world emerged that were influenced by settler-colonial forces and European presence, but the Cherokee worldview did not necessarily change or disappear. Rather, it went underground, maintained by traditionalists and spiritual leaders. This worldview—the relationship-based approach to governance—surfaces throughout history in response to radical social change and exerts its force on governmental leaders.

One significant element of this worldview, however, remained overt and palpable: communal ownership of the land. The fundamental principle of land as inalienable, to which the nation possessed common title, undergirded Cherokee state-building and represented an outward projection of traditional values. Perdue (1998, 155) asserts, "The Cherokee national government's commitment to the preservation of common title to realty was perhaps the most important way that the early Cherokee republic embodied a feminine ethic in its legal code." Laura E. Donaldson (2010, 50–53) extends this interpretation to say that land dispossession, by way of its ability to strip away the domain of women's authority and sever relationships with nurturing *Elohi* (Earth), was in fact considered an act of matricide. Upholding common title to land, in turn, symbolically and literally upheld Cherokee women's status and rights. Furthermore, national common property was an impediment to market forces. Private property had become a central feature of nascent free market capitalism, and the restrictions on this institution by the National Council represented a significant resistance to full capitalist incorporation.

By the time of Removal, Cherokees had formed a new type of relationship with the land. While they always knew where their territory was in relation to other indigenous nations, the need to formally demarcate it with fixed, mapped, precise lines arose in response to drastic circumstances brought on by settler colonialism. This state–territorial relationship carried over to the lands west of the Mississippi in the Indian Territory. But to Cherokees, land continued to be more than just territory. Thus, while those who travelled along the Trail of Tears entered the western lands as an already mapped space, their political relationship to the land was accompanied by the need to develop additional and more intimate connections to a new place.

CHAPTER 2

Shaping New Homelands

Landscapes of Removal and Renewal

STORIES OF ENVIRONMENTAL CHANGE—whether implicitly or explicitly—
are often stories of changes in human interaction with the environment.
Significant accounts of environmental change in recent history have
involved competition between differing ideals of the human relationship with the nonhuman world (e.g., Cronon 1983; Merchant 1989). This
chapter tells the story of how Cherokees developed relationships to new
lands in the west after Removal (circa 1839–61) and how colonial interference by non-Indian intruders and the U.S. government influenced
and disrupted these relationships during the Civil War and Allotment
Era (circa 1861–1914). I discuss this process in terms of both "cultural
landscapes," or how a culture group imbues the landscape with meaning, and "normative landscapes," or how a group views the landscape in
terms of its utilitarian and aesthetic value. In this light, I describe how
Cherokee relationships to the new lands assumed material, spiritual,
and political forms and how these relationships shaped the land in distinct ways.

Drawing on their extensive work with American Indian communities in the U.S. Great Basin, anthropologists Richard Stoffle, Rebecca
Toupal, and M. Nieves Zedeño (2003, 99) write, "The concept of cultural landscape derives from the notion that the land exists in the mind of
a people and that their imagery or knowledge of the land is both shared
among them and transferred over generations." The term is useful for
explaining how people develop connections to certain places or landscapes through material and spiritual experiences to the point where
land and identity become intertwined. Cultural landscape also suggests that the development of environmental knowledge plays a large
role in establishing intimate connections to place. In the first part of
this chapter, I discuss how the rolling hills in the eastern part of western

Cherokee lands (presently northeastern Oklahoma) have inscribed themselves on Cherokees, due to both their topographical familiarity to the southeastern homelands and the historical and spiritual events that have taken place there. Additionally, I discuss how the transference, adaptation, acquisition, and development of environmental knowledge in the western lands have all served to imprint a Cherokee identity onto the land.

The concept of normative landscape, as Lynn Huntsinger and Sarah McCaffrey assert, describes how people biologically manipulate lands and natural resources in order to produce specific goods and services (Huntsinger and McCaffrey 1995, 157).[1] The clashing of two or more normative landscapes in the context of unequal relations of power (e.g., colonialism) often leads to profound ecological change. In the second part of this chapter, I explore ethnohistorical descriptions of the environment so as to understand how Cherokees viewed, used, and manipulated the early Indian Territory landscape in aesthetic and pragmatic ways. Cherokees readily shaped the new land through customs, laws, agriculture, and especially fire. The reestablishment of the Cherokee state in the Indian Territory continued to uphold the system of communal land ownership, and the relational values that underpinned this system served to define Cherokee environmental governance during this time.

In the aftermath of the U.S. Civil War, Cherokee resource control decreased progressively. The railroad and timber economies of the Industrial Revolution infiltrated Cherokee lands and created significant environmental changes. In the midst of these changes, the federal allotment policy drastically altered the Cherokee land tenure system, thus altering the entire nation's relationship to its territory.

Nevertheless, Cherokee resistance applied continual counterpressure on what amounted to fractured and incoherent (even if ultimately enacted) settler-colonial projects. This counterpressure exerted its own influence on the environment, once again invoking environmental *production* as an ongoing process of making and remaking landscapes, dictated by both human and nonhuman forces and shaped by the ever-present roles of power, politics, and time. Examining the history of Cherokee environmental production in the Indian Territory illuminates the various and changing norms and expectations with regard to natural resources, as well as the backdrop of colonialism that Cherokees continue to confront today.

Place-Making and Environmental Adaptation

The Cherokee lands west of the Mississippi are in many ways similar to the southeastern homelands, but they retain some distinct characteristics of their own. The eastern part of the territory includes the westernmost portion of the Ozark Highlands and Boston Mountains ecoregions, which although much less dramatic, resemble the familiar hills and valleys of the homelands. This area is also characterized by broadleaf deciduous forests, encompassed by the Ozark Broadleaf Forest / Meadow Province and the Eastern Broadleaf Forest (Continental) Province (Bailey 1995). Yet, while there are many common species of vegetation between the two areas, the forests in the west are notably less luxuriant (Hewes 1978, 15). The western Ozark forests receive less annual precipitation and are mainly composed of drought-resistant oak/hickory woodlands with intermittent stands of pine. Moving further west, the terrain becomes mostly prairie flatlands, located in the Central Irregular Plains ecoregion and the Prairie Parkland (Temperate) Province (Bailey 1995). Overall, the eastern homelands are vaster and more diverse than the western Cherokee territory, with higher elevations and a wider range of ecoregions represented (see Figure 4). Nevertheless, Cherokees have made them home.

By the late eighteenth century, Cherokees had come to know the Ozark area well. Russell Thornton (1990, 43) suggests that Cherokee people had inhabited lands west of the Mississippi River by as early as 1721. The depletion of game in the homelands caused by the deerskin trade had most likely led eastern Cherokee hunters to travel into Arkansas territory since the 1780s. Further, the migration of the Chickamauga Band in 1794, along with a sizeable group of traditionalists who wanted no part of conflict with Europeans, added to the western population. As the population grew with increased emigration from the east, the group became known as the Western Cherokees and later as the Old Settlers. Due to a jumbled series of treaties made between the U.S. government and the Western Cherokees (much to the opposition of the Cherokee Nation proper, which was still residing in the homelands), they were gradually forced further west and eventually settled the area that became the Cherokee lands of the Indian

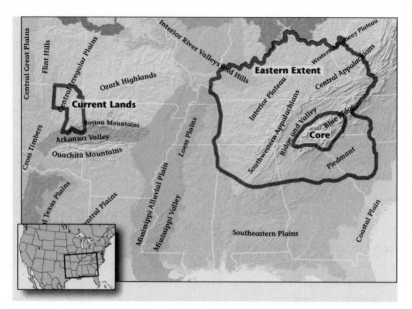

Figure 4. *Ecoregions and Cherokee territories. Adapted from US-EPA Level IV Eco-regions. Map by Mark Lindberg.*

Territory (Mooney 1900, 136–41).[2] By the time the Ross party arrived in 1839, Cherokees had inhabited the ecoregion for more than a century.

The early inhabitation of the region was not without conflict from the other Indian peoples residing there. The land was the home of the Qua-paws and Osages (both Siouxan tribes). Not surprisingly, the Osages and Quapaws saw the Cherokees as invaders. From 1805 to 1807, warfare between the Cherokees and Osages/Quapaws erupted over the use and settlement of the territory. The U.S. government attempted to regulate the relations between tribes, but this was mostly unsuccessful. In October of 1818, the Old Settlers and the Osages signed a treaty, but the Osages later abandoned the agreement because of the increasing amount of Cherokees and other Indians (relocated Shawnees, Delawares, and Oneidas) moving into the area. Warfare between these parties continued until around 1824 (McLoughlin 1986, 263). Such tensions between the Cherokees and the original peoples of the area likely precluded any exchange of local environmental knowledge.

R. Alfred Vick (2011) provides a comprehensive survey of the differences in plant species between the eastern and western lands, and he finds that

Cherokees were deprived of one-third of their culturally significant plants due to Removal. Moreover, Vick notes that the plants left behind in the homelands consisted of many of the most important species in the practice of Cherokee medicine and crafts. Nevertheless, the prolonged presence of the Old Settlers in the Ozark region, combined with the existence of vegetation similar to that in the homelands, made for a working knowledge of the environment. Of course, Cherokees continued to learn about their new lands, generating new environmental knowledge through the powers of observation. On a practical level, healers would have been able to deduce similar medicinal applications for plants that may have been the same genus but a different species.[3] In some cases, this process involved extended observation, such as watching how certain animals interacted with specific plants. In other cases, it involved seeking guidance through dreams or divination. Some believe that many medicines of the new country were shown to the people through communication with animal spirits, the Little People,[4] or even *Unehlanvhi,* the Creator. An account from the Doris Duke Collection of American Indian Oral History tells of Cherokees receiving medicinal plant knowledge in the new country directly from God:

> Mr. John Silk told this story from memory . . . It's a story that took place shortly after the Cherokees arrived in the new territory. And the location of this event is somewhere between Bell Community and [the] Arkansas state line, on one of the peaks, [the] high points. This event came about due to the sickness that was existing in the Cherokee [Nation] in this particular village of the Cherokees after the forced march from North Carolina.
>
> The leaders of this particular village decided that they should try to pray so that they might be able to receive guidance from God. They chose, as I said, one of the highest peaks to perform their rituals. They stretched out a deer skin. Upon the deer skin, they placed their most sacred tobacco, and they did the ritual over the tobacco and the deer skin, and began to smoke their peace pipes and send the white smoke to the heavens. [This was] a message to God; that they were in dire need of his guidance at this time. [Amid] their turmoil and their problems, the only one they could remember for assistance was God.
>
> After some time of performing their rituals, I would say half of the evening, two hours or so, they began to hear winds, far away

winds, as if [a] low thunder and tornado was coming their way. But [the sound] was so far away that it was [hard] to think that they were going to get anything that night. To their surprise, the noise grew louder and louder, and seemingly [it came] closer and closer to them. They did not see a thing, but just before the noise was about to fall upon them, silence fell over the atmosphere, and then a voice from the air asked the people: "What do you want? What may I do for you?"

[They said,] "We have asked for you because there's sickness in our village, lack of food, the children, the orphan children, are crying for their mother, their father, and all [in] all we are [experiencing] the most difficult times of our lives. For this, we ask you for guidance." This was the answer that the Cherokee people, the medicine men, gave to the voice in the air.

The voice in the air then returned their answer, and said, "All you have to do is look at the earth, look at the trees, look at the grass, and all of the plants that I have placed upon this planet. You will find the medicine if you will look. Again I will repeat, look to the earth, look to the grass and trees, and all the plants I have placed on this planet. You will find your medicine there." This was the answer that God gave to his people. And the answer that Indian people are following today—not Indian people in one location, but Indian people all throughout the Cherokee Nation.[5] (Silk 1967)

To clarify, an alternate version of the same story ends with the line: "Then the seven wise men went back to the people. They could see medicine everywhere they looked, all along the way," thus implying that they had received the knowledge of specific medicinal plants through a divine act (Spade and Walker 1966, 10–13).

Another story about the origins of plant knowledge in the west is one of prophecy. The story recounts how a group of medicine men, having prophesized the forced removal of the Cherokees, traveled to the lands west of the Mississippi long before Removal took place. On this journey, they transported cherished medicinal plants from the east in order to distribute them throughout the new country. To this day, some credit the existence of many important herbs in northeastern Oklahoma to the actions of these prophetic wise men (Vanbuskirk and Vanbuskirk 2000). One such plant is American ginseng (*Panax quinquefolius*), a mysterious and controversial plant due to its numerous medicinal properties and its high market value. The demand for American ginseng (mainly from China, where it is believed to compliment the Asian variety of the plant) since the early 1800s has caused its near depletion in the forests of the southeast (Johannsen 2006; Taylor 2006).[6] To Cherokees, the plant has a sacred status as a "cure-all," and it is perhaps the most important ingredient in medicinal formulas. Although its presence in northeastern Oklahoma (both historical and current) is highly doubted by botanists, Cherokees maintain that it was once plentiful in certain areas. Still today some claim to know where it grows, but it is extremely hard to find.

Whether through observation, divination, or prophecy, Cherokees developed intricate knowledge of the new environment. They thus made the hills of the western Ozarks *home*, and these stories illuminate this process. Regardless of which story is "true" (they could all be), they serve to explain the process of developing a new connection to place. The divination story (Silk 1967) differs significantly from the more familiar "Origin of Disease and Medicine," as recorded by anthropologist James Mooney with the eastern Cherokees in the late 1800s (Mooney 1900, 200–252). Although the version recorded by Mooney is still referenced by contemporary Oklahoma Cherokee storytellers, the new story is meant to fit the historical experiences of the new land. Whereas Cherokees likely had a working knowledge of the flora of the western Ozarks (again, many species were similar, if not identical), receiving such knowledge from the Creator imbues it with special meaning. Telling the story acknowledges this gift and the Creator's blessing of the Cherokees' new home. Transporting "roots" could be read in a similar light: Metaphorically, roots are the stuff of cultural or social grounding in a place.[7] Transporting roots not only established important medicines; it established a cultural connection to the land. Through these stories that depict material and spiritual experiences, the western Ozarks became a Cherokee cultural landscape. Cherokees have maintained this cultural landscape, and to this day, the northeastern Oklahoma hills are an important marker of identity.

Political Reunification in the New Lands

Yet while Removal resulted in the need to establish new relationships to place, it also required Cherokees to reestablish relationships with each other. Ross Party Cherokees, who numbered around fourteen thousand people, relied on the knowledge and help of the Old Settlers in the initial period after the Trail of Tears when, for many, survival meant reverting to deerskin clothing and the old skills of fashioning tools and weapons from strictly natural materials (McLoughlin 1993, 35). However, despite the Old Settlers' generosity toward their brothers and sisters, politically speaking, Cherokees were deeply divided. The Old Settlers, who numbered only about five thousand people, had set up their own government, complete with a tribal council and principal chief. Also present in the western lands was the small Treaty Party, who had arrived shortly after signing the fraudulent Treaty of New Echota in 1835. McLoughlin notes that "the removal crisis so divided the Cherokees that they did not find real unity until after the Civil War, if then" (5). Nevertheless, after a short period of readjustment in the new lands, Principal Chief John Ross began negotiating the terms of reunion between the two groups. He knew very well that the existence of two Cherokee political bodies was an extremely dangerous situation, potentially leading to civil confusion or, worse, the federal government exploiting this situation by playing one party against the other (11).

But reunification proved difficult. Tensions were high between the Ross and Treaty parties. As delineated by Cherokee Nation law, the signers of the Treaty of New Echota were individually murdered for ceding the lands in the east. Further, the Old Settlers insisted on maintaining their government and representatives, while the leaders from the east did not show signs of compromise. The eastern leaders asserted that those who had migrated west—separate from the official Cherokee Nation—had relinquished their rights as citizens, and thus the burden was on the Old Settlers to negotiate reacceptance within the nation. This stalemate continued until two prominent Cherokee figures stepped forward to help deliberate the terms. With the help of Sequoyah, the charismatic orator and inventor of the Cherokee syllabary who had been residing with the western Cherokees since 1824, and Jesse Bushyhead, another charismatic leader known for his integrity among the eastern Cherokees, a people's council convened on July 1, 1839 (14). This was the first of many meaningful dialogues on reunification, which resulted in the adoption of a new Cherokee constitution on September 6, 1839. This new version only differed from the former 1827 constitution in that the principal and second principal chiefs were now elected by popular vote, rather than by the council (21).

Although the eastern and western Cherokees were symbolically reunited under the new constitution, intense factionalism and infighting continued between the Treaty and Ross parties for the next seven years. Retaliation ensued from the murders of the treaty signers in the form of numerous outlaw gangs throughout the Indian Territory and neighboring Arkansas. Unable to accept the validity of the Treaty of New Echota, John Ross made multiple trips to Washington to protest its terms and the price of $5 million for the ancestral homelands. Yet, once again, the political survival of the Cherokee Nation lay in the maintenance of national unity, and Ross ultimately realized that he must compromise in order to achieve this. The violent actions of the outlaws had raised concern among the federal government, and it issued threats of intervention to control the "lawlessness." In an act of concession, Ross agreed to enter into treaty negotiations with the Cherokee factions and the federal government, and in August of 1846, an arrangement was made that ended the bitterness between the parties and allowed for the true unification of the Cherokee Nation (56–58).

The Treaty of Washington, as it was called, paved the way for the reconstruction of Cherokee government and communities in the new homeland from the ground up. In one of the treaty's provisions, fee simple ownership of the land was granted to the Cherokee Nation, once again making Cherokee lands the common property of the nation. Another provision authorized the per capita payments owed from the federal government for Removal, creating the financial means for reconstruction. The town of Tahlequah was named the new Cherokee Nation capital, and a courthouse, jail, and male and female seminaries were erected—the first institutions of higher education west of the Mississippi. This period of relative prosperity (circa 1846–61) has been called the "Golden Age of the Cherokee," wherein "economic, cultural, and social institutions that had begun to flower before removal now came to fruition" (Strickland and Strickland 1991, 114).

The Produced Environment in the Indian Territory

Upon arrival in the Indian Territory, many Cherokee settlements from the east reestablished themselves among the rolling hills of the Ozarks located in the eastern part of the new Cherokee Nation. Geographer Leslie Hewes (1978, 16) notes that, although it was certainly not the homelands, many Cherokees did not view the region as poor country. The combination of "small areas of productive soil, open woods, small prairies, and abundant sources of water" made for quite hospitable land according to Cherokee aesthetics and lifestyle. Many families made their homes in the valleys (or "hollows"), with proximity to flowing water for streamside farming. The western parts of the new lands, however, were slow to be settled. The expansive prairies were unfamiliar and inhospitable. Wood and water were harder to find than in the forested eastern areas, and the Osages who resided in and around this area were not welcoming to the Cherokee newcomers. In addition, the Trail of Tears had deprived the majority of basic necessities, and the contractors who were in charge of disbursing rations were located across the Arkansas border to the east. But even after the nation regained a sense of well-being, the western areas remained sparsely populated until after the Civil War. Hewes states, "The Cherokees left familiar country reluctantly" (18).

Accounts of the environment in the Cherokee Nation lands of the Indian Territory are scattered throughout the Indian-Pioneer Papers and the Doris Duke Collection, which contain interviews from the 1930–60s that capture entire generations of experience and memory.[8] Virtually every account on the environment in these collections tells of abundance in wild edibles and game. Even if one allows for a certain level of nostalgia reflected in these reminiscences, the consistent picture that emerges is significant. One account, given by E. F. Vann (aged 68 years, born 1870) in 1938, asserts,

The country of the Cherokee Nation was thinly populated and wild game was abundant. . . . In the Flint District and in surrounding districts, except in the clearings which were being tilled, the country was still in its original condition, a hill country of forest with small areas of prairie scattered through it. It seemed the entire country abounded in wild game, deer, bear, opossum, raccoon, wild hogs, wild cattle, wild horses, bobcats, squirrels, rabbits, wild turkeys, quail, prairie chickens and wild pigeons.[9] . . . All species of soft water fish were abundant in the creeks and rivers. . . . Wild bees were common and the Indians could have plenty of honey by cutting down a "bee tree" and robbing the bees of their treasure. Each fall many nuts were gathered such as pecans, walnuts, hazelnuts, and chinquapins as well as hickory nuts. . . . Some orchards were planted but not many because there were plenty of wild fruits and berries such as plums, grapes, seedling peaches, dewberries, huckleberries and a number of others.[10]

The "wild hogs" and "wild cattle" were a result of free-range animal husbandry that was widely practiced at this time. Speaking more specifically of this, Elinor Meigs (aged 75 years, born 1862) stated in 1937,

> I can remember when there were dense canebrakes in the river lowlands which afforded wonderful winter range for cattle, also a shelter for the stock from the severe winter weather and a refuge for game. There were also wild fruit [sic] in abundance, such as wild plums, strawberries, dewberries, blackberries, raspberries and huckleberries. Game was plentiful, such as deer, turkey and prairie chicken. . . . The prairie grass in those days were [sic] as tall as a person's shoulder and grew in every nook that was not covered with trees, and it was free and open range for stock. But that also, like everything else we once had, is gone.[11]

Allowing stock to roam free throughout the woods was a custom afforded by the Cherokee land tenure system, in which all land was considered public domain. Fences at that time were almost nonexistent, save for rudimentary "zigzag" rail fences that surrounded family plots of about 20–25 acres (Hewes 1978, 28). The accounts of dense canebrakes and shoulder-high prairie grass indicate an ample supply of wild fodder (which also included "mast," or wild nuts), eliminating the need for manufactured feed. Instrumental in creating this condition was the human use of fire.

In their inhabitation of the lands west of the Mississippi, Cherokees came across a lived environment. In addition to the Quapaws and Osages, Wichita and Caddo peoples had once inhabited parts of what would become the Cherokee Nation lands in the west (Baird and Goble 1994). Indigenous fire regimes had helped to define the character of the western Ozarks at that time: park-like old-growth forests with interspersed grassy meadows. As anthropologist Albert Wahrhaftig (1978, 421) documented in the 1970s, "Cherokees say that, when they first came to the area, the Ozark forests had trees so big and so widely spaced that through them you could see a man on horseback a quarter-mile away." In the eastern homelands, Cherokees had become very familiar with fire as a management tool; naturally, they would also find this practice useful in the western lands (Fowler and Konopik 2007, 168–70). In addition to the documented evidence of Cherokee burning in the Ozarks, the preceding accounts—in their descriptions of abundant berries and game and large meadows and canebrakes—suggest that a regime of controlled burning continued in the Indian Territory.

Studies on anthropogenic fire in North America have shown that, throughout the continent, Native Americans used fire to open up the forest by freeing it of underbrush (Pyne 1982; Stewart 2002). One main reason for this was to aid in human mobility through the woods and allow for better visibility while hunting. Additionally, burning generated fresh growth in meadows and fields, which in turn attracted game to forage in these sites. Thus the practice simultaneously encouraged a healthy population of game and aided humans in hunting them for subsistence (Lewis 1993). The use of fire also made gathering forest resources easier. Setting frequent, light, controlled fires cleared understory species that could otherwise prevent easy access to berry bushes and nuts (in the Cherokee case, this benefited both humans and their livestock). Further, under these conditions, berry bushes thrived—the light fires kept fungus and insect pests at bay and "stimulated the production of fruits" (Huntsinger and McCaffrey 1995, 166). Yet another reason, especially in the south, was to control the undesirable tick and chigger populations.

Thomas Blackburn and Kat Anderson (1993, 19) assert that fire was also used by Native Americans for "creating and sustaining vegetational mosaics." The accounts of dense canebrakes, scattered prairies, and open forests in the Indian Territory indeed may describe examples of such mosaics, sustained by the Cherokee use of fire. Frequent light fires also stabilized forests by regularly burning off the "ladder fuels" that can carry fire into forest canopies, resulting in devastating "crown fires" (Huntsinger and McCaffrey 1995, 163). The time of year that one burned also factored into the efficacy of fire as a management tool. Oral accounts from my fieldwork say that burning the hills was an annual early-fall activity. To this effect, the Cherokee Nation, as early as 1841, established a law that prohibited "any person or persons, to set the woods on fire, from the fifteenth of October to the first of March, in each year" (which implies that early spring was also an acceptable time to burn; Cherokee Executive Committee 1969, 48–49). However, scientific research on river cane (*Arundinaria gigantea*) shows that longer burning intervals of 7–10 years would have been necessary to maintain large canebrakes (Platt and Brantley 1997;

Figure 5. Photograph by Dr. Leslie Hewes taken in the 1930s showing possible remnants of prestatehood environmental conditions. This figure shows grassy, open woods in southern Adair County. Copyright University of Nebraska Board of Regents. Reproduced by permission of owner. All rights reserved.

Brantley and Platt 2001), which suggests that Cherokees employed a nuanced application of fire for different vegetational zones.

Agriculture in the early Cherokee Nation was primarily subsistence based. As stated before, Cherokee farms averaged 20–25 acres. In this regard, Cherokees also employed fire to clear their fields for planting. Large trees in a field plot were girdled, left to dry out, and then burned (Hewes 1978, 21). Among the eastern part of the nation (the Ozark hill country), a community-based way of life was predominant, exemplified by another practice for clearing farm plots, called "rail maulings." Similar to the old *gadugi* work crews that Cherokee communities once formed to help families in need (see Fogelson and Kutsche 1961), rail maulings were social events designed to help neighbors and friends. According to a description by Lynch Sixkiller (aged 58 years, born 1879) in 1937,

> [W]hen a man wished to make a new farm, he would invite his friends to meet there at some specified day and bring their axes,

Figure 6. Photograph by Dr. Leslie Hewes taken in the 1930s showing possible remnants of prestatehood environmental conditions. This figure shows a Cherokee subsistence farm in the Jenkins Creek area, Adair County. Note the "zig-zag" rail fence and the deadening girdled trees in the field. Copyright Economic Geography. Reproduced with permission of John Wiley and Sons, Inc.

wedges and mauls. Sometimes the man who wished the land cleared would have mauls and gluts made so that the work would not be hindered if the extra ones were needed during the day and sometimes he would have some timber already cut the length of rails in order to get more rails made. The whole family came along with the men for it was a day of enjoyment as well as work. The visiting women always assisted in preparing the big meal for the noon hour. There were always prizes given and the one who could win the first prize was highly honored. The man who made the most rails during the day received first prize of one dollar in money; the one who made second received a plug of Star tobacco; and the one who scored third received a cake. Many times there would be a party given the night following the rail mauling.[12]

Many similar accounts of this time show a strong communal ethic. To this effect, money was rarely needed or used. Another account from the Indian-Pioneer Papers given by Phillis Pettit (aged 76 years, born circa 1861) in 1937 states, "We didn't have a hard time making a living then. We raised our corn and our meat and molasses. We had our own garden truck, and if one family had hard luck and didn't raise enough to do them, other families in the neighborhood would divide with them."[13] Yet class differences in the Cherokee Nation did constitute differences in agricultural production. More affluent Cherokees, who either owned slaves or employed white migrant workers, often farmed the more expansive eastern prairies on a larger scale. Regardless, the early Cherokee Nation agricultural economy consisted of minimal exports (Hewes 1978, 24–30).

By as early as 1841—just two years after their forced removal to the western lands—the newly reestablished Cherokee state began to exert an influence on environmental affairs. Because of the Cherokees' communal system of land tenure, the tribal government saw the need to pass numerous regulations on the use of the public domain—most notably on the export of resources to U.S. citizens. For example, the sale of timber to U.S. citizens was strictly prohibited, and the use of salt wells and salt springs was regulated by short-term leases and limited to Cherokee citizens. Mineral resources such as coal and lead, although extracted on a very small scale, were also regulated and restricted to citizen use only (Hewes 1978, 29). In 1841, a law was passed that prohibited the felling of pecan trees—a common way of harvesting the nuts had once been to cut down the entire tree. The same act regulated the burning of the woods as mentioned before.

This type of state regulatory activity differed drastically from the type of statecraft evolving in Europe, which James Scott (1998, 11–52) has documented through the origins and development of the cadastral survey. As historian Rose Stremlau (2011, 96) notes, "Part of the Cherokee government's trust was to manage the communal resources of the people, including minerals, timber, and grass as well as land and to raise revenue to support services for its citizens."[14] Instead of a system of authoritative governance that relied on the simplification and legibility of land and people, Cherokees had built a system based on ideals of representative power, egalitarianism, and communal ownership in land. Communal ownership in land was the foundation of Cherokee environmental governance, and the Cherokee state served to protect and maintain this common resource. In doing so, the Cherokee state continued to uphold the traditional value system as it had in the east before Removal. Stremlau writes, "Communal landholding engendered a political ethic and concern for social welfare that distinguished the Cherokee Nation from other governments of its time." Yet while resource development did raise funds for the Cherokee government, they were minimal. Meager funds, combined with the small size of the Cherokee state, made the enforcement of environmental regulations difficult. This issue, along with increasing class divisions within the Cherokee Nation, would later result in serious problems for the nation, for which the U.S. Civil War served as catalyst.

Threats to the Public Domain

The Civil War left the Cherokee Nation in a state of devastation; however, numerous accounts depict a rapid reconstruction. In as few as four years, most Cherokees had restored their farms and livestock (Hewes 1978, 33). Although Cherokees would once again enjoy a short time of prosperity, the Treaty of 1866—signed with the United States as a response to Cherokee involvement in the fight against the Union—contained harsh stipulations that would soon be set in motion. The Treaty of 1866 opened up the Cherokee Nation to railroad companies, and with them came intensive resource exploitation and settler encroachment. In 1871, railroad tie cutting began in the northeastern part of the nation. Mainly post oak was harvested for this purpose; however, the industry soon realized the abundance of quality timber for export and convinced local Cherokees to sell stands of old growth black walnut (Bays 1998, 82). Although the Cherokee Nation passed laws to inhibit the sale of hardwood timber, Brad A. Bays notes that "the trade was a prime example of the ineffectiveness of Cherokee law and federal administration to control railroad exploitation and intruder spoliation in the Indian Territory" (ibid.). Despite the efforts of Cherokee lawmakers to protect tribal resources, the forces of capitalism (through timber export) and colonialism (through settler and railroad encroachment) had created circumstances that were changing the land and Cherokees' relationship to it.

The railroad and timber industries, working in concert with each other, marked the onset of the Industrial Revolution in the Indian Territory. A different kind of fire emerged on the Cherokee landscape during this time.

High intensity, stand-replacing fires accompanied logging activity, as felled areas were often burned to prepare them for grazing livestock (Fowler and Konopik 2007, 170). Sparks from passing locomotives could also ignite exposed, dry, clear-cut areas. These activities changed the character and composition of the Ozark forests by eliminating old growth hardwoods and pines. Large fields eventually replaced many of the park-like expanses of forests that had once defined the Cherokee Ozarks. The disturbance also drastically affected important forest resources, such as huckleberry bushes. In 1969, the interviewer of J. D. Whitmire (aged 78 years, born 1891) gave the following account:

> He recalls a long time ago when they looked forward to huckleberry time. Then families would go into the woods and gather the berries by the washtub full. The bushes would be so loaded they just set the tub under them and strip the berries off the limbs. But then came the whiteman and his timber cutting and burning of woods and another pleasure and suffice of the Indian went. . . .
> This at one time was a good timber country [present-day Adair County], and many carloads of ties and lumber were shipped from Addielee. A sawmill operated there for many years. When the railroad was taken out the town quickly died. He says the railroad was taken out because the whitemen mismanaged the cutting of timber. No reseeding or planting for the future was done and even today the once plentiful pine and hardwoods have not returned.[15]

The agricultural landscape in the Cherokee Nation was changing too, and this change primarily reflected class differences in agricultural production. An increasing population of noncitizen white tenant farmers, combined with increased agricultural activity among an elite Cherokee planter class and intermarried whites (who were considered citizens), resulted in illegal enclosures becoming more of a problem. Before 1875, the only legal fences in the Cherokee Nation were the previously mentioned zigzag rail fences—intended to enclose a small family plot (the legal amount was no more than fifty acres per family member). Regardless, by the early 1870s, numerous types of fences dotted the landscape, including board, barbed wire, hedge, and stone. In 1875, the Cherokee Nation government legalized board, hedge, and stone fences, among others (due to their benignity), but maintained the illegality of barbed wire. With barbed wire, one could cheaply enclose a vast amount of land, and this was the predominant practice on the larger Cherokee prairies among white and elite Cherokee farmers (Hewes 1978, 40). Speaking of these large enclosures, Hewes states, "It was not a Cherokee landscape. . . . Monopoly, contrary to the Indian ideal, prevailed" (50).

Although social factions had come to divide the Cherokee Nation culturally, politically, and spatially, the retention of communal land ownership represented a value to which all citizens could adhere. The communal land use system, better described as "use-right land tenure" (Bays 1998, 10), was based on the assumption that all members of the tribe had full rights to unused land within the Cherokee Nation land base. While the land was considered to be owned in common by the Cherokee Nation, any improvements on the land were regarded as strictly the property of the individual laborer, which could be sold or inherited (Bloom 2002, 498). Khaled Bloom notes that, in theory, this system could be seen as a relatively pure form of Lockean natural-right property (499). But this system differed from Locke in that the soil was not alienable. Whereas Locke writes of *possession* of the land itself,[16] in the Cherokee system, once worked ceased, only a year's time would transfer the land back to the public domain. Land itself was not necessarily property as it was territory, and one could not territorialize more than one could work.

Unsympathetic American visitors and governmental officials perceived this communal system of Cherokee land use as inefficient, backward, nonsensical, and a hindrance to Cherokee progress. Whereas the majority of Cherokee citizens enjoyed a humble but comfortable life under communal land tenure,[17] the disruption to the system caused by elite Cherokee entrepreneurs was the highlight of outside attention. The elite practice of hiring cheap outside labor (previously done by slaves) was beginning to create many problems for the Cherokee Nation, as more and more poor white laborers began settling within its borders and elite landowners continued to grow rich from their plots of nontaxable property. But this issue was not met without opposition from common Cherokees.

The conservative faction of the Cherokee Nation, represented by smaller-scale and community-oriented Cherokee farmers (in contrast to the larger-scale and commercially oriented whites and elite Cherokee farmers), reacted strongly to the illegal enclosures. In 1875, a member of the National Council named Oochalata led a movement representing common Cherokees to protest the perversion of the traditional communal land tenure system. Traditionalists saw the actions of whites and elite Cherokees (who were still in the minority) as leading to corruption and greed, which violated the core values of the nation. Nevertheless, Oochalata saw the Cherokee Nation still as one people, albeit with a class that had been corrupted by Euro-American values. He believed that the Cherokee people could be reunited if they returned to the traditional value system that had sustained Cherokee relationships with the land and with one another for generations (McLoughlin 1993, 341–42). Communal land ownership underpinned this value system. Land was the substance that connected everyone to each other; it was the foundation on which Cherokee relationships stood. As Stremlau (2011, 95) highlights, "Home was not the place where one Cherokee family lived but where all Cherokee families lived in relationship with one another."

The traditionalists that Oochalata represented were fighting for the preservation of this value system, which was being compromised by elite Cherokee farmers. His movement, which McLoughlin calls "the full-blood rebellion of 1875," was by and large contained within the Cherokee political system through the traditionalist majority in the National Council. This entailed political maneuvering (e.g., reinvigorating the traditionalist-led Downing party) and the articulation of ancient Keetoowah principles that condemned "monopoly of the public domain for speculative purposes" (McLoughlin 1993, 323–24). Keetoowah, or *giduwa*, was the name of the Cherokees' mother town (place of origin) in the east, and the term signified allegiance to the original teachings handed down to the Cherokees at the time of their creation. The Keetoowah Society, which had originated during the Civil War as a traditionalist organization that opposed slavery (and to which Oochalata belonged), reorganized in 1876 and lent their support to Oochalata's cause. Their influence—representing the majority interests of the nation—helped Oochalata to win the election for principal chief in 1876, which marked the second time a full blood had been elected to this position since 1827. By reasserting Keetoowah principles of common land-ownership and egalitarianism, Oochalata and the Keetoowah Society had demonstrated another instance of dialectical tension between the Cherokee polity and traditionalists that had influenced the direction of Cherokee state transformation. This time, instead of acquiescing to elite leadership for the purpose of national unity (as in White Path's rebellion), traditionalists sought to take the helm of the nation's political structure in order to steer it back to the fundamental values that defined Cherokee culture.

Yet even with this bold approach to redirecting Cherokee political development, settler-colonial forces strained the ability of traditionalists to carry out their agenda. With land reform and a redistribution of wealth in mind, upon his election, Principal Chief Oochalata proposed strict labor permit laws to curtail the practices of the elite few and ensure the expulsion of laborers and tenants who remained illegally in the Cherokee Nation after the expiration of their leases. However, because of the large amount of white laborers already living and working within the nation, Oochalata's administration did not have sufficient means to enforce this law, and it was soon repealed (349). To make matters worse, the problems with land and labor monopoly had turned Indian sympathizers against the Cherokee system on the grounds of social injustice. They saw an elite few taking advantage of loopholes in the system to the detriment of disenfranchised, incapable "full-bloods"—even though Oochalata himself was a "full-blood" principal chief. Thus the Cherokee Nation found itself criticized on every front: progressive-minded businesspeople and the federal government viewed actions like Oochalata's permit law as blocking the path of progress and exemplifying "regressive traditionalism," and American populists condemned what they saw as elite control over Cherokee affairs (ibid.). Furthermore, ethnocentric and exaggerated caricatures of the property situation in Indian Territory produced reports of the "un-American" and "communistic" characteristics of the Cherokee customs by government officials. Just as Andrew Jackson had done in the midst of the removal crisis, the federal government exploited this situation in order to intervene in Cherokee affairs, which conveniently fit along with its other policies of Indian assimilation and land expropriation.

Senator Henry Dawes from Massachusetts made trips to the Indian Territory to survey and report on Indian land use. His reports simultaneously praised and criticized the Cherokee property system. Angie Debo (1940, 21) writes, "The most partisan Indian would hardly have painted such an idealized picture of his people's happiness and prosperity . . . but, illogically, the Senator advocated a change in this perfect society because it held the wrong principles of property ownership." In Dawes's words,

> The head chief told us that there was not a family in that whole nation that had not a home of its own. There was not a pauper in

that nation, and the nation did not owe a dollar. . . . Yet the defect
of the system was apparent. They have got as far as they can go,
because they own their land in common. . . . [T]here is no enterprise to make your home any better than that of your neighbor's.
There is no *selfishness,* which is at the bottom [i.e., foundation] of
civilization. Till these people will consent to give up their lands,
and divide them among their citizens so that each can own the
land he cultivates, they will not make much more progress. (21–22;
emphasis added)

This passage highlights the founding principles of the General Allotment Act of 1887. The concept of "selfishness" expressed by Dawes
reflects the influence of economist Adam Smith's writings on self-interest
as an inherent human trait (Smith 1901 [1776]). Further, the objective in
this discourse was to define the Cherokee system as inherently "backward," thus standing in the way of progress. Tropes of backwardness
rationalized the expropriation of "unused" land. The Allotment (or
Dawes) Act proposed the "allotment in severalty" of communally held
Indian lands into 160-acre tracts for each (male) head of household, 80
acres for unmarried adults, and 40 acres for each child (Debo 1940, 23).
The unallotted "surplus" land was purchased by the federal government
and opened up to non-Indian settlement. This policy was assimilative in
nature, whereby American Indian people were encouraged to do as their
newfound settler neighbors did and farm their plots as European-style
yeoman farmers. Hence the policy was designed to break up communal
land ownership among tribes and, in the process, break up communities
and traditional subsistence patterns.

The Cherokee Nation staved off the Allotment Act until 1898. And
while the majority of the nation opposed the policy, a small "progressive" group (i.e., citizen whites and elite Cherokees) was in favor of the
concept, albeit by very different means. They proposed that the solution
to the perceived problem of "unused" land in the Cherokee Nation was
to simply allot the entire land base to citizens only. There would be no
"surplus" land for outsider settlement, and "the [federal] government
would not dare to take from individual property owners the land that
these outsiders wanted" (McLoughlin 1993, 280). The problem with this
proposal was that, while it might inhibit white encroachment, the land
would become alienable. This struck the nerve center of conservative

faction—to Cherokee traditionalists and patriots, collectively owned land was the crux of national survival.

Cherokee Resistances to Allotment

Most Cherokees firmly supported their existing system of communal land tenure, despite its purported flaws and problems. In opposition to allotment, both Western-educated Cherokee statesmen and Cherokee traditionalists articulated distinct forms of resistance. In analyzing such counternarratives and resistances, one can see how allotment policy hit a deep nerve in Cherokee society, challenging the basis of national sovereignty and identity.

Cherokee statesmen relied on their knowledge of the U.S. political system and their ability to engage in public debate (via publications and lobbying) to construct counternarratives to the allotment policy. Their arguments insisted on clarifying the Cherokee system of property and often did so in relation to their view of the dominant system. In response to incoming criticisms, officials questioned and criticized the dysfunctional and visibly unequal American system of private property (Denson 2004). In Principal Chief Dennis Bushyhead's words, "The only difference between your land system and ours is that the unoccupied surface of the earth is not a chattel to be sold and speculated in by those who do not use it. . . . So long as one acre of our domain is unoccupied, any Cherokee who wishes to cultivate it can do so, and make a home, which is his" (1881, quoted in Denson 2004, 225). Cherokee statesmen were able to counteract negative accusations by maneuvering within the political discourse and uncovering the hypocrisies of American ideals. Furthermore, the Cherokee state allowed for more effective confrontation on the moral grounds of "civilization." Through mimicry, Cherokee institutions were not merely "customary" structures that could be coopted. Rather, their resemblance of the federal models provided an ethically formidable entity to dismantle, and they required incredible leaps of irrationality in order to justify their termination. State structures also served as a vehicle for articulating foundational Cherokee values toward the land that most citizens shared. Stremlau (2011, 100–101) writes, "The adoption of a republican-style government modeled after that of the United States did not replace traditional Cherokee culture but perfected it."

The Redbird Smith movement, as described by Robert K. Thomas (1961), was the culmination of the traditionalist resistance to allotment. For many years during the proposals and planning for allotment, the Keetoowah Society held meetings to discuss these issues. Traditionalists saw allotment much in the same light as Cherokee statesmen; however, their concerns about Cherokee autonomy had a more deep-seated religious significance. The concept of balance was an important part of traditional Cherokee life. Allotment, through its proposed coercive measures, directly violated treaties held between the Cherokees and the U.S. government. The potential breaching of these treaty agreements—which Keetoowahs considered sacred agreements—signified a loss in the natural balance of life. A faction of the Keetoowah Society, which became known as the Nighthawks, reacted by withdrawing from political affairs and turning to their old religion.

The Nighthawks appointed Redbird Smith, a staunch traditionalist and skilled leader, to revive the old ceremonies that had been forgotten or lost as a result of Removal. Smith traveled throughout Indian Territory, conversing with Creek and Natchez traditionalists and discussing the meanings of sacred Cherokee wampum belts on which ceremonial meaning had been inscribed. Soon Cherokees throughout the nation were reviving the ceremonial dances. To these traditionalists, ceremony worked to restore balance to a world they felt was increasingly filled with turmoil. The wampum belt collaboration resulted in the Four Mothers Society—a confederation of traditionalists from all the "Five Civilized Tribes" (Cherokee, Chickasaw, Creek, Seminole, and Choctaw) into one resistance organization. In a shift from previous political withdrawal, the Four Mothers Society acquired lawyers for their cause and even sent delegates to Washington to fight allotment (Thomas 1961, 164).

Yet both forms of resistance—governmental and traditionalist—failed to overpower the underlying goal of allotment: the continued expropriation of Indian lands. White settlers in the neighboring states of Kansas and Arkansas wanted land, and federal policy makers were in the position to oblige them. The problem of intruders in the Indian Territory had already gotten out of hand, and as McLoughlin (1993, 364) states, "federal refusal to honor the requirement of removing intruders was to be the means of forcing the Indian nations to do what they did not want to do." By the time the Curtis Act asserted federal plenary power over the Five Tribes in 1898, the Dawes Commission was poised to allot the Cherokee Nation.

Under these harsh circumstances, in 1902 the Cherokee Nation negotiated the allotment in severalty of tribal lands (Stremlau 2011, 155).
Allotments were assigned to individual tribal members by means of a
pseudocensus called the Dawes rolls. Indian blood quantum—a federal
invention designed to manage the racial composition of Indian people—
was determined for each individual, and those with one-half degree of
Indian blood or more were restricted from selling or leasing their land
because of a presumed lack of economic competence. Redbird Smith
and other Nighthawks were arrested and forced to enroll for their allotments. This delivered a fatal blow to the movement, and many of Smith's
followers submitted to enrolling themselves as well (Thomas 1961, 164).
The Dawes Commission was terminated in 1906, but the allotment of the
Cherokee Nation would last until 1914. According to the report of the U.S.
Department of the Interior, by 1911, of the original 4.42 million acres of
land once owned in fee by the Cherokee Nation, approximately 4.35 million acres were allotted to 40,196 Cherokee citizens, and 72,000 acres were
sold, opened up to white settlement, or annexed for railroad right of way
and townships (United States Department of the Interior 1912, 389).

Despite the ultimate imposition of allotment policy, both groups of
opposition had voiced a conception of what it meant to be Cherokee,
albeit in different ways. Traditionalist Cherokees initiated an effort to
retain cultural and spiritual meaning throughout attempts to divide the
Cherokee land base. This movement represented a response to the allotment policy in terms of peoplehood, and it is indicative of how Cherokee
had retained their identity as a *people,* imbricated with the nationalistic
stance of Cherokee statesmen. Whereas tribal officials articulated Cherokee nationhood and sovereignty in response to encroachment, a Cherokee
notion of peoplehood—individuals joined together through an interconnected matrix of language, land, sacred history, and ceremony (Holm et
al. 2003)—had essentially gone underground and was maintained by religious societies like the Nighthawks. A general concept of peoplehood was
still an important facet of a traditionalist Cherokee worldview that surfaced in the form of resistance or rebellion when aspects of it were being
threatened. White Path's rebellion in the 1820s and Oochalata's movement in 1875 had been for similar purposes: Cherokees were losing their
way by succumbing to "corrupt white intruders and their alien values"
(McLoughlin 1993, 341). Further, Oochalata had made these calls from
the position of principal chief and as a fierce nationalist. Thus nationhood

and peoplehood—although distinct ideas of "community"—informed, strengthened, and overlapped with each other. To Cherokee statesmen and religious leaders alike, resistance to allotment meant a refusal to "break their bond to the land [and] to each other" (Stremlau 2011, 152).[18]

Conclusion

The transfer of environmental knowledge and practices from the southeastern homelands and the development of new environmental knowledge through observation and divination shaped the western Cherokee lands and created both cultural and normative landscapes. This process manifested materially through controlled burning and subsistence agriculture and spiritually through storied experiences of divine communication. In rebuilding their state structures in the west, Cherokees were able to maintain their foundational value system despite intense pressures that resulted from increasing class divisions and white encroachment. The foundation of this value system, and what could be called the foundation of Cherokee environmental governance during this time, was communal land ownership. Cherokees who adhered to this value system—including both Western-educated and traditional, "mixed blood" and "full blood"—asserted the difference of their political system from that of the United States through this relationship-based approach to governance. As in the east, the Cherokee state developed from this relationship to land. It also evolved through the ardent defense of territory.

Internal class conflict and colonial encroachment changed the way Cherokees related to the land by compromising subsistence economies and forcing market-driven exploitative practices. Whereas the railroads had opened up the Cherokee Nation for incorporation into the capitalist market economy, the implementation of the allotment policy effectively territorialized tribal lands. Formerly, Cherokee farm plots, settlements, and towns had been seemingly scattered and nonuniform as a result of Cherokee communal land tenure. Because land was not taxed or deeded to individuals, there was no need to uniformly map land claims. A look at pre- and postallotment U.S. Geological Survey maps shows that boundaries to land claims and agricultural fields preallotment were more determined by natural features rather than arbitrary invisible lines. With the imposition of allotment, surveyors needed to divide and map individual plots of land in order to assign them to tribal citizens. Thus the postallotment map is a series of uniform square grids that transect natural boundaries. It represents former "experienced" space as imagined, "abstract" space (Vandergeest and Peluso 1995, 388–89). Doing so virtually erased established plots and facilitated land expropriation. It also forcibly changed the way the Cherokee Nation as a whole related to its land by supplanting one property system with another.

These changes in Cherokee relationships to the land caused by the clashing of differing normative landscapes in a context of unequal power relations in turn resulted in extreme environmental changes. In addition to burned, clear-cut forests, by the 1920s, animal populations had significantly decreased (likely due to clear-cutting) and soil runoff from the sale and settlement of surplus lands had led to severe erosion (Stremlau 2011, 210). Environmental production is a process, and the degree of control over this process by Cherokees decreased gradually after the U.S. Civil War, throughout the Allotment Era, and up to Oklahoma statehood in 1907. As the somber notes of loss and land degradation in many of the accounts from the Indian-Pioneer Papers and Doris Duke Collection attest, this resulted in a produced landscape that was undesirable to most Cherokees. My discussion of environmental production in the Cherokee Nation continues in the next chapter, wherein after the revitalization of Cherokee political structures beginning in the 1940s, Cherokees proceeded to take this process into their own hands once again.

CHAPTER 3

The "Greening" of Oklahoma

State Power and Cherokee Resurgence after the Dust Bowl

IN HER EXTENSIVE ARTICLE, Yaqui legal scholar Rebecca Tsosie offers an assessment of contemporary American Indian environmental management and governance. Her acute analysis of the multifarious and complex challenges American Indian nations face with regard to cultural revitalization, economic development, and environmental protection (and how all are intertwined) informs her notion of environmental self-determination—"the right to exercise sovereignty and autonomy over reservation lands and resources" (Tsosie 1996, 227). Referencing the dramatic shift in federal Indian policy through the Self-Determination and Education Assistance Act of 1975, Tsosie argues that the movement toward *environmental* self-determination "has enabled the tribes to overcome or mitigate the impacts of earlier federal environmental statutes designed to exploit tribal natural resources and incorporate Indian tribes into the larger market economy of the United States" (330). However, she continues, "True environmental self-determination . . . depends upon the ability of Indian nations to preserve their land bases and engage in economic development according to their own policies and values." In this light, the right to maintain indigenous relationships with the land really boils down to the right to live as free people.

This chapter explores the development of Cherokee political structures that have contributed to contemporary environmental self-determination for the Cherokee Nation. I explain how Cherokees rebuilt their political structures after allotment and Oklahoma statehood in tandem with reasserting jurisdiction over land and resources and thus how Cherokee state transformation—and the dialectical process that continued to shape it—both informed and necessitated Cherokee environmental self-determination. With the communal land base divided into individually owned parcels and tribal governmental operations severely hindered by colonial rule, Cherokee governance may have momentarily ceased in a formalistic way, but it continued to play out along customary and religious lines in Cherokee churches, ceremonial grounds, and among community elders (Wahrhaftig 1975c).[1] In fact, I assert that grassroots activism and organizing born out of this type of governance reinvigorated Cherokee political development by sparking dialectical tension with those who sought to reassemble the tribal government.

In the first part of this chapter, I discuss how allotment and its aftermath contributed to the displacement of the Cherokee normative landscape and, concomitantly, the increasing restriction of Cherokee access to forest resources. The infiltration of the Cherokee Nation by federal land-management agencies, along with the development of Oklahoma state agencies and their assumption of control over former Cherokee lands, resulted in more environmental changes. The national fire suppression era of the 1930s combined with the Great Depression dealt blows to Cherokee subsistence lifestyles and interactions with the land. Later, the creation of man-made lakes by the Army Corps of Engineers in the 1940s and 1950s in order to promote the state of Oklahoma's outdoor recreational tourism agenda literally flooded many Cherokee settlements.

Cherokees were not passive bystanders to these policies and restrictions. In the second part of this chapter, I describe the actions that Cherokee political and community leaders took to resist federal and state hegemony. Cherokee political leaders began to reassert political autonomy in the 1940s by reestablishing a council-style system of representation. In the late 1960s, a grassroots community group called the Original Cherokee Community Organization (OCCO) formed as a reaction to restrictive Oklahoma hunting laws and subsequently called into question the federal control over the Cherokee political apparatus. More recently, the self-governance compact of 1990 under Principal Chief Wilma Mankiller played a large role in reclaiming control of Cherokee land and resources. In this context, I discuss the creation of the Cherokee Nation Natural Resources Department and the Office of Environmental Services around this time. These institutions initially took over the responsibilities of the Bureau of Indian Affairs (BIA) and mimicked federal agencies. Over time, however, they began to develop their own institutional identities, and today they are beginning to assert control over the process of environmental production in the Cherokee lands of northeastern Oklahoma.

In the third part of this chapter, I discuss how the legacy of imposed state and federal policies affects both contemporary tribal citizens and tribal resource managers and, further, how that legacy affects the relationship between the two groups. I discuss resource access in relation to the two levels of state dynamics in the Cherokee Nation: the relationship of the Cherokee Nation to the U.S. state and the relationship of Cherokee citizens to the Cherokee state. Access to natural resources is something that the Cherokee Nation, as a federally recognized tribal government with a distinct relationship to the U.S. government, can aid tribal citizens in acquiring. However, as a state, the Cherokee Nation can also grant or deny tribal citizens access to resources through the gate-keeping of tribal lands. I explore these dynamics of indigenous state practice in the context of access theory (Ribot and Peluso 2003), which acknowledges the contingencies in human–government–land relationships. Further, following Robbins (2000), I focus on "knowledge alliances"—networks and cross-scale interaction that constitute actual practice among local and state actors. I conclude with a discussion of the elders' advisory group and how it addresses some of the inherent challenges in indigenous state transformation. The chapter as a whole demonstrates how environmental production in a settler-colonial context has created overlapping and conflicting normative landscapes, which Cherokees are reconciling and counteracting through a resurgence of indigenous ecological sovereignty.

Resource Restrictions and the Production of Oklahoma's "Green Country"

Around the turn of the twentieth century, resource conservation and scientific forestry were becoming the dominant frameworks for U.S. land management policy. As a reaction to the destructive actions that accompanied railroad construction and industrial logging, the conservation movement advocated the professional management of natural resources to ensure sustained yields. This movement is often credited to the first chief of the U.S. Forest Service and the founder of American professional forestry, Gifford Pinchot. Due to the recent large-scale annexation of tribal lands by way of allotment (i.e., the creation of thousands of acres of "surplus" land), it is not surprising that tribal forests were included in this movement. After a brief period of turf wars between the Forest Service and the BIA, the Act of March 3, 1909 (35 Stat. 783), established BIA jurisdiction over forests on tribal trust lands under its Division of Forestry. In the absence of tribal governance institutions (a convenient fact that was also a consequence of allotment), the Omnibus Bill of 1910 (36 Stat. 857) named the BIA the official managing body of Indian forests. In this capacity, the BIA oversaw trust property timber harvests, including the finances of these operations, which were also held "in trust." At this point, Indian forests became "part of a national, conservation-based forest management program that would assure a steady supply of timber and protection of watersheds" (Huntsinger and McCaffrey 1995, 171).

According to this new management regime, the key to ensuring the availability of timber was the suppression of fire. Whereas this position was aimed at eliminating catastrophic industrial fires, all forest fires were judged a threat to valuable national resources, including customary small-scale fires that cleared the underbrush (Fowler and Konopik 2007, 171). The combination of past clear-cut logging and catastrophic fires with the new fire suppression policy that eliminated small controlled burns caused significant environmental changes in the western Ozarks that impeded Cherokee access to natural resources. The buildup of underbrush that accompanied the second-growth forests decreased the ease of hunting and gathering by obstructing formerly open forests and providing ample habitat for pests like ticks and chiggers. Wild game populations likely diminished as a result of fire suppression (combined with an increased human population), as Huntsinger and McCaffrey (1995, 175) have documented.

After Oklahoma statehood in 1907, increased state infiltration of the former tribal land base imposed new laws and jurisdiction on Cherokee people, including land use and hunting restrictions. "Hog-fencing laws" ended open-range practices (Wahrhaftig 1978, 450), and non-Indians began to erect enclosures on former resource-gathering areas. The Great Depression in the 1930s, along with severe droughts in 1935 and 1936, made matters worse; while the restrictions to forest resources increased, so did Cherokees' reliance on them. During this time, Albert Wahrhaftig notes, "Cherokees were increasingly blocked from their generalized utilization of the woods and streams, deprived of sufficient cash supplement to capitalize even a subsistence farm, and confined to the tiny island of their allotments. Cherokee self-sufficiency had seriously declined by the time World War II arrived" (ibid.).

The Depression had caused the migration of the few white families with whom Cherokees had developed neighborly relations. Eventually, those who became known as "land hawks" consolidated many of the lands abandoned by these families into large ranches (420–21). The interviewer of Ross Bowlin (born 1909, aged 60 years) gave an account in 1969:

> For Ross much of the country has changed in his time. New roads and fences have been one of the big changes, which came with the white man who owns nearly all of the land now. As we drive around the hill country, Ross points out different places where he used to hunt, but now it is all fenced, although few people live here. He finds it hard to understand that the whitemen don't live here, but comes and fences up the land and refuses to let anyone hunt. This is the story most Indian[s] tell—the loss of their hunting right, their way. We pass a couple of whitemen driving new pickup trucks with stock racks, but there is no exchange of greeting . . . Over on a stretch of woodland Ross tells that it was once the finest huckleberry place in the country. But no one is allowed in there now, and the "Warning! Keep out!" signs on the new fence bespeak the landowner's greedy wishes. Speaking as one of them, Ross says that the Cherokees have never liked to see outsiders come into their country and destroy the woodlands, but the government has seen to it that there is nothing they can do about it. He says there is no longer any Cherokee Nation.[2]

Cherokee distrust and bitterness toward whites was heightened by the fact that many had directly deceived Cherokees and robbed them of their lands. The term *grafter* belonged to those who dealt in the business of Indian land. These individuals exploited the land policy left behind by allotment. "Restricted land" referred to land allotted to Cherokees of one-half or more Indian blood. Under this system, the land was exempted from property taxes, and the U.S. government held the title to the land in trust. Grafters "helped" restricted allottees with the process of taking their lands out of restricted status—often aided by the Indian agents (Wahrhaftig 1978, 424, 449). Once this was achieved, the land was easily acquired by manipulating the bureaucratic system that was unfamiliar to many non-English-speaking Cherokees.

The allotment policy had dire repercussions for the generation of Cherokees that immediately followed it. Cherokees who were born after the closing of the Dawes rolls in 1906 (referred to as "too-lates") never received allotments. Although they often inherited land from a deceased relative, allotment policy called for the removal of restrictions upon the death of the original allottee. Because the removal of restrictions exposed the land to taxation—an expense that many Indian families could not afford—these allotments were often sold through the county courts, leaving the "too-lates" landless. In many cases, such families resorted to squatting on other restricted lands. One report describes an old woman and original allottee in the Nicut area who accommodated six families living in small shacks on her 60-acre allotment.[3]

As a reaction to the Dust Bowl and the Depression Era, the Oklahoma State Planning and Resource Board (formed in 1935) began the construction of dams throughout the state. With the help of the Army Corps of Engineers, the Bureau of Reclamation, and the Grand River Dam Authority, numerous lakes were formed throughout northeastern Oklahoma. The lakes were designed to provide flood control, a steady water supply, hydroelectric power, and opportunities for outdoor recreation (Johnson 1998, 4). As time went on, the area, with its large lakes and rolling green hills, became known among other Oklahomans and the surrounding states as a place for recreational tourism. In an effort to capitalize on the region's new image, northeastern Oklahoma was dubbed "Green Country." The establishment of a special organization in 1965—Green Country, Inc.—spearheaded this campaign and served to "coordinate [the] promotion and development of sixteen northeast Oklahoma counties" (Stauber 2007). Writing in the early 1970s, Wahrhaftig (1978, 421) commented that the name *Green Country*

> evokes a new future for the region, as a paradise of woods, lakes, bass, legions of free-spending tourists and vacationers, second homes for Tulsans and Dallasites—the playground of Texas and Kansas. This image submerges the old realities: Indians, lawlessness, failed farms, poverty, cultural and economic backwash. The new image, and the national advertising that is merchandising it, has the timeless ring of God-created wilderness, revealing that Oklahomans are apparently oblivious to their impact on the environment. In less than a century it has been transformed, certainly to the disadvantage of the Cherokees and, perhaps, to that of everyone else.

Also to the disadvantage of the Cherokees, as Wahrhaftig notes, was the flooding of numerous Cherokee settlements by the new lakes. Entire communities were relocated, and family and community cemeteries had to be excavated and moved. Speaking with animosity toward the rapid rate of "progress" throughout Cherokee country, Wahrhaftig notes, "The price Cherokees have paid for Green Country is scrub-choked, tick-infested, second-growth forests; fishing lakes that have drowned former Indian settlements; and a displaced Cherokee population which is either on welfare or in California" (ibid.).[4]

Whereas Oklahoma statehood had geopolitically subsumed the Cherokee Nation, the making of Green Country attempted to complete the incorporation of the Cherokee Nation into the state of Oklahoma through the superimposition of regional boundaries. Although the campaign was welcomed in some parts of the Cherokee Nation as a source of economic development, this proved to be for all the wrong reasons. Instead of promoting sustainable, locally based economic opportunities, white Oklahomans were more interested in resource exploitation (fish and game) and shallow cultural tourism that presented Cherokee people as remnants of the past (430–32). The Oklahoma Office of Tourism and Recreation maintains the image and boundaries of Green Country today, along with five other tourism regions such as Kiamichi Country (i.e., the Choctaw Nation) and Arbuckle Country (i.e., the Chickasaw Nation). From the same entity comes the term *Oklacolor* to describe the geographical and cultural diversity of the state, and Green Country's tag line in a promotional video asserts, "Green Country: We've got all the Oklacolors of the rainbow waiting for you in northeast Oklahoma. Go for it."[5]

Settler colonialism, manifested in structures and policies such as scientific forestry, fire suppression, fence laws, allotment restrictions, hydroelectric dams, and recreational tourism, directly impacted Cherokee lives and the degree of people's interaction with the land. In time, the social and environmental changes that resulted from these policies and institutions compelled Cherokees to organize politically. As with Cherokee resistances to allotment, this political organization took different forms— Cherokees organized on both national and local levels in response to the increasing encroachments on Cherokee sovereignty and the right to live.

Cherokee Political Resurgence and Grassroots Activism

Around the time regional developers were attempting to "rebrand" Cherokee lands into Green Country, tribal leaders began to reassert Cherokee political autonomy. Although the Curtis Act of 1898 had declared the tribal government null by colonial fiat, the Five Tribes Act of 1906 had reinstated the functions of tribal governments "in full force and effect." The phrase is dubious, considering that the federal government proceeded to appoint Cherokee chiefs without the vote of the people, but nevertheless, the Cherokee Nation government continued to exist—at least on paper.

In 1938, Cherokee attorneys negotiated a ten-year contract with the U.S. Court of Claims to begin the process of litigating compensatory claims against the federal government. One of the first of many Cherokee claims cases involved reparation for the forced cession of the Cherokee Outlet during the turn of the century—6,022,000 acres of Cherokee land that was located along the northwest border of Oklahoma.[6] Although this case would not be resolved until 1962, the claims process created a substantial opportunity to rebuild the Cherokee Nation government. Also in 1938, several existing Cherokee organizations came together to form an ad hoc council, and in 1941 this body selected Jesse Bartley Milam as candidate for principal chief. Marking a significant shift in the presidential appointment process, President Roosevelt approved Milam for the position (Mankiller and Wallis 1993, 177).

Principal Chief Milam was an influential figure in Cherokee politics. A member of the Keetoowah Society, Milam was a keen advocate for Cherokee culture and language. He was also the first chief to begin the process of buying back tribal lands that had been lost during allotment. This process was carried out via congressional funding and entailed two major land reacquisition projects. Toward the northern part of the Cherokee Nation in what had become Delaware County was the Kenwood project, named for the predominantly full-blood community that it surrounded and totaling roughly 17,000 acres. Toward the south in what had become Adair County was the Candy Mink Springs project, named for a prominent local community leader and consisting of approximately 15,000 acres.[7] These land reacquisition projects are evident in current maps of Cherokee Nation trust lands (refer to Figure 2).

Milam also played a major role in organizing the Tahlequah national convention of 1948 that, according to Wilma Mankiller and Michael Wallis (1993, 179), "was a major step toward the return of the tribal-council form of government for the Cherokee Nation." The 1948 convention convened under the auspices of both Principal Chief Milam and the U.S. Commissioner of Indian Affairs to reunite numerous Cherokee groups as one polity and, with this unity, continue the claims process against the U.S. government. Filling to capacity a large auditorium on the campus of Northeastern State University in Tahlequah—the site of the old Cherokee Female Seminary—Cherokees gathered and passed a resolution that formed the Cherokee Executive Committee. The committee consisted of twelve members: the principal chief (acting as the ex-officio chairman), nine members representing the districts of the old Cherokee Nation, one member representing Cherokees outside of the original tribal boundaries, and one member representing the Texas Cherokees—a group with historical continuity that had members living in both Texas and Oklahoma.[8]

Principal Chief Milam passed away in 1949, leaving behind a strengthened sense of Cherokee political autonomy and more than 30,000 acres of reacquired land. His successor, William Wayne Keeler, continued to work toward Milam's goals of rebuilding the Cherokee Nation government through the 1970s. The Stricklands (1991, 130) describe Principal Chief Keeler as "the most powerful, enigmatic, and controversial Cherokee tribal leader since John Ross." Coming from a prominent mixed-blood family in Bartlesville, Oklahoma, Keeler had served on the Cherokee Executive Committee as the representative for the Texas Cherokees. At the time of his appointment to principal chief, he was an oil executive for Phillips Petroleum. Keeler was a skilled businessman and savvy politician, and because of this, he has been criticized for not understanding the needs of common Cherokees (Wahrhaftig 1975b, 64). Yet many accounts of Keeler from traditionalist Cherokees praise him as a good leader and someone who connected with the people (Mankiller and Wallis 1993, 181).[9] Regardless of these conflicting opinions of his character, Principal Chief Keeler was able to put his business and political skills to work for the Cherokee people, and the Stricklands (1991, 130) note that "there is no question that when Keeler retired as chief, the Cherokee Nation had become a vital force once again."

Upon his appointment by President Truman in 1949, Keeler further developed the Cherokee Executive Committee to resemble a more representative tribal council (Lowe 1996, 118). In 1952, using his personal funds, he established the Cherokee Foundation, a nonprofit entity that could obtain and administer funds to Cherokee communities. This foundation would lay the groundwork for many of the social service programs operated by the Cherokee Nation today (120). In 1962, under Keeler's leadership, the Indian Claims Commission followed through on its commitment and awarded $19 million to the Cherokee people in Oklahoma, which produced small per capita payments to the individuals or their heirs listed on the Dawes rolls. The remainder of the funds, in combination with another settlement regarding the Arkansas Riverbed (totaling about $2 million), was used as seed money to continue rebuilding the Cherokee Nation (Strickland and Strickland 1991, 128–29).

With these funds, Keeler oversaw the construction of a hotel and restaurant on tribal lands to create jobs for Cherokees and generate revenue for the tribe. He created housing and job programs for tribal citizens in need of assistance and erected the first buildings of what would become the Cherokee Nation tribal complex (later named the W. W. Keeler Tribal Complex). At that time, however, the BIA operated their Tahlequah offices from this location. Principal Chief Keeler also held community meetings throughout the Cherokee Nation to inform people about governmental activities and to encourage leadership and involvement in the renewal of the Cherokee Nation government. He asked each community to appoint a spokesperson to act as a liaison for tribal affairs, reinvigorating a sense of community representation in Cherokee government (Lowe 1996, 122). Finally, the passage of the Principal Chiefs Act (P.L. 91-495) in 1970 authorized the people of the Five Tribes to select their principal officer by popular vote, and in 1971, Keeler became the first principal chief of the Cherokee Nation to be elected by the people since 1903.[10]

Cherokee communities were also organizing themselves politically during this time. Anthropologist Albert Wahrhaftig carried out extensive ethnographic fieldwork among Oklahoma Cherokees in the 1960s and 1970s and experienced these dynamics firsthand. In November 1965, he was asked to serve as the English-language recorder for the burgeoning Five County Northeastern Oklahoma Cherokee Organization, which later became the Original Cherokee Community Organization (OCCO).[11] The OCCO organized as a reaction to restrictions on Cherokee hunting and fishing practices. Wahrhaftig, writing with his wife Jane Lukens-Wahrhaftig, states, "Interference with Cherokee hunting and fishing [in the form of impounding game, confiscating firearms, and levying fines] by Oklahoma state game officials . . . finally induced Cherokees to gather and seek redress of their grievances" (Wahrhaftig and Lukens-Wahrhaftig 1979, 230). With the blessings of their elders, a group of younger Cherokee men sought to stage a "hunt-in" in order to challenge Oklahoma state hunting laws en masse. As a result, in 1966, a Cherokee man named John Chewie was charged for hunting out of season and without a state license. Chewie appeared in court in Jay, Oklahoma, and admitted to the charges without apology, asserting that he was a Cherokee, that he had hunted on Cherokee land, and that he had done so to feed himself and his family. The case drew a great deal of attention, as four hundred purportedly armed Cherokees showed up the morning of Chewie's court appearance (Steiner 1968; Conley 2005b, 214). Nevertheless, the case was held over that day and sent to a federal district court in Tulsa, where, Wahrhaftig (1975c, 144) laments, it was "buried in legal procrastination" and ultimately dismissed.

Regardless, as an organization, the OCCO later "developed into a loose confederation of committees representing counties, individual settlements, and special interest groups . . . [and served as] an instrument of the Cherokee people as a whole" (Wahrhaftig and Lukens-Wahrhaftig 1979, 233–34). Wahrhaftig (1975a, 145) describes the OCCO as "the most comprehensive and impressive of modern Cherokee institutions." Indeed, as a uniquely Cherokee act of resistance, this organization was a special moment in recent Cherokee history. Hunting, and by extension the maintenance of proper relationships with the rest of Creation, was at the core of the movement: "Cherokee perception and protest of economic, political, and social exploitation became focused only in reference to this specific and critical issue" (Wahrhaftig and Lukens-Wahrhaftig 1979, 230). Wahrhaftig and Lukens-Wahrhaftig elaborate on the significance of Cherokee hunting:

> The issue of hunting strikes at the very core of Cherokee existence. It affects all—young men who actively hunt, old men who remember Cherokee national sovereignty and understand life sacredly,[12] and women who not only understand the need for game protein as a crucial supplement to family diet but also appreciate the need for hunting as a validation of male proficiency. Beyond this, Cherokee hunting and the United States–Cherokee treaties which guarantee Cherokee hunting rights are fundamental symbols of the meaning of Cherokee life. Hunting is, in effect, a reality-test of proportions basic to the Cherokee worldview. Cherokees believe that their Creator intended for them to be permanently a part of the world; therefore, game was placed on the earth to sustain them. Through all their turbulent history, hunting has persisted among Cherokees not only as a subsistence activity but also as a demonstration of the Cherokee peoples' covenant with their Creator. (ibid.)

The OCCO and the moral and political foundations on which it stood "roused members of Cherokee settlements from the fifty-year period of dormancy which had persisted since Oklahoma statehood" (238). By asserting Cherokee treaty rights and the need to maintain connections to the land through subsistence practices, the movement contested Oklahoma state hegemony over natural resources and the management thereof. To this day, the hunting and fishing rights of Cherokee citizens are still legally untested and ambiguous with regard to Oklahoma state game authority on nontribal land, although Cherokee citizens continue to hunt and fish without licenses on tribal land and waterways within the Cherokee Nation fourteen-county jurisdictional area.[13]

Wahrhaftig claims that the OCCO came to an end in 1973 due to the disillusionment of its members and a lack of funds (240). In terms of its larger efforts to represent marginalized Cherokees and seek redress for their grievances, he views the organization as an unsuccessful endeavor doomed by the reorganization and assertive presence of the initiative's hired non-Indian lawyer. Yet there are aspects of the organization's legacy that Wahrhaftig fails to recognize as positive contributions in the development of the modern Cherokee Nation. He notes that the OCCO forced the nascent Cherokee Nation government to grant official recognition to rural Cherokee communities and to relate directly to them for the first time (Wahrhaftig 1975b, 144–45). This resulted in the creation of what is now called the Cherokee Nation Office of Community Services, with hired positions for Cherokee community representatives. Wahrhaftig views this as the cooptation of the OCCO's efforts, but I argue that this demonstrates the purpose and efficacy of the group when viewed in the appropriate political-economic and historical perspectives.

Wahrhaftig's work on the OCCO is a useful account of the development of a Cherokee institution. He argues that the process revealed primordial forms of Cherokee social organization—"the same processes . . . which led to the formation of the historic Cherokee Nation" (Wahrhaftig and Lukens-Wahrhaftig 1979, 224). Thus he suggests that the development of the OCCO represented a "resurrected state"—the true Cherokee Nation (242–43). But his analysis is couched in his biased view of the Cherokee Nation tribal government of this time—what he labels the "Cherokee Establishment." His disdain for the Cherokee Nation tribal government of the 1960s is best exemplified in statements like the following: "The present Cherokee tribal government was created, and is directed, by white Americans of Cherokee descent who are legally recognized as Cherokee ... the tribal government is a component of an entirely illegitimate and alien society which exists only by virtue of its unilateral abrogation of federal treaties. ... [It] explicitly pledges allegiance to the laws of the United States and the state of Oklahoma and to institutions which in the past and at present sanction the theft of Cherokee lands and assets" (225, 229).

This racialized analysis situates "white Americans of Cherokee descent" as neocolonizers who have created a pseudogovernment from scratch through which to exploit and oppress their darker-skinned, culturally pure, distant brethren.[14] Yet this perspective seems to me a product of both the antiestablishment/antiauthority climate of the 1960s and trends in the field of anthropology at that time that sought to locate primordial peoples and "protect" their culture—a tradition that would later be discredited by works such as Eric Wolf's *Europe and the People without History* (1982). Additionally, Wahrhaftig assumes that the dissolution of the Cherokee Nation as a result of Oklahoma statehood had been valid, when in fact no laws have ever confirmed this. On the contrary, the 1906 Five Tribes Act (which Wahrhaftig fails to mention) reaffirms the continued existence and authority of tribal governments in Oklahoma (Strickland and Strickland 1991, 123). More radically, the belief in the dissolution of the Cherokee Nation assumes that the U.S. government has the ability to perform such an act, thus validating federal "plenary power," which runs contrary to the foundations of tribal sovereignty.[15] As Robert Conley (Cherokee) writes with regard to Principal Chief Milam's refusal to reorganize the Cherokee Nation government under the federal Oklahoma Indian General Welfare Act of 1936 (a correlate of the Indian Reorganization Act designed especially for Oklahoma tribes), "The Cherokee Nation was already in possession of its inherent sovereignty" (Conley 2005b, 205).

Wahrhaftig claims that the political situation in the Cherokee Nation during this time was distinct from the dynamics in other Indian communities throughout the United States. He asserts that whereas other Indian nations were experiencing internal factionalism (made up of factions of more and less acculturated individuals), Cherokees were witnessing oppression by complete outsiders (the "white Americans of Cherokee descent").[16] Moving away from this racialized and essentialist framework, we see that the OCCO represents a reoccurring historical pattern—a social movement in response to dire circumstances. Other movements such as White Path's rebellion, Oochalata's movement, and the Redbird Smith movement illustrate earlier instances, and all of them are in some way a reaction to the loss of control over tribal institutions due to federal (colonial) intervention. These movements represent the dialectics of Cherokee state transformation, or the push and pull between bureaucratic and traditional authority. In this context, mixed-blood elite Cherokees in the 1960s did not simply assume, as Wahrhaftig portrays, the role of the colonizers. Rather, their task was to rebuild the Cherokee Nation government, and they did so with significant support from full-blood leadership. Dorothy Milligan recounts that in 1954 Principal Chief Keeler sought to resign from his position in favor of a full-blood and fluent Cherokee speaker. She writes, "Much to his surprise the full-bloods of the Cherokee Nation petitioned the Department of the Interior to keep Keeler as chief" (Milligan 1977). I make this point not to deny any unequal relations of power that existed within Cherokee society along racial lines; rather, my intent is to reframe the analysis of historical events in order to move beyond overly and inaccurately racialized conceptions of Cherokee politics, and to acknowledge the positions of multiple and internally diverse actors.

The degree to which the Cherokee Nation is able to work out these internal issues by its own accord affects the success of such movements. The efforts of the OCCO and the resulting recognition of the subordinated status of rural Cherokee communities by the Cherokee Nation government represented an acknowledgement of problems in Cherokee society that needed to be addressed. The creation of a system of community representatives marked a significant development in the rebuilding of the Cherokee Nation during this time. One could argue further that this movement led to future changes in the tribal government, including demographic shifts in the tribal leadership starting in the 1980s that are more representative of rural Cherokee communities (see Sturm 2002, 98–107). Thus the movement served its purpose and was successful in prompting social change, but it did not become a permanent fixture in Cherokee politics.[17]

Interestingly, Wahrhaftig (1975a, 136–39) makes a very similar claim elsewhere about other Cherokee institutions that did not "get off the ground." In a paper titled "Institution Building among Oklahoma's Traditional Cherokees" (1975a), he describes a Cherokee community church that had lost control over its functions due to a newcomer preacher who promoted "white" Christian ways and ceased the use of the Cherokee language during services. The old men of the church formed a coalition with the local non-Christian Four Mothers Society in order to build a new institution—a Sunday school—for teaching the written Cherokee language outside of a religious context. As the discussions between the old men of the church and the leaders of the Four Mothers Society began to lead to actual plans, word got around to the rest of the church congregation. The congregation saw that the partnership between the church elders and the Four Mothers leaders represented a sign of withdrawal—a definitive act of disapproval in Cherokee society. Sensing the unrest as a threat to the existing institution (the community church), the congregation officially replaced the new "white-oriented" preacher with one who was well known for promoting Cherokee values and the Cherokee language. The Sunday school proposal never materialized, and things went back to normal at the community church. Wahrhaftig argues that instead of viewing this prospective institution as a failure, it should be viewed as serving its purpose by affecting the outcome of events—namely, a return to the syncretic Cherokee way of Christian worship. This anecdote (and even the rest of Wahrhaftig's paper) is in line with my thesis here—that the membership of the OCCO never saw the organization as a "resurrected state." Rather, the OCCO served a purpose by forcing the tribal government to react to it in ways that addressed its demands.

The OCCO was a form of Cherokee activism—a forum through which members could gather to envision a Cherokee society unhindered by the oppression and exploitation of settler colonialism. It protested both the state of Oklahoma and the federally controlled Cherokee Nation government and called for the recognition of rural Cherokee communities and their rights. The case of John Chewie had called into question the legitimacy of Oklahoma state authority in the Cherokee Nation, and the grassroots movement that became the OCCO reasserted the voice and influence of Cherokee communities in the Cherokee Nation government. Although incorporation into the state of Oklahoma and the production of "Green Country" had resulted in a seemingly typical rural American landscape throughout the Cherokee Nation, the actions of the OCCO reclaimed the western Ozark Plateau as the cultural and social heart of the Cherokee Nation.

While today Cherokees are still outnumbered by the local white population, cohesive Cherokee communities permeate the region—many of which, as Wahrhaftig (1968) documented, have persisted since Cherokee arrival in the Indian Territory. Wahrhaftig's work (see 1966a) also documented the intense poverty of the region, and this by and large continues today. However, much has also changed since the time of Wahrhaftig's fieldwork that has positively affected Cherokees and their standing in the larger regional social milieu. Cherokees have been reasserting their authority in northeastern Oklahoma through the increasing sophistication of tribal governance structures. Many of these strides have been made in the realm of resource control. At the time of Wahrhaftig's research, the Cherokee Nation had little to no control over tribal lands, yet in the 1980s and 1990s, the Cherokee Nation would regain this power by reclaiming institutions designed to protect and manage tribal natural resources.

Environmental Self-Governance and the Reclamation of Resource Control

With the election of W. W. Keeler as principal chief by the people in 1971, the Cherokee Nation once again directed the affairs of its government. Although the degree of Cherokee sovereignty differed significantly from that of pre-Oklahoma statehood, leaders began to focus on reforming the tribal government from a "paper" institution back to a constitutional government. Keeler began this process by appointing a small group of community representatives to work on a new Cherokee Nation constitution, but he resigned from politics in 1975 after a short four-year term. His successor, Ross Swimmer, went on to spearhead the new constitution. Also an affluent businessman, Swimmer's approach to restructuring the Cherokee Nation government was based on efficiency and corporate models. In his view, the more efficiently the Cherokee Nation government administered services to the Cherokee people, the better off Cherokee communities would be. As such, the tribal council created by the new constitution in 1976 was based on a unicameral corporate model, despite early discussions about recreating the bicameral legislature of the 1839 constitution (Lemont 2006, 291).

Eric Lemont asserts that the unicameral legislature was a product of the circumstances: "For almost seventy years, the Nation had had no enrollment and no government . . . Instead of creating a government, Swimmer simply wanted to organize a system for the improvement of the delivery of services to individual Cherokees" (ibid.). While it may be true that the bicameral form was abandoned due to the need to efficiently administer services to Cherokees in need, this does not mean that the product of the

1976 constitution was not a government. The 1976 constitution had also reestablished the tripartite governance system, including the judicial and executive branches. Furthermore, although Lemont criticizes the style of governance created by the unicameral system, its goals and purpose matched those of the historic Cherokee Nation government to "extend hospitality to its citizens" (Stremlau 2011, 96). This "concern for social welfare," as Rose Stremlau notes, was what made the Cherokee system unique from other governments of its time. Therefore, while the unicameral form was indeed a product of the circumstances, by staying true to these foundational values (even in the absence of communal landholding), those who were rebuilding the Cherokee Nation government nevertheless were able to maintain some continuity with past forms.

For the next twenty years, the Cherokee Nation thrived under its new constitution, and Cherokees developed a strong reputation from their stable and influential tribal government. Following Swimmer's ten-year term, in 1985 Wilma Mankiller was elected principal chief of the Cherokee Nation—the first woman to serve in this position. The Stricklands (1991, 132) note that this accomplishment "[brought] forward and fulfill[ed] a tradition of leadership that dates back to the 'Beloved Women' leaders of the precontact and preconstitutional eras." They further recount, "Speaking of her electoral victory, Mankiller said that the most important thing about her election was not that she was a woman, but that she represented a different kind of Cherokee, from a new background, with a different agenda. She did not have a national power base, profession, or position of wealth, but rather she was an Indian from an Indian community who had worked with Indian needs from within the Indian nation." This observation highlights the demographic shift in tribal leadership noted previously. Although Mankiller had been raised in the San Francisco Bay Area for much of her life, she had returned to her home community to work on a grassroots level and had already initiated important changes in Cherokee community development. In 1981, she helped establish and then was named the first director of the Cherokee Nation Community Development Department, which, much like Keeler's Cherokee Foundation, served to procure and administer funding for rural community projects (Mankiller and Wallis 1993, 233).

One such project entailed the installation of a water line in the rural Cherokee community of Bell, located in Adair County. Bell had been "a community in utter decline" (234). The area was very poor—at least a quarter of the households had no running water, in addition to limit-ed access to clean water. Mankiller spearheaded a community self-help project through a partnership with Bell community members and the Cherokee Nation. Acting as a community liaison, Mankiller secured fund-ing through grants, while the people of Bell provided all the labor for the project as volunteers. The Bell project was a tremendous success, and it became a model for Cherokee Nation community work, as well as com-munity development programs throughout Indian Country. Through this project, Mankiller strengthened her skills at community organizing, affirmed her belief in collective problem solving and community inter-dependence, and met her future husband, Charlie Soap. The project had also left a definitive imprint on her political consciousness—its focus on social-environmental issues would inform the development of Cherokee Nation environmental programs that arose out of the self-governance pol-icies during her tenure as principal chief.

In 1987, due to increasing frustrations with federal Indian bureaucracy, American Indian tribes throughout the United States began to question the efficacy of the then twelve-year-old Self-Determination and Education Assistance Act and called for significant policy amendments. While the Self-Determination Act had promoted American Indian control over their own affairs, the BIA had been reluctant to step down from its paternalistic role. Many institutions, including Indian Health Service facilities and tribal forestry programs, were still operated by Department of Interior personnel (Johnson and Hamilton 1994). Along with pressure from the tribes, a BIA fiasco in Arizona that received wide media coverage prompted congressio-nal action.[18] "Self-governance" became the new emphasis in federal Indian policy, and in 1988, new amendments to the Self-Determination Act cre-ated Self-Governance Compacts by which Indian tribes could "administer and manage programs, activities, functions and services previously man-aged by the Bureau of Indian Affairs" (Self-Governance Communication and Education Project [SGCEP] 2006, 22). The legislation also acknowl-edged the authority of tribes to "redesign those programs and services to meet the needs of their communities, within the flexibility of allocating funds based on tribal priorities."

On October 1, 1990, Principal Chief Mankiller signed such an agree-ment on behalf of the Cherokee Nation and "put the Tahlequah BIA agency out of business."[19] Under self-governance, the Cherokee Nation began to assume control over the former BIA trust programs, which included loblolly pine silviculture, cattle-grazing leases, and noxious weed suppression on the 45,000 acres of Cherokee tribal trust land. The Cherokee Nation Natural Resources Department (NRD) emerged as the new tribal entity for managing these activities. Also around this time, the Cherokee Nation Office of Environmental Services was established in an effort to mirror the activities of the U.S. Environmental Protection Agency on tribal trust lands. Later renamed Cherokee Nation Environmental Programs (CNEP), its duties entail environmental monitoring (water and air quality), as well as environmental cleanup and remediation (illegal dumpsites, brownfields, and superfund sites). In 1992, the CNEP developed and launched the Inter-Tribal Environmental Council, which provides environmental services and training programs to forty-one member tribes in Oklahoma, New Mexico, and Texas (see http://www.itec.org). This era marks another significant step forward in contemporary Cherokee Nation governance, as tribal programs were reclaimed from the paternalistic hand of the federal government. It also marks a significant development in contemporary Cherokee state transformation, as these new tribal departments and programs began to form a more complex, sophisticated, and bureaucratic state structure.

The Cherokee Nation also began passing important legislation with regard to environmental issues. In 1993, the tribal council passed the Environmental Quality Act (later renamed the Environmental Quality Code) in order to "establish and implement a Cherokee Nation policy which will encourage productive and enjoyable harmony between human beings and their environment" (63 CNCA §301). The act also aimed to "promote efforts which will prevent or eliminate damage to natural resources and the environment and to enrich the understanding of the ecological systems and natural resources important to the Cherokee Nation." Moreover, the act established the Cherokee Nation Environmental Protection Commission, composed of environmental specialists and scientists who serve as an advisory board to the Cherokee Nation government. This flurry of activity in the environmental sector in the early 1990s earned the Cherokee Nation recognition as a leader in this regard throughout Indian Country. It also speaks to the concomitant processes of environmental protection and state transformation in the Cherokee Nation. Through these acts, the Cherokee Nation clearly stated the importance of environmental issues. As governmental actors worked to establish bureaucratic offices and programs that would administer environmental monitoring and natural resources, the articulation of "harmony between human beings and their environment" conveyed values that still permeated Cherokee perspectives of land and their relationship to it.

In 1994, after her third term as principal chief, Mankiller decided not to run for office due to increasing health issues and the desire to see new leadership emerge. The election that followed proved to be the most controversial in contemporary Cherokee history, culminating with a political crisis in 1997 that entailed SWAT teams, "goon squads," and national news coverage.[20] In the midst of this crisis, the Cherokee Nation was experiencing a significant attempt at governmental reform. A clause in the 1976 constitution required that the tribal government submit to Cherokee Nation voters the question of a proposed constitution convention at least every twenty years. In 1995, Cherokee Nation citizens had voted to hold such a convention. With plans under way, the organizers faced the difficult task of bringing the Cherokee people together under the conditions of intense divisiveness caused by the political crisis. In a lengthy and delicate manner, the small group that made up the convention rules committee managed to form an independent Constitution Convention Committee that maintained a stance of political neutrality. By 1998, the committee had received formal approval from the entire council, along with an initial budget of $250,000 to begin the process of reform, and by 1999, the committee had formed a group of seventy-nine delegates that represented all political factions. On February 26, the delegates convened for the first day of a nine-day convention held on the campus of Northeastern State University. This momentous occasion produced the 1999 constitution, under which the Cherokee Nation operates to this day (Lemont 2006, 295–98).[21]

The convention produced lively debate on many issues, most notably on "the growing disconnect between the [1976] constitution's corporate model of government and the Nation's phenomenal growth in population, diversity, and assumption of governmental responsibilities over the preceding three decades" (300). Lemont states, "Between 1970 and 1999, the Nation's population had grown from 40,000 to more than 200,000. The government had contracted or compacted with the U.S. government in a host of different areas, including housing, health, economic development, elderly programs, education, and environmental management. As a result, the Nation's budget had ballooned from $10,000 to $192 million" (ibid.). In this regard, the four main debates centered on bicameralism, strengthening the judiciary branch, providing representation to nonresident Cherokee Nation citizens, and requiring a minimum blood quantum for the office of principal chief. As a result of these debates, delegates strengthened the former Judicial Appeals Tribunal and named it once again the Cherokee Nation Supreme Court. They also created positions for two at-large council representatives. Ultimately, the delegates denied the proposed requirement for a minimal blood quantum for the principal chief, as well as the proposed return to a bicameral legislature. Interestingly, despite an informed and energetic debate, delegates denied the proposal for reinstating the bicameral legislature on the basis of cost (302). The 1999 constitution also established the position of secretary of state and the offices of attorney general and marshal. A formal statement of Cherokee Nation territorial jurisdiction is included as Article II, and Article XVIII requires that the constitution be printed in both the Cherokee and English languages.

The convention had strengthened and solidified the Cherokee constitution amid turmoil, and this period of intense political development had hardened the foundation for contemporary Cherokee state transformation. The Cherokee Nation has since continued to advance in the areas of health care, community services, economic development, and regional and national political influence. Still true to its roots, the Cherokee state operates as both a governing body and an instrument for social welfare; however, certain departments must increasingly navigate the social costs of this political form. Not surprisingly, many of these predicaments have manifested in the realm of natural resource management, an area central to modern state practice. The situation is further compounded by the complexities of allotment's legacy and the lingering paternalistic oversight of the federal government.

While the Cherokee Nation worked to extend tribal control over environmental programs in the 1990s, it inherited a complex land management bureaucracy that persists to this day. Checkerboarded tribal lands and the red tape that accompanies them cause difficulties in jurisdiction and property maintenance. Messy land deeds and property lines tell the story of grafters and land hawks. Multiple heirs of individual allotments complicate ownership beyond comprehension and inhibit any effective use of the property through agreement. And the enduring system of blood quantum to determine "restricted" land status continues to racialize property issues in the Cherokee Nation (see Leeds 2006). Furthermore, although self-governance had deemed the Cherokee Nation in control of its own resource management programs, the BIA retained some authority in the form of "trust evaluations." Outlined in the Permanent Self-Governance Act of 1994 (P.L. 103-413, section 403[d]), the trust evaluation "allows the United States to exercise the necessary supervision or oversight relative to its obligations to the Tribe and to individual Indians. An escape clause is provided whereby the United States may assume direct management of the physical trust assets, upon proper notice to the Tribe, if the trust assets are in imminent jeopardy. Imminent jeopardy is defined as significant loss of devaluation of the physical Trust asset, caused by the Tribes' action or inaction" (SGCEP 2006, 45). By establishing regulations and normative "best practices" that are guided by the assumption that lands must be made profitable, trust evaluations attempt to maintain BIA land management hegemony. In the Cherokee Nation, former BIA land management practices that are continued in the present include loblolly pine silviculture, the leasing of tribal lands to cattle ranchers for grazing, and fire and weed suppression to enable the two former practices.

These management responsibilities often put undue strain on NRD personnel, who, while they are charged with maintaining the former BIA programs, also have a professional duty to respond to Cherokee Nation citizen input (as they are tribal employees and, in most cases, tribal citizens themselves). Often the two tasks are entirely at odds with each other. For instance, tribal citizens frequently complain that their use of forest resources is jeopardized by NRD silvicultural activities— programs that are carried out per BIA "best practices" guidelines. Loblolly pine silviculture eliminates the oak/hickory forest in place of monocrop stands, a practice that decreases species diversity in both flora and fauna and thus negatively impacts hunting and gathering activities. There is also an intrinsic value to the hardwood forests that is compromised by these activities. At a community meeting in Kenwood (located in Delaware County, where there is an abundance of tribal trust land, about 1,100 acres of which is being used for silviculture), one participant expressed his regret about seeing the habitat for birds and other animals disappear along with the hardwood forests. With a tone of voice that conveyed a deep familiarity and respect for the area's remaining hardwood stands, he said, "I would just hate to see them go."[22] With regard to leasing tribal lands for cattle grazing, important medicinal plants like milkweed (*Asclepias* L.) are threatened due to the fact that they cannot compete with the Bermuda and fescue grasses that are seeded on native prairies to achieve "improved" pastures. Furthermore, herbicide spraying makes healthy milkweed specimens harder to find.

These practices, and the citizen responses they have triggered, show that while the resource-based approach to environmental governance has established a greater degree of authority over tribal lands, the inherited land management programs are inadequate when it comes to representing traditional Cherokee ways of relating to land and nonhumans. Not surprisingly, the resource-based approach has created tension between tribal citizens and NRD personnel. The NRD's response, however, shows how Cherokees mediate this tension and how the dialectical process it generates has come to characterize Cherokee state transformation.

Resources, Relationships, and the Dynamics of Indigenous State Practice

Since roughly 2004, the NRD has begun to deviate from BIA protocol, stemming largely from its response to the citizen input exemplified in the previous section. Loblolly pine monocropping has decreased in the last two years, and as I indicated in the introduction, the NRD has begun to reconsider the use of herbicides on prairies in favor of brush-hogging (clearing by mowing). While brush-hogging would inevitably cut back some culturally significant prairie plants, NRD staff has discussed reserving areas of important plant growth for cultural use. Further, harmful chemicals would be eliminated from land management practices.

The reduction of BIA activities has been accompanied by the initiation of culturally inspired land management activities. In recent years, NRD staff has launched numerous "cultural forestry" projects that prioritize the cultivation and reintroduction of culturally significant species. Most notable among these projects are the large-scale planting of Shagbark Hickory trees (*Carya ovata*), an important species for food, crafts, and medicine that has become increasingly scarce, and Osage Orange trees (*Maclura pomifera*), which have long been used by Cherokees in the western lands for making strong bows. NRD staff has also begun to focus on nonwood forest products, which include the medicinal, edible, and crafts-based herbs, forbs, and grasses that have no significant "value" from the perspective of BIA forestry programs. Rivercane (*Arundinaria gigantea*), used for numerous traditional crafts, and ginseng (*Panax quinquefolius* L.), an extremely important medicinal herb, have been key species in these efforts.

Figure 7. Author and NRD staff planting ginseng and goldenseal roots. Photograph by author.

Figure 8. Two-year-old ginseng root. Photograph by author.

Figure 9. Ginseng sprouts after one year. Photograph by author.

Figure 10. Goldenseal sprout after one year. Photograph by author.

These cultural forestry projects, although inspired by citizen input, also stem from the larger trend of cultural revitalization within the Cherokee Nation government (see Sturm 2002, 104). Such a political climate has allowed NRD staff to devote some of their time to the maintenance and protection of cultural resources and to explore alternative management practices. The work directly informs a key policy initiative—the Cherokee Nation Integrated Resource Management Plan—with the goal of identifying and cataloging cultural resources for conservation purposes. The ethnobotany initiative that began in 2004 and the inception of the elders' advisory group in 2008 are components of this strategy. As a result of the work done with the elders' group, in 2009 the NRD produced a small booklet titled *Wild Plants of the Cherokee Nation* (Figure 11), which currently serves as a supplementary text for biology lessons in the Cherokee-language immersion school. Printed in Cherokee and English, the goal of the booklet is to raise awareness among Cherokee citizens of the richness of their cultural heritage and to encourage the continued application of such knowledge through land-based gathering activities. The elders' group is also working with the NRD to establish numerous areas of contiguous tribal land on which to carry out management programs for medicinal wild plants. This two-pronged approach to cultural forestry—(1) identifying, cataloging, and planting culturally significant plants and (2) creating physical and institutional space for the continued transmission of traditional knowledge—clearly deviates from the norms established by BIA forestry programs and indicates exciting new directions in tribal natural resource management.

Of course, the NRD's new approach to land management is not without obstacles. NRD responsibilities are not limited to forestry and range management activities: The department is often stretched thin by demands from other Cherokee Nation departments that rely on NRD staff expertise in areas like land appraisal and GIS technology. Further, at the time of my fieldwork, the interest in ethnobotany rested with only two staff members, which made the "cultural" element of their work more of a sidebar than a central priority. There is also a certain amount of hesitancy in renouncing BIA "best practices" in favor of activities that promote cultural resources. Not only do land leasing and monocrop silviculture contribute to tribal revenues, but per the "trust evaluations," the BIA technically can still assume management of tribal lands if they are in "imminent jeopardy." On multiple occasions, the NRD supervisor indicated to me that the trust

CHEROKEE NATION®

GWY Ꮑ ᎢᎾᎢ ᏝᏚᎠᏁᎢ ᎠᏐᎮ ᏛᎲᎤᏚᏢ ᏝᏚᏅᏝ ᏚᎤᎬ

Wild Plants of the Cherokee Nation

Figure 11. Wild plants booklet published by the NRD as a result of consultations with the elders' advisory group.

evaluation process does cause him anxiety with regard to the cultural forestry projects that contradict BIA forestry conventions.

Reinstating cultural practices on the land also poses difficult issues. Although the NRD has been known to aid and supervise small burns on tribal citizens' property, when I asked about reestablishing controlled burns on a large scale, the NRD supervisor replied that the idea was a "bureaucratic nightmare" due to the checkerboarded land ownership and federal and state restrictions.[23] Yet another obstacle is simply the paucity of lands over which the Cherokee Nation has control. A small land base not only limits the ability to create space for tribal management activities but also puts the NRD in the unfortunate position of having to govern access to tribal lands. Thus resource gathering, although still practiced throughout the Cherokee Nation, remains a controversial issue on trust lands. While the right to gather on trust land is open to all Cherokee citizens, locked gates restrict access to many of these tracts, and one must request a key from the NRD. This has caused tension between NRD staff and tribal citizens when, because of repeated instances of overharvesting, the staff insist on opening the gates in person and remaining until the gathering is finished.

The overharvesting of plants and animals by some Cherokees is a real problem, even though this tendency is considered a deviation from traditional ideals. Many Cherokees are aware of overharvesting activities, and some elders assert that the decline of traditional knowledge is a direct cause of this. Bloodroot (*Sanguinaria canadensis*) has become a highly sought-after plant that is used for making a natural red dye for baskets, but it is also a potent medicine. In the course of my fieldwork, elders have commented that younger craftspeople mistakenly gather large amounts of the root when only a small portion is needed to make a good quality dye. The overharvesting of bloodroot by craftspeople limits its availability for those who seek the plant for medicine.

This topic has been raised during the elders' advisory group meetings with regard to issuing gathering permits to individual tribal citizens, but so far there has been no resolution. Elders themselves have been stopped and questioned by the Cherokee Marshal Service when gathering plants on tribal lands, leading the advisory group to advocate a way to distinguish between those who have been properly trained to gather and those who may still need guidance or teaching from a knowledgeable source (i.e., an elder). Yet myriad complications arose concerning who would have the authority to issue such permits and whether the program would be effective. When approached with the idea of gathering permits, many tribal council members considered the proposal to be contradictory to their responsibility toward all citizens and were not in favor of a program that would grant special rights to individuals.

I will take up the issue of gathering rights and permits in more detail in chapter 5. For now, I focus on how NRD personnel have had to negotiate between the incorporation of relationship-based approaches to environmental management and the resource-based approach that settler-colonial indigenous state dynamics demand. Political ecologists have countered past presumptions of *a priori* state-versus-local opposition in which nonlocal "experts" always represent state agencies that disenfranchise or displace local peoples and their respective environmental practices and knowledge (Dove 1994; Sivaramakrishnan 1999; Robbins 2000). Similarly, in the Cherokee Nation—where environmental management is carried out on a relatively small scale—framing the analysis in terms of networks and alliances illuminates the interpersonal relationships that exist on the ground between Cherokee state actors and ordinary tribal citizens. The small-scale interactions between NRD field workers and Cherokee community residents, combined with the long-term and site-specific nature of NRD activities, create a high level of accountability. Even if a resource manager is not "local" in the sense that he or she was not reared in a Cherokee community, credibility among the communities is very important because of the understood "soft" authority that communities have in their respective areas. Additionally, the general congeniality that is characteristic of rural social interactions, as well as the pride and dedication to the people that many individuals feel in working for the tribal government, are indicators of atypical "statist" tendencies (at least in James Scott's [1998] "high modern" sense). This assessment not only bolsters other scholars' calls for viewing social organization and environmental politics in terms of *heterarchy* (Crumley 2003) and *networks* (Robbins 2004) as opposed to hierarchical chains; it also displays aspects of the Cherokee state (notably its small size and unobtrusive role) that distinguish it from other states.

Nevertheless, despite the Cherokee state's relatively benign posture, there are areas from which community-based citizens feel increasingly alienated. While access to authority is fairly "open" (and a tribal citizen can call or visit the director and staff of the NRD with relative ease), the job responsibilities of Cherokee Nation staff are often structured in a way that does not guarantee a citizen's ability to meaningfully influence the outcome of events. As political ecologists Jesse Ribot and Nancy Peluso (2003) remind us, legal or official rights have no value without the ability to *do* what those rights stipulate; the right to resource access means nothing when the gate is locked. But just as the land base was diminished by forces beyond the control of the Cherokee Nation, so was its government. Not surprisingly, for the Cherokee Nation the reclamation of land and resources have gone hand in hand with the transformation of governance institutions. The elders' advisory group, which has made tribal land reacquisition one of its central concerns, thus represents the formation of a significant alliance. Although the group has coalesced around the subject of traditional plant knowledge, the forum is used to voice related concerns, as exemplified in the gathering-permit issue.

The alternative style and setting of the elders' group meetings illuminates issues of *process*—ways of making decisions and getting things done—and the contrast between bureaucratic methods and traditional ones. The group meetings also call attention to changing perspectives on knowledge and authority. Group meetings in the rural areas have shifted the focus from Western scientific knowledge obtained by college degrees to local traditional knowledge. This has not been a superficial "seat at the table" given to traditional experts; rather, the meetings have quite literally moved the table itself—or the chairs, in the case of when NRD staff must bring folding chairs to the meeting sites. Accordingly, the elders' group represents the creation of an alliance that has enabled certain people to gain direct access to multiple forms of authority. Ribot and Peluso (2003, 170) note that access to authority plays a large role in the ability of groups to benefit from resources. Through the group meetings, the elders have gained access to land management authority, and the proposal for creating gathering permits demonstrates the ability of the group to potentially influence land management decisions in very concrete ways. NRD staff has gained access to the elders' traditional authority—specifically in the form of plant knowledge but also in the ability to sanction or condemn others' potentially harmful activities on the land. The dynamics created by this situation have spurred a healthy amount of caution with regard to the group's activities. Group members are cautious about "throwing their weight around" and instead have advocated for laying a foundation of spiritual values that would define the group's purpose as for the benefit of the community at large. Rather than purporting to speak for all, the group has emerged as an "advisory council." They have created a forum in which to meaningfully express concerns to the tribal government from a traditional and spiritual perspective—a discursive space that one could argue has been lacking in Cherokee governance structures since before allotment (i.e., with the end of the bicameral system).

Conclusion

In the midst of landlessness, paternalism, and environmental degradation, Cherokees reestablished their government, and in the process, they reestablished their relationships to one another and to the land. While the loss of the communal land base had struck a huge blow to Cherokee ideals of governance, Cherokees retained the "political ethic and concern for social welfare" that had underpinned common ownership in land (Stremlau 2011, 96). On this foundation, and through dialectical tension among official and grassroots organizations, the Cherokee state reemerged in a distinctly modern form. Whereas official forms of organization stressed political sovereignty and the reinvigoration of the tribal government, grassroots struggles explicitly dealt with the right to maintain subsistence practices. The combined result of these efforts regenerated a significant degree of political and territorial sovereignty, reaffirmed a Cherokee way of life and subsistence economy, and restored in Cherokee governance the traditional ideals of sociopolitical organization embodied in semiautonomous communities.

The development of the modern Cherokee state once again came with compromises. As an identifiable modern state practice, natural resource management revealed to Cherokees the social costs of the state form. Nevertheless, the actions of the NRD and the elders' advisory group highlight how the process of negotiating the dynamics of indigenous state practice is an integral aspect of Cherokee state transformation. In other words, while NRD staff has negotiated the settler-state paternalism of BIA trust evaluations in tandem with its own regulation of citizen access to sparse tribal lands, the process of asserting the relationship-based approach via cultural forestry projects has produced a unique partnership that addresses inherent challenges of the state form. And although the elders' group is not a movement per se, through its assertion of traditional authority, it displays historical continuity with formations such as White Path's rebellion, Oochalata's movement, and the OCCO. The elders have created a forum through which they can articulate important concerns about the way decisions are made, specifically with regard to the non-human world. One might say that this embodies Rebecca Tsosie's (1996, 227) notion of "true" environmental self-determination.

In chapter 5, I provide a more detailed look into the negotiations that surround indigenous state transformation, drawing from my experiences in carrying out the tribal ethnobotany project from 2004 to 2008. This project was unique in that it was directly connected to policy and governmental operations. In this attempt to merge culture with bureaucracy, roadblocks arose that were based in the historical and social context of Cherokee medicinal knowledge, bringing to light the politics of plants and the stakes of contemporary cultural revitalization.

CHAPTER 4

Indigenous Ethnobotany

Cherokee Medicine and the Power of Plant Lore

"YOU SEE, IT'S LIKE APPROACHING A WOLF," he said. "You have to get them to come to you." This was advice a friend gave me in a conversation about how best to broach the topic of plant medicine with elders.[1] He is, in fact, an elder himself, and currently he is involved closely with the elders' advisory group, although this conversation took place three months before the first group meeting. We had been driving rural dirt roads in Adair County, stopping along the way to observe and discuss the plants growing on the roadside and often venturing into the woods as he saw more familiar plants that he wanted to show me. I had subtly expressed my frustration about how difficult it was to get people to participate in the tribal ethnobotany project due to the secrecy surrounding Cherokee medicinal plant knowledge. At the time, he was one of the few who had faith in the goals of the project and was willing to take time out of his day to drive around and teach me about what he knew. His advice that day hinted at the protocol of indirectness that permeates much of Cherokee social interactions. Simultaneously, it spoke to the care with which one must carry out a project of this sort. In theory, one must not only approach a wolf with caution, respect, and indirect behavior but also—if successful in getting the wolf to come to you—maintain the trust that has been given. One false move and it can never be obtained again.

During the course of my work on the project, I had been told by some peers that "you just don't talk about medicine." This statement seemed to close off the topic in a knee-jerk reaction to cultural taboo. But I persisted in inquiring about plant medicine, perhaps partly out of stubbornness, but also out of the belief that if done the right way—with respect and caution—I could generate a meaningful conversation about this hugely significant part of Cherokee culture that is fading rapidly. Working for the tribal government made things more difficult, but this is another area in which I decided to persist. I had been advised by many observers to take the project out of the government if I wanted it to thrive. They claimed that others would be reluctant to participate if "the tribe" controlled the project. As the project is clearly concerned with cultural preservation, my informants wanted to ensure that it was available for use by "the people," and they thought this goal would be hindered if cultural knowledge was tied up in a web of bureaucracy. But as much as this was a worthwhile suggestion, I was disheartened by the opportunity that would be lost. With a project like this one—inherently tied to the Cherokee Nation's environmental programs—we had the chance to engage with this issue and change things for the better, rather than take for granted the current situation and ignore the deeper problems.

The resurgence of the Cherokee government in the 1970s and the development of increasingly sophisticated state structures for environmental management in the 1980s and 1990s had worked to extend protection over tribal lands and natural resources. But while these structures had attempted to articulate broad Cherokee values of environmental stewardship (as seen in the Cherokee Nation Environmental Quality Act of 1993), they had not fostered within them the cultural processes that ensured the respectful treatment of traditional knowledge. In other words, relationship-based approaches that account for interpersonal trust, cultural protocol, and accountability were lacking. This presented problems when tribal resource managers (and unwitting interns) sought to fill this cultural gap and "incorporate" traditional knowledge into tribal policy. However, the ethnobotany project, and its unavoidable association with the topic of traditional medicine, proved to be a fitting approach for addressing these problems. As Albert Wahrhaftig (1975b, 146) writes with reference to the interpersonal dynamics of traditional healing practices, "The corpus of Cherokee medicine emphasizes *relationship*" (emphasis added). What better area to work toward relationship-based approaches to environmental governance than that of traditional medicine?

As such, this chapter discusses the cultural and historical significance of Cherokee medicinal plant knowledge and therefore provides context for understanding what exactly it means to "do" ethnobotany in the Cherokee Nation today. As I state in the introduction, the paradox surrounding this work was that although people wanted to see this knowledge revitalized, many of them had reasons for not talking about it. This chapter attempts to give the reader an idea of the many sources of those reasons. First I discuss some historical and ethnographic literature on Cherokee plant lore, including its place in the larger realm of Cherokee healing practices and beliefs, as well as the controversy surrounding its past publication. Next I give a description of some contemporary Oklahoma Cherokee perspectives of medicospiritual knowledge, including its structure, how it is acquired, and what it means to "have" this knowledge. I then bring in a discussion of the process of carrying out the ethnobotany project and the social roadblocks I encountered along the way. In addition to a self-reflexive discussion on issues of race and identity, I look at the issues that have arisen surrounding the publication of *Wild Plants of the Cherokee Nation*, the educational booklet mentioned in chapter 3. While the booklet has been a success in terms of its community impact and goals for cultural revitalization, its publication has been plagued with intellectual property concerns and the lack of control over its reproduction and dissemination. These incidents prompted the elders' group to form an editorial board in order to establish controls over the booklet and its use—the process of which contributed significantly to the overall incorporation of the group as a recognized advisory council to the Cherokee Nation government. These issues illuminate within cultural revitalization efforts the parallel stakes of environmental governance and sovereignty. Ethnobotany emerges both as a tool for cultural revitalization and as an object of critique in the context of settler colonialism and the cultural politics of knowledge.

Historical and Ethnographic Accounts of Cherokee Plant Lore

As with many indigenous cultures, Cherokees and plants go way back. As recounted in chapter 1, Cherokee oral tradition tells of how the plants came to the people's aid despite the disrespectful acts committed against the animal world, and Cherokees will forever owe a debt of gratitude for these deeds. Anthropologists alike have noted how the use of plants as medicine has long been a major component of Cherokee culture, to the point of claiming that the depth and significance of this relationship exceeds that of other indigenous peoples. Writing at the turn of the twentieth century, James Mooney stated, "The vegetable kingdom . . . holds a far more important place in the mythology and ceremonial of the [Cherokees] than it does among the Indians of the treeless plains and arid sage deserts of the West, most of the beliefs and customs in this connection centering around the practice of medicine, as expounded by the priests and doctors in every settlement" (Mooney 1900, 420). Consequently, the vast subject of Cherokee medicinal plant lore has received much study, most notably by Mooney himself (Mooney 1891; Mooney and Olbrechts 1932).[2] Since Mooney's time, most of the work on this subject has been with the Eastern Band of Cherokees (Witthoft 1947; Witthoft 1960; Hamel and Chiltoskey 1975; Garrett 2003; Banks 2004; Cozzo 2004; Hall 2006). But despite this substantial body of work, ethnobotanical studies in the Cherokee Nation (i.e., northeastern Oklahoma) are few and far between. The materials that do exist are mostly small, locally published works (Cowan 1975; Cochran 1983).

Although Mooney collected large amounts of ethnobotanical data, the majority of this material actually went unpublished.[3] Moreover, his published materials on the subject, *Sacred Formulas of the Cherokee* (1891) and *The Swimmer Manuscript* (1932),[4] have been described as only "peripheral" ethnobotany (Hall 2006, 20) due to their emphasis on Cherokee healing incantations, or *idi:gawésdi.*[5] Subsequently, these incantations, and the cultural practices and beliefs surrounding them, have attracted important scholarship (Fogelson 1975; Kilpatrick 1997). Studies of these "sacred formulas" reveal the wider world of Cherokee medicomagical beliefs and illuminate a philosophy of healing that includes the use of plants but also encompasses the spiritual and "supernatural" realms of conjuring, divination, witchcraft, and love medicine.

Anthropologist Raymond D. Fogelson (1975, 113) highlights that in the old Cherokee belief system, death or disease was rarely thought to be a product of accidental or natural causes. While Mooney's (1900, 250–52) version of the "Origin of Disease and Medicine" shows how medicine originated in response to vengeful attacks from the animal clans, the belief system included a significant role for human beings in the instigation of disease and death. "Man-killers," or *anididá:hnese:sgi,*[6] occupied one such role and were generally thought of as benevolent members of the community who nevertheless had the ability to retaliate through preternatural means when they had been wronged or insulted (Mooney and Olbrechts 1932, 29). Occupying another point on the spectrum were witches, or *anitsgili,* who are to this day believed to be humans (male or female) that intentionally do harm to others out of purely malevolent intentions. Fogelson (1975, 119) characterizes *anitsgili,* or "night-walkers" (*svnoyi anida:i*), as community parasites—"irredeemable beings whose true existence falls outside the realm of humanity." "Conjurors," as they were known in the past, served to counteract harmful spirits and witchcraft through the use of specialized knowledge, spiritual ability, and, of course, *idi:gawésdi*. Today, this role is occupied by medicine people, or healers (*anidida:hnvwi:sgi*), who, although they do not commonly refer to themselves as "conjurors," may still claim to employ the act of "conjuring" to heal their patients. Wild plants can help in this process, but they are not always the central focus in healing rituals. Other spirits, including helpful animal spirits, are often called on for their abilities to counteract a particular ailment.

Although strict ethnobotanical work among Oklahoma Cherokees is lacking, the study of *idi:gawésdi* in the Cherokee Nation has been given much attention by Cherokee ethnographers Jack and Anna Kilpatrick.[7] A married team, the Kilpatricks collected a vast amount of Cherokee oral stories and written documents in the 1960s (Kilpatrick and Kilpatrick 1964, 1965a, 1965b, 1967, 1970). Much of this material pertained to medical texts, including many private notebooks of individual healers written in the Sequoyan syllabary.[8] The Kilpatricks' (1965b, 1967, 1970) publications of these materials provided translations and explanations of the texts, including the scientific names of any plants mentioned therein. More recently, their son, Alan Kilpatrick (1997), published a comprehensive account of Oklahoma Cherokee witchcraft and "sorcery" using his late parents' notes and his own further research on the subject.

While the Kilpatricks' efforts have preserved a wealth of Cherokee cultural knowledge (and one could view the primary documents as the foundation of a Cherokee national literature),[9] many Cherokees were upset by the publication of these materials—"sacred" as they are. The adverse reaction largely concerned the Kilpatricks' bold act of making available this knowledge to anyone wishing to read it. Albert Wahrhaftig foretold of the impending controversy in a review of their first volume of formulas published entirely in English (Kilpatrick and Kilpatrick 1965b). With regard to the fact that this volume is a collection of love incantations (used to attract and seduce), Wahrhaftig (1966b) states, "To have reproduced these texts in the Sequoyah syllabary, or in transcription with literal interlineal translation as some scholars might demand, would certainly have created a panic among nubile Cherokees and consternation among their parents, for indiscriminate use of this medicine is a serious matter." Perhaps to the surprise of many, the Kilpatricks' later publication of *Notebook of a Cherokee Shaman* (1970) was indeed a transcription with literal interlineal translation (much like Mooney's publications). The subject matter of this work includes the more severe topics of medicine and witchcraft. Although the authors maintained that the formulas were "dead" well before publication (85), other accounts have suggested otherwise, claiming that the *idi:gawésdi* still possess some of their magical powers and are therefore dangerous if used by someone with improper intent (Conley 2005a, 38).

Heidi M. Altman and Thomas N. Belt (2009), on the other hand, state that the act of publishing the formulas is what "neutralized" them and suggest that this in itself was disrespectful. (Mooney's publications are included in their criticism.) They write that "translating or diverging from the proper use of the language for healing is considered [by Cherokee traditionalists] an act of profanity" (12). Another account voiced the concern about the elder Kilpatricks profiting from this activity, saying that the medicine would eventually come back to harm those who mistreat it by "using [the formulas] to make money for themselves" (Mails 1992, 292).[10] Alluding to their untimely deaths, the informant said, "They were not capable of handling all the power that goes with such knowledge." The bitterness toward the Kilpatricks' work lingers today among Cherokees in northeastern Oklahoma. This sentiment was repeatedly expressed to me in the course of my fieldwork through both indirect references and direct comments. Although many of the claims have been conflated to the point of hyperbole, the controversy around the improper divulging of medico-spiritual knowledge remains salient.

Despite its controversy, the elder Kilpatricks' work has proven helpful on multiple accounts in the course of my efforts on the ethnobotany project. In their translation and analysis of each incantation, the authors meticulously list minute details, including the scientific names of any plants mentioned. This information has helped to solve some mysteries (and confirm some educated guesses) regarding the identification of medicinal plants referenced by elders. Often practitioners of Cherokee medicine are more familiar with the Cherokee or common names of the plants they use, and because certain plants are becoming ever scarcer, it is hard to find specimens to identify. With the context and detail that the Kilpatricks provide, Natural Resources Department (NRD) staff and I have been able to correctly identify some of these rare plants and target them for conservation. On another level, their work provides, through its own "peripheral" ethnobotany, documented contemporary instances of the adaptation of environmental knowledge. One occasion of this deals with the substitution of a rare and potent plant of the east for another rare and potent plant of the west (Kilpatrick and Kilpatrick 1967, 87–88). Since the original plant cannot grow in Oklahoma, Cherokees recognized the efficacy of an alternate, native plant in performing the same functions.[11] As Fogelson (1975, 116) points out, the Kilpatricks' work in Oklahoma "is especially crucial in revealing continuities and changes in belief structure as the Western Cherokees adapted to a new ecological and social situation."

Contemporary Oklahoma Cherokee Approaches to Medicine

Cherokees today continue to view medicine in a range of contexts, as reflected in the multifarious applications of idi:gawésdi presented by Mooney, Fogelson, and the Kilpatricks. As such, medicine concerns not just physical illness but also mental and spiritual well-being, including the well-being of one's relationships.[12] Furthermore, the physical "stuff" of medicine includes more than just plants. To many Cherokees, stones, soil, water, animals, insects, and plants all have "medicine." As Cherokee spiritualists and healers say, this medicine is identified as the spirit that runs through all Creation, put there by the Creator himself.[13] Identifying this spirit in a plant or a particular mineral (a stone or crystal) and communicating with it allows the healer to use these material substances to cure injuries and sicknesses. Thus, to Cherokee healers, "medicine" is also a philosophy, or a particular way of seeing the world. Included in this philosophy is keeping a "good mind" (duyukdv).[14] The practice of medicine begins with maintaining a positive outlook on everything, without any negative forethought. Just as the plants and minerals were given a spirit by the Creator, so were human beings—each person has this spirit within. As I was told by prominent Cherokee healer Crosslin Smith, recognizing this common spirit throughout all Creation is the first step in understanding Cherokee medicine.[15]

In the cases where plants are employed in healing, many healers emphasize the importance of matching specific plants with a person's spirit. Hence there are different medicines for each patient. This applies to individual specimens, not just particular species. Thus one must find not only the right species of plant to cure the particular ailment of a particular individual but the specific plant that offers its spirit to the healer for that purpose. This illuminates that often the chemical or biological makeup of a plant used in healing is only one aspect of the Cherokee view of plant-based medicine. That a plant's physical substance will interact chemically with the human body and help in some way could be seen as "level one" of this perspective. Often, botanical analyses of these plants show that the remedies are well founded, such as the astringent properties of elderberry (*kosuk*, or *Sambucus nigra*) leaves or the suppressant qualities (e.g., for hacking cough) of a mixture of hickory bark (*wanēi*, or *Carya spp.*) and wild cherry bark (*gitāya*, or *Prunus virginiana*).

"Level two" of this perspective assumes the spiritual foundation of Cherokee medicine—that the spirit of the plant is what aids in healing, and one must communicate with that spirit in order for the medicine to work. Just as often, anthropologists have found that the presumed healing qualities of plants used in Cherokee medicine have no "scientific" basis with regard to chemical composition. This was documented numerous times in Mooney and Olbrechts's (1932, 53) work, and they consequently disregard such remedies as "matter[s] of coincidence and chance" (writing in the typical fashion of early anthropologists). Yet such plant medicines that contain no active chemical compounds are understood to do their work through "the spirit," which for many Cherokees is just as effective. This distinction between "levels" is not necessarily an inherent facet of Cherokee ethnobotanical knowledge; I only intend this construction to display some of its dimensions. Most Cherokees who practice plant-based medicine (even the "laity") believe that spirituality is inseparable from any form of healing.

From a more emic perspective, Unanetlv, a friend and elder, once described the structure of Cherokee medicinal knowledge as comprising four separate (but interconnected) stratums, or fields (demonstrated by my own representation in Figure 12). In this depiction, each successive field of knowledge encapsulates a more complex and spiritual realm, with the smaller the circle and the darker the shade signifying the more special- ized and less-accessible knowledge.

The first or baseline field is considered common Cherokee knowledge and is transmitted mainly by older family members during childhood. This type of knowledge is useful for extended excursions into the woods (e.g., when exploring as children or, later in life, while out hunting and/ or fishing). For example, in the spring, the young shoots of the smooth sumac (*qualōg*, or *Rhus glabra*) can be eaten as a natural "energy bar," com- mon ragweed (*gūg*, or *Ambrosia artemisiifolia*) will help repel ticks when mashed up and rubbed on one's clothes, and crushed elderberry (*kosŭk*, or *Sambucus nigra*) leaves will soothe insect bites. The second field is more specialized knowledge that must be learned from an expert. Individuals

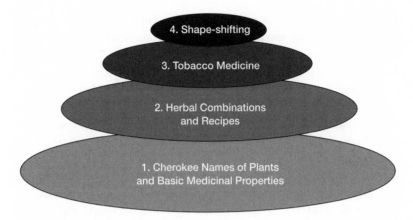

Figure 12. "Fields" of Cherokee medico-spiritual knowledge.

who exclusively deal with this type of knowledge may consider themselves "herbalists" rather than medicine people. This level of knowledge is the art of mixing various herbs, barks, or roots to cure minor ailments like colds and coughs or scrapes and bruises.

The third field is sacred knowledge that only skilled medicine people are sanctioned to use. Tobacco (*jōla agayvli*, or *Nicotiana rustica*) is considered a sacred plant by the Cherokee and must be treated with the utmost respect and caution.[16] As Crosslin told me, the proper way to use tobacco does not entail smoking it but using it in its dried form for blessings or offerings (sprinkling a small amount into a fire, in a body of running water, on the ground, etc.). Although some believe that the plant can be "fixed" or "remade" by skilled healers for specific remedies that require the right *idi:gawésdi*, it was stressed to me that because tobacco was given to the people directly by the Creator, it is already endowed with divine medicine and should therefore not be tampered with. Nevertheless, this level of knowledge can be dangerous when used inappropriately, potentially causing serious harm to the individual who does not know how to properly handle it.

The fourth field—shape-shifting—is the most specialized and secretive realm of knowledge. This area of knowledge is often associated with witchcraft; however, when performed correctly, it is believed to be an important tool for trained medicine people. This practice involves transforming into animals by spiritual means. In theory, a medicine person may want to check up on a patient, but without driving or walking to their house. Transforming into a small bird may be one way they choose to do this. Individuals who are knowledgeable of the third and fourth fields are understood to have extensive knowledge of all previous fields.

The process of acquiring specialized medicinal knowledge is dictated by many factors. Many believe that those who are born with special characteristics have the highest ability to retain and practice medicinal knowledge. Babies born with a thin veil-like membrane covering their faces (often referred to as a "caul," said to be a sign of those "born behind the veil") and twins are more prone to this disposition. Sometimes medicine people will have visions about whom to impart their knowledge (Mails 1992, 306). Other, less mystical signs may be simply that a child is attentive and possesses an advanced capability for retaining information. Adults are expected to pay attention to these signs. Often children are inadvertently exposed to the knowledge and thus take an interest in it. Many medicine people practicing today purport to have absorbed a lot of their knowledge from overhearing the conversations of their parents or grandparents, who were knowingly exposing them to this realm by not censoring their discussions.[17]

Some stories recount how individuals who have been chosen by "the spirit" are called back home to help administer medicine to the people. In one case, a young man had left home and traveled all over the country, living in many different places. He ended up in southern California, and although he had lost touch with the Cherokee community in Oklahoma, he often socialized with other local Indian groups native to the area. One day he was discussing with some California Indian friends how he knew of a way to cook a traditional food in the ground by building a "pit oven." When asked if he would demonstrate how to do this, he agreed, and the next day he began the process. Yet when he was done, he began hearing voices telling him to go back home and help his people. The act of preparing traditional food had triggered within him a sense of responsibility to pursue what he was "chosen" for. Later he said that he had been running away from the responsibility of medicine all his life, but the spirit had found him, and that is why he ultimately moved back home and began his study of medicine.[18]

The advanced study of traditional medicine comes from apprenticeships, which take years of training if a healer agrees to teach his or her knowledge.[19] Further, it is generally expected that even if one has completed an apprenticeship, a person is not ready to practice traditional medicine independently until their hair turns gray and they have a family of their own (Mails 1992, 306). Apprenticeships are commonly kept within the extended family, although this is not a requirement. Gender may play a minor role in terms of knowledge transmission and patient treatment; however, this is not as prevalent as it once was. Throughout history, male and female Cherokee healers have possessed an equal status, although individual abilities among healers may sometimes differ along gender lines. (Men may possess knowledge specific to treating men, and the same holds true for women.)

Knowledge is central to the practice of medicine, and "gaining knowledge" is an emphasized and complex process. Anthropologist Robert K. Thomas (1958, 7–8) exemplifies the importance placed on viewing the practice of medicine (and, more broadly speaking, life) in this way:

Cherokees come to manipulate their fate and the world not through power but through "knowledge." One cannot acquire power through dreams, one must study for the "priesthood" and learn a general theory and many techniques in order to be powerful. New techniques can be acquired through dreams, such as a new herb, a short formula, or some small ritual. But power, itself, cannot be acquired directly. Cherokees "gain knowledge" as it is said in Cherokee, they do not acquire power. When two medicine men come together they will say, "What do you know?" To say, "He knows a lot," is a compliment in Cherokee. Knowledge is almost a commodity and one can be called stingy with "what one knows." And one does not "gain knowledge" just by learning the "medicinal" techniques and formula alone. One can experiment with new herbs or one can gain new insights into purposes of technique by seeing a new relationship between the parts of the general theory or between a technique and another part of the theory. So a man becomes more knowledgeable by experimentation and a kind of "rational" thinking, a very different process from acquiring power.

Thus the adage "knowledge is power" has a literal meaning for Cherokees. In the realm of Cherokee medicine, one could view knowledge as having autonomy as a living thing. This is evinced in the inherent "power" of the written *idi:gawésdi* and is a main reason for the controversy surrounding the Kilpatricks' work. Knowledge is vulnerable to exploitation, yet it has its own agency—when mistreated, or used in an improper way, it can "come back on you" and inflict harm (similar to the Buddhist concept of karma).

The loss of Cherokee medicinal knowledge has been lamented since Mooney's time. Yet, while many have noted the decline of this knowledge, it is significant that the practice of Cherokee medicine continues today. In the late 1950s, Fogelson (1980, 69) remarked that "one should be hesitant in sounding the death knell for Cherokee conjuring. Mooney, Olbrechts, Bloom, and Witthoft all mourned the passing of eminent practitioners with gloomy predictions of the imminent disappearance of Cherokee medicine and conjuration. Yet somehow, younger men always seem able to take up part of the slack, and today conjuring is far from dead." This is largely true today, and I hesitate to describe the current state of Cherokee traditional medicine too dismally. However, from the perspective of the elders' group, the status of this knowledge is in poor condition compared to even the recent past. This perspective was illustrated to me as I was sitting with Unanetlv shortly after our first group meeting in October 2008. He drew a large circle in the dirt (about one foot in diameter), which represented the entire body of Cherokee plant knowledge (all that has ever been known). Then he drew a very small cutout of that (less than an inch in diameter) and said it represented what Cherokees know now.

The attrition of such knowledge can be attributed to many factors, including (1) the influence of the mainstream educational system on Cherokee youth, followed by a general disinterest in the subject by younger generations; (2) an increasing reliance on Western medicine; (3) the destruction of ecosystems and important plant species through development activities; and (4) what Luisa Maffi (2001, 7) identifies as the "'extinction of experience': the radical loss of the direct contact and hands-on interaction with the surrounding environment that traditionally comes through subsistence and other daily life activities." Karen C. Hall (2006, 2) also notes how economic factors play a large role due to the amount of time it takes to specialize in this knowledge and the absence of paid apprenticeships. Unlike the old days, becoming a healer—although more demanding than any wage labor—is not a "career option."

It is not difficult to see how these factors are products of settler-colonial forces. Educational agencies that legitimize the settler state (see Abrams 1988, 76–77), capitalist incorporation and the resultant suppression of subsistence economies (see Kuokkanen 2011), and the environmental degradation and restricted resource access discussed in chapter 3 have all contributed to the attrition of traditional ecological knowledge. Further, as Wendy Makoons Geniusz (2009, 105; Cree) asserts, the psychological effects of colonialism have had a significant effect on the transmission of traditional knowledge, in which many indigenous people "no longer see the strength of our indigenous knowledge. Our minds have been colonized, along with our lands, resources, and people."

In light of these broader causes, most Cherokees agree that the principal cause for knowledge loss is simply not using it. Returning to the concept of knowledge as a living thing, it is understood that the knowledge "dies" when it falls out of use. During our first meeting, Ganohalegi, a member of the elders' group, related the situation to the properties of water. Paraphrasing him, "We all know what happens to standing water: it grows algae and becomes dirty—unhealthy to drink. But running water runs clean and clear and purifies the mind and body. So if we all just sit still and do nothing, the knowledge will become like standing water and will not be used. But if we are active and make a difference, we will have health and clarity for the future."[20] The analogy of running water is especially fitting because of its significance to Cherokees. Bodies of running water are viewed as living things. A river is referred to as *yv:wi ganvhi:da* ("long person"), in contrast to ponds, which have no inherent life force. Many Cherokees view natural spring water as medicine in itself (and, to some, it is also necessary for making medicine). According to Ganohalegi, the water from a spring contains its own medicine, simply because it passes over so many medicinal roots in the course of its flow to the surface.[21]

In this light, Ganohalegi's statement about running water articulated a sense of purpose that bridged Cherokee theory and practice. By equating properties of knowledge with those of water, he had put cultural revitalization in the context of the Cherokee belief system. "Sitting still" and allowing the attrition of medicinal knowledge to carry out its course would not only result in cultural loss but negatively impact Cherokee health by severing connections to the nonhuman world. Later, he described this situation as moving away from the "animal spirit" and toward the "computer spirit"—another "nonhuman" realm, but one with consequences for the place of human beings among the rest of Creation. He said, "Our people have come from North Carolina to Oklahoma, and we've maintained the animal spirit. But we're starting to walk away from it. Any minute, God will take that away." To him, maintaining traditional knowledge given to Cherokees by the Creator is a responsibility that serves to uphold the relationships Cherokees have with the plant, animal, and spirit worlds. To neglect this responsibility is to disrespect the Creator's gifts. Linking knowledge disuse and environmental change, he gave the example that hazelnut trees (*yūgid,* or *Corylus americana* Walter) had ceased growing near his home because people were not using them. In his words, "We need to strengthen our way and lift it back up to the Creator so that he can be pleased with what we're doing."[22]

Ganohalegi's perspective characterizes the new direction the ethnobotany project took as a result of the first elders' group meeting. But achieving the endorsement and participation of elders and knowledge-keepers was a long process that deserves some discussion. In the next section, I go into detail about the process of carrying out such a project in the context of the preceding cultural and historical information.

Doing Ethnobotany in the Cherokee Nation

Cree scholar Wendy Makoons Geniusz (2009, 8) highlights that the fundamental difference between indigenous-led ethnobotany and that conducted by outside nonindigenous researchers is *intent:* "Our priorities in recording or reclaiming this information differ from those of non-native researchers, who often view their research on us as: a preservation effort, a final attempt to save strands of a dying culture, a bringing of native knowledge to the rest of the world, or a means of gathering data to prove some academic theory. Instead, our priority is to revitalize this knowledge within our own lives so that it will be there for our children and grandchildren and their children and grandchildren." Her statement is a useful and warranted critique of the practice of ethnobotany. Central to Geniusz's own work in indigenous ethnobotany is acknowledging the colonial origins of the study of "ethnoscience" while decolonizing this approach in practice as a tool for cultural revitalization. The dynamics of ethnobotanical research change when this tool is in indigenous hands.

Yet, even so, the *process* of carrying out a tribal ethnobotany project has not garnered much attention. Here I explain the micropolitics that I had to address in the course of my work, emphasizing the need to attend to relationships as a core part of the process of ethnobotany. Again, what makes this project unique is its association with tribal bureaucracy and policy, and so while cultural revitalization is still the central goal, these other elements add layers of complexity that one must account for. My intention is to discuss this complexity through firsthand experience in hopes that others might draw from the lessons I learned. As a point of clarity, specialists would likely construe the "type" of ethnobotany that we employed as simplistic—our goals did not include gathering physical specimens for lab research or the creation of a herbarium. Rather, our methods included identifying culturally significant plants, documenting their local English and Cherokee names, photographing specimens, and discussing cultural knowledge about each plant to the extent our informants chose to divulge. I kept an encrypted database and log of the ethnobotanical information, which remains in the possession of the former NRD director (now the director of the Administration Services Department), who still serves as the liaison between the elders' group and the Cherokee Nation.

A clear picture should be emerging with regard to the depth and significance that Cherokees ascribe to traditional medicine and the use of wild plants. The combination of spirituality and taboo attached to this corpus of knowledge made for a daunting task when I was asked to design and carry out the ethnobotany project from scratch in 2004. In short, because plant knowledge is associated with medicine, and because medicine is inherently connected to spirituality (and can cross over into witchcraft), people were hesitant to participate. Embedded within this perspective were a number of other concerns, including (1) the concern that such knowledge could be used for illicit profiteering; (2) the concern that such knowledge could be published or copyrighted and "owned" by others (i.e., the concern for intellectual property); (3) the concern that if used improperly and unsupervised, such knowledge could lead to harm of others or themselves (which also includes the belief that if medicinal knowledge is improperly divulged, it can "come back to you"); and (4) the fact that Cherokees often guard such knowledge because they feel that it is one of the few cultural possessions yet to be stolen by outsiders. Yet another underlying cause was that in the not-so-distant past, "Indian medicine" was ridiculed outside of the community.

As an employee of the Cherokee Nation, an "outsider" for all intents and purposes (despite my tribal citizenship), and later a university researcher, I potentially represented—at least at first glance—many of the sources of these concerns. I could accept my position as an outsider, and I knew that because of this I would have work to develop meaningful relationships based on mutual trust. But what I had not anticipated was the level of skepticism toward the tribal government. In fact, I had imagined the project would be considered much more ethical working for the tribe than for an outside agency that would be subject to federal Freedom of Information Act (FOIA) policies. Regardless, the project got off to a slow but promising start. The first summer of work culminated with a successful "river trip"—a method I had borrowed from advisors and mentors at the University of Arizona who had worked closely with American Indian people of the Colorado River Corridor, among many others (Stoffle, Halmo, and Austin 1997). I had managed to recruit two able-bodied elders (both in their late fifties / early sixties) to accompany myself and three staff members (from the Cherokee Nation Environmental Services Office and the Natural Resources Department) on a rafting trip down the meandering Illinois River. Along the way, we made frequent stops to discuss the plants growing on the banks. The excursion was well-received by the participating elders, and both expressed a willingness to continue their participation in the project. Although this was the only time I employed this method (due to the time and resources it requires), I would seize any future opportunities to replicate this experience.

Over the course of two subsequent summers (2005, 2006), the project gained momentum, and I continued to visit communities in order to explain its purpose and goals. When the opportunity presented itself, I conducted open-ended, informal interviews with elders who would sometimes show me around their homes or family land in order to discuss specific plants. In the meantime, I worked in the office developing the computer database and researching previous work on Cherokee ethnobotany. Although the work seemed to go slow, I realized that at that point, maintaining an involvement in community life (i.e., just "being there") was much more valuable than acquiring "information." Later, in the course of my official dissertation fieldwork, I learned that a man who I thought barely recognized me strongly supported the project because I had "been around a while." Another man—an influential figure both at the tribal complex and in the communities—described the way that many rural Cherokees figure out whether or not someone is worth talking to as "the code of the hills." No matter how nice an outsider may seem, information of a sensitive nature is never given until the person who is approached has had a chance to ask other members of the community about them. Perhaps most important, sometimes the process of ethnobotany requires *not doing ethnobotany.* Building trust with one elder required lending a hand with needed labor—sometimes menial (e.g., picking up trash in the yard) and sometimes exertive (e.g., hauling firewood). This was not a spoken requirement of building trust but an intuitive process of demonstrating reliability and character. To other ethnographers, the concept of "building rapport" would seem commonplace—an expected part of carrying out a research project. But I stress this aspect of the process so as to underscore its importance—even (or perhaps especially) when the projects are based in the tribal government.

Another closely related element is the necessity of time: Building trust is time intensive. As a graduate student during the bulk of this process, I had the luxury of ample time, although I was still "on the clock" as a Cherokee Nation employee for a significant portion. The project benefitted greatly from my supervisors' confidence (and patience) in my goals and approach, allowing for irregular schedules and informal project reports. Their perspective, of course, demonstrated their familiarity with the sociocultural dynamics and protocols of work in Cherokee communities, and I cannot understate the importance of this outlook.

My initial experience with the project also included issues of racial phenotype. As anthropologist Circe Sturm has shown in her book *Blood Politics* (2002), race in the Cherokee Nation is, paradoxically, an elusive but pervasive topic. While she demonstrates that in the Cherokee Nation there is more to racial identity than just phenotype, she also finds that phenotypical judgments are commonplace. Such judgments tend to classify a person along a "spectrum of Indianness" (my phrase) in terms of physical appearance. As a light but "olive-skinned" mixed-blood Cherokee, I have received many such judgments on both sides of the spectrum. I have found that this is often a matter of context; in the course of my fieldwork, the more acquainted I was with an individual from a Cherokee community, the more likely they would say that I "look Cherokee." Conversely, as a stranger, I have often been regarded by community folks as a "white guy." Nevertheless, racial phenotype is a very real issue for a project like this, considering the distrust that continues to be harbored by community-based Cherokees against white people generally (Cherokee or not). Thus, when well-meaning light-skinned individuals attempt to discuss sensitive topics like plant knowledge, often outward appearances get in the way. The following situation seems to sum up the overall viewpoint.

One afternoon at the tribal complex, I was having a discussion with my supervisor (Pat, a Cherokee citizen in his forties who is light-skinned and blonde/blue-eyed) regarding who would be good potential interviewees for the project. He decided to call a coworker in another department (James, "half" Cherokee and in his late thirties) to see if his father (a "full blood") would be willing to participate. On speaker phone, the conversation went something like this:

PAT: I've got this student from Berkeley here—he's a Cherokee citizen—and we wanted to ask you a question. Say we were trying to talk with some old-timers about their general knowledge of wild plants—do you think your dad would be willing to help us out? Do you think he'd talk to us?

JAMES (doubtfully): He might talk a little, but probably not.

PAT: What about this guy from Berkeley who's doing most of the interviews? He's a young guy—do you think he'd talk to him?

JAMES: What does he look like?

PAT: Uh, well, I guess you'd say he looks like a white guy.

JAMES: Well, probably not. See this knowledge is kind of a Native American thing that is passed down through family members.

PAT: And we all know it's not being passed down anymore.

JAMES (concedingly): Uh, yeah.[23]

In another situation, Perry ("half" Cherokee and in his midfifties) acknowledged and openly discussed the evolution of his acceptance of me. When I first went to visit him in 2004, he "shut me down" due to the nature of my visit and questions. (In this case, "shutting someone down" simply means pretending not to know anything.) He said that I had been too forthright and that I had approached him all wrong. Yet, when I visited him in 2008, he was a different person completely. Not only did he present himself as knowledgeable and willing to share his knowledge, but he gave off a completely different air of intelligence and competence (before he had seemed to play the role of the "backward hillbilly"). He even offered an apology and said that he didn't really mean to be rude—it's just that he was brought up to behave that way toward intrusive outsiders. I had been perceived this way, even though I don't remember being pushy. Later he explained that you will never get a response from a Cherokee the first time you ask about something like plant medicine. First of all, you have to ask in a nonintrusive way. Second, do not expect a "yes" or a "no" on the spot—the individual will have to "think on it" some. He said that after seeing my face around for a while (and passing me off to other, more "accessible" people), he finally thought that my approach was acceptable. Besides time and persistence, other things that helped when I visited him in 2008 were a referral from another reputable person and being accompanied by a student intern who happened to look more "Indian" than I. When I asked if it was really all about "looks" (i.e., racial phenotype), he said that it was probably 70 percent looks. There was a slight pause, and then he revised his statement and said that it didn't have to be all about looks if the approach was right; in that case, you could probably change it to be 30 percent looks and the rest about approach (a complete reversal of percentage!).[24]

The conversation between James and Pat also highlights one of the paradoxes inherent to doing ethnobotany in the Cherokee Nation: While most everyone realizes that the knowledge is not being passed down as it once was, the tendency to withhold this knowledge remains strong. This tendency goes beyond issues of racial phenotype—the "identifiably Indian" student intern mentioned before recalled that it was difficult to get her own grandmother to speak to her about this topic. Her point of view was that people were just "being stubborn" about it—and this is partly true. In Cherokee society, the high value placed on the knowledge one has "gained" (as elaborated by Robert K. Thomas previously), combined with the history of exploitation, has created a cultural system wherein knowledge is indeed a commodity. As Thomas writes, "one can be stingy with what one knows." Crosslin once described how recently he was being approached by many people (not associated with this project) who wanted to acquire his knowledge "like they're going to Wal-Mart." Yet, while one aspect of this cultural system (knowledge transmission) is changing, Cherokees are realizing that they must find ways to adjust the rest of the system in order to keep the knowledge alive. One of these adjustments involves, under the right conditions, the willingness to speak openly about the subject.

Cultural Property and the Politics of Knowledge

The elders' advisory group created in 2008 has taken the first step toward speaking openly about plant medicine. As I stated in the introduction, the first meeting was coordinated with the hopes of bringing together the individuals I had been visiting separately in the course of my work on the project. Since that time, the group has continued to meet frequently. The meetings involve a mixture of socializing, storytelling, sharing plant knowledge, and discussing the organization and goals of the group. A significant accomplishment has been the publication of the afore-mentioned booklet, *Wild Plants of the Cherokee Nation* (Figure 11). The group requested the booklet as a way to promote the revitalization of Cherokee ethnobotanical knowledge. In its first printing, it contains descriptions of eighteen plants, along with basic knowledge. Publishing baseline or "field one" knowledge was approved as a way to reinvigorate people's interest in the subject and to highlight the efforts of the group in "starting the conversation." Although the group fully supports the booklet, it contains no names. The elders requested this so as to maintain a level of humility about the initiative. In this way, no one can view those associated with the project as seeking personal gain or enhancing their reputation. Currently, the booklet has been translated entirely into the Cherokee syl-labary, and a second edition is in the works with more than one hundred plants listed (including fungi and cultivated heirloom crops). As stipu-lated by the group, the booklet is provided free for Cherokee citizens.

As for the knowledge represented in the booklet, one elder remarked, "It's just enough information to keep it interesting." The significance of the publication is not lost on the group—they all realize that the book-let is a huge step forward in overcoming the taboo of widely distributing this knowledge. That this is being done under the supervision of an elders "council" is what makes it different. While everyone understands the potential risks of publishing this information, they all agreed that any time something is put out in the world, it runs the risk of being used for unin-tended purposes. In response to this, one elder asserted that if someone tries to "get rich" off the booklet, such a negative act would "come back on them," and they will soon find themselves broke. With regard to the medicinal applications of the plants listed, the group feels that because they did not provide the sacred formulas for making medicine (i.e., the prayers and/or *idi:gawésdi*), the potency of the remedies is nullified and therefore protected from exploitation. This, in itself, "protects" the knowl-edge from exploitation. Such beliefs in the nature of this knowledge have maintained a sense of confidence in the group's efforts.

Nevertheless, despite such confidence, a recent incident surrounding the printing and distribution of the plant booklet has prompted the group to reassess its stance on the issue. In October of 2011, the booklet was found for sale in the Cherokee Nation Gift Shop, located next to the tribal complex in Tahlequah. Additionally, the booklets that were on display were versions that had been reprinted in China. (The original booklets had been printed by a Cherokee-owned company in Oklahoma.) For a multitude of reasons, this incident caused bewilderment among the group. From the beginning, group members had articulated the importance of not selling the booklet for fear that this would constitute the marketization of Cherokee culture and would tarnish the vision of the overall initiative. Selling the booklet in the gift shop further exposed the knowledge to consumption by tourists, when its targeted audience was Cherokee youth. Its printing in China was perhaps the more surprising act, seeing as it added insult to injury: Not only was the booklet being sold, but it was further commodified and devalued as a product made in China.

Many had not anticipated the booklet's success, which had led to its appearance on the Cherokee Nation Gift Shop's bookshelf. Shortly after its initial printing, the director of the Natural Resources Department received a request for five hundred copies of the booklet from a Barnes & Noble Booksellers store in Phoenix, Arizona (which he declined). How the booklet made it that far from the Cherokee Nation was not explained; however, the previous distribution of the booklet at an open tribally sponsored conference during the 2009 Cherokee National Holiday may have been responsible. At issue was not the open distribution (since the conference was aimed at participants in the Cherokee National Holiday, who are predominantly Cherokee) but the lack of any process of consultation with the elders' group. This was an unfortunate result of not associating any names with the booklet, as well as printing it with tribal funds. In short, the booklet was treated as property of the Cherokee Nation, which is to say that tribal officials took for granted their ability to freely distribute it.

The editing and layout of the booklet had originally been performed by the Cherokee Nation's Communication Department, but through an agreement with the NRD in 2010, a Cherokee nonprofit foundation acquired the master electronic file of the booklet in order to begin translating it completely into the Cherokee language. Sometime later, a private individual who had seen the booklet and recognized its educational value donated funds to the foundation for additional printing. To maximize the quantity of booklets produced from the donation, the foundation's leaders independently decided to contract with a printing company in China and made 1,500 copies. The director of the foundation then purportedly consulted with one member of the elders' group about selling the booklet at the gift shop, with all proceeds from the sales going to a restricted fund for tribal projects related to ethnobotany.

When the elders' group heard the whole story, many voiced that it had been overall a learning experience and a part of the group's "growing pains." Without the proper channels of communication, things had gotten out of hand. Apparently, the group member whom the director of the nonprofit foundation had approached had been asked in the context of a large gathering. When he expressed agreement about selling the booklets and storing the proceeds in a restricted fund, the director forwent any additional consultation with other group members and entered into the contract with the Cherokee Nation Gift Shop to sell a small amount of booklets. Yet it is likely that this particular elder, who is in his mideighties, misunderstood (or misheard) the nature of the director's request. With this knowledge, the group realized that no ill will had been intended by the nonprofit's director. But despite the group's ultimate clemency, the incident had compromised the participation of at least one member, who later openly admitted to almost withdrawing from the group entirely. And while the topic was on the table, another group member expressed concern about seeing the booklet in other questionable settings, including a Cherokee gift shop in North Carolina.

The situation illuminated the need for the group to form an organizational structure in order to have some control over the future printing and distribution of the booklet. To this end, the group's subsequent meetings focused on the formation of an editorial board that would oversee the Cherokee Nation's publication of ethnobiological information. After consultation from the Cherokee Nation Attorney General's office, the group drafted an executive order that proposed the establishment of the Cherokee Nation Ethnobiology Publications Board, consisting of three members of the elders' group who would act in an advisory capacity with regard to the contents and distribution of Cherokee ethnobiological materials. Principal Chief Bill John Baker signed the executive order in March 2013, and since this time, the publications board has successfully reviewed numerous requests for the plant booklet. At the time of writing, they are in the process of reviewing the next edition of the plant booklet, which contains information for more than one hundred plants.

The significance of the plant booklet cannot be overstated. Despite its turbulent past, the first edition has had a profound effect on tribal citizens, especially those who reside outside of the Cherokee Nation and who constitute what are referred to as "at-large" Cherokee communities. For at-large citizens, many of whom maintain strong relationships with kin and community in Oklahoma, feeling a connection to the Cherokee Nation as a place is paramount. In one case, the booklet motivated an at-large citizen to come "home" and work for the people. Although this person grew up outside of Oklahoma, he had watched his aunt react so strongly to the familiar plants of her childhood represented in the booklet that it moved him to create his own connections to place and community. He is now the new director of the Cherokee nonprofit foundation mentioned previously, and he was able to tell this story to the publications board during one of their meetings.

While the elders' group experienced firsthand the messiness of controlling published knowledge, they also took measures via the publications board to ensure its more respectful treatment. As this case shows, the stakes entailed reconciling extreme measures of guarding cultural knowledge (not talking about it) with taking risks to disseminate it in order to ensure its revitalization. To reinvoke Ganohalegi's metaphor, with the publication of plant booklet, the elders had taken the first steps to remove the dam that restrained the flow of ethnobotanical knowledge. The stream that resulted may have been forceful and unpredictable at first, but the act had ultimately enabled its continued vitality.

Conclusion

In tribal hands, ethnobotany is a useful tool, but one that needs to be employed cautiously because of the social and political setting in which it is required. The many roadblocks that I experienced as a researcher, and that the elders experienced as a group, point to the colonial origins of ethnobotany, which once sought utilitarian values of plants over relational values that respect the teachings of the plants themselves (Geniusz 2009, 43; see also Kimmerer 2013). The existence of the ethnobotanical project itself is a product of the times in which we find ourselves. "Cultural revitalization," as a project that tribes must undertake, is part and parcel of the ongoing forces of settler colonialism. But the process of overcoming these roadblocks is equally significant. As a tool, ethnobotany can help American Indian people arrive at desired outcomes. In the case of the Cherokee Nation ethnobotany project, these outcomes amount to no less than the maintenance of our relationships with, and responsibilities toward, each other and the nonhuman world. Thus tribally led ethnobotany (and by implication, "ethnobiology," which includes the animal realm) is much more than "science": It entails attending to relationships, which make up the center of many indigenous ontologies. The process of such projects—from building trust, gathering and documenting knowledge, and ensuring its proper treatment—illustrates the complexity and significance of advancing relationship-based approaches to environmental governance.

Tribal community health, although not an explicit focus of this chapter, is implicated here, in that we must not only revitalize the knowledge of traditional medicine; we must use it, too. Although few would contend that traditional medicine is the sole answer to tribal community health, demonstrating the value of traditional knowledge by incorporating it into one's life is a statement in itself. As Geniusz (2009, 161) writes, "If we cannot recognize that plants and trees have the ability to help us reclaim our balance, hope, and sense of self-worth, then our revitalization programs will never be fully effective." Although once labeled a central facet of Cherokee life, plant medicine went underground after periods of ridicule, abuse, and exploitation. Revitalization programs—no matter how much they attend to relationship-based approaches—cannot rescue us from the effects of oppression if we don't get behind them. The elders' group has provided a platform on which to advocate for the continued transmission of traditional ecological knowledge, but more broadly, they seek to reinforce foundational spiritual guidelines that inform the practice of this knowledge. The next chapter focuses on how they have articulated this larger project and how we might envision its realization.

CHAPTER 5

The Spirit of This Land

Terrains of Cherokee Governance

ON A COOL AND SUNNY late winter day in February of 2010, the elders' group is gathered for their seventh meeting inside the nonprofit's small cabin nestled in a secluded hollow. As usual, everyone has brought a variety of foods, including homemade stews, cornbread, and pies. Crosslin's wife, Glenna (an expert of Cherokee cuisine), has brought the traditional winter comfort food, *kenvchi*—a delicious "soup" made of mashed and strained hickory nuts with hominy. Perhaps in part due to this delicacy, the atmosphere is especially jovial. Also as usual, conversation has tended to center on Crosslin, who is adept at spinning tales that both intrigue and amuse. He drifts in and out of Cherokee, and despite my linguistic shortcomings, I am entranced by his oratory skill and his ability to captivate others. Sometimes I can only smile while the rest of the group laughs heartily about one of Crosslin's remarks. But rather than feel out of place, I am at ease and contented to be a part of another successful gathering.

As the meeting progresses, English begins to overshadow Cherokee, and more serious business emerges in place of the lighter conversation. The plant booklet had come out only a few months earlier, and deep into the meeting, the group continues to cautiously pore over the act of disseminating such information. Sensing such caution, one member points out the paradox that has been created in the course of the discussion. She asks, "Why we are being so cautious with this knowledge when, as Crosslin says, it is meant for everyone?" In response, someone says that certain aspects of the knowledge could still be misused. "But," she persists, "if we keep thinking this way, our fears will work against our goals for keeping the knowledge alive." Another woman chimes in and says, "What separates us is the spirit of the group. Our efforts and labor will be blessed if we have this good frame of mind, so we should go ahead and move forward." Finally, Crosslin says, "There's nothing we can do about what other people try to do with this work. That's just the way it is. That can't keep us from doing the work we are doing with the spirit—somebody's got to do it. We have to do something to honor the spirit of this land. If that is lost, then all hell breaks loose."

Years later, these words stick with me: *Honor the spirit of this land.* The words speak to how Crosslin views the work of the group as a matter of upholding relationships with the nonhuman world, with place, and with the Creator, or "the spirit." Doing this entails passing on the gifts that the Creator gave Cherokees—embodied in both the ancient knowledge that remains from the homelands and the "new" knowledge that Cherokees received and developed after their arrival in the western lands. It entails maintaining the responsibility to act as caretakers of a place that, while it is not *the homeland,* is nevertheless *a homeland.* To forget the knowledge and practices that tie the people to the land would be to ignore or disgrace its spirit. This would result in the loss of a key component of Cherokee cultural identity, leading to psychological distress and spiritual chaos. To honor the spirit of the land is to acknowledge and act on the responsibilities that come with being indigenous, displaced from original homelands or not. As Steven Feld and Keith Basso (1996, 11) write in their volume *Senses of Place,* "Indeed, displacement is no less the source of powerful attachments than are experiences of profound rootedness."

As I will explore in this chapter, Crosslin's teachings about "the spirit" embody the relationship-based approach to indigenous environmental governance. In asserting this approach, the elders' group is contributing significantly to the process of indigenous state transformation in the Cherokee Nation. This chapter seeks to describe empirically what this process looks like and how the elders' group is influencing the way Cherokee Nation state actors and agencies "make sense of the world" (to return to Philip Corrigan and Derek Sayer's aphorism). For many indigenous communities, making sense of the world entails ascribing to "Original Instructions" or "Natural Law" (see Nelson 2008). In Crosslin's words, it boils down to distinguishing between "Creator-made laws" and "man-made laws." Creator-made laws encapsulate ethics of respect and reciprocity toward the land and all life, and they guide the knowledge and practices embedded in traditional subsistence-based ways of life. This perspective—more appropriately, this *worldview*—has required translation when interfacing with the Cherokee Nation bureaucracy. The need for translation arises out of the way the Cherokee Nation has tended to structure its relationships with rural Cherokee communities as a product of corporate forms of governance. The elders' group's experiences and subsequent deliberations in reaction to this tendency both critique and offer alternative perspectives to the current scenario.

First, I discuss the value of indigenous subsistence in today's world, its place in contemporary Cherokee life, and its relevance to environmental governance. Next, I explore the recent history and present character of relationships between the tribal governmental bureaucracy and rural Cherokee communities, looking specifically at how corporate forms of governance have influenced the way they interact. I illustrate these dynamics with a case on the politics of resource access in order to show how these issues play out on the ground. I then describe how the elders' group has voiced its concerns about this structuring and how traditional teachings of spirituality and group unity can inform tribal governance today.

Indigenous Subsistence and Oklahoma Cherokees

Like most indigenous peoples, Cherokees defy romantic stereotypes of the "ecologically noble savage" and other notions that have flowed from within the American environmentalist movement and New Age spiritualism (see Nadasdy 2005). But land-based subsistence practices to this day encompass key features of what it means to be Cherokee, founded in a connection to place and in observations of seasonal cycles. Through subsistence comes relationship, and through relationship comes ethics. Such ethics comprise ideal ways of interacting with both fellow humans and nonhumans, and as ideals, it follows that Cherokees do not always adhere to them. Nevertheless, as should be clear in what I have termed the relationship-based approach to environmental governance, traditional teachings seek to uphold and promote the responsibilities that Cherokees have to one another and to the land.

In addition to traditional teachings like Crosslin's, individual and collective experiences on the land are what constitute a Cherokee "land ethic" (to quote Leopold 1989 [1949]). Cherokee attachments with the nonhuman world arise largely through lived experience. Elders have recounted to me their childhood memories of roaming the woods all day, armed mostly with the knowledge passed on to them from their elders regarding which plants can treat a cut or scrape and those that are edible for snacking. Communities and families relish in seasonal subsistence practices that, while they may not account for the majority of Cherokees' caloric intake, are a large part of understanding one's identity as a Cherokee. One could describe elements of a Cherokee "seasonal round" with the appearance of ripe hickory nuts (the main ingredient in *kenvchi*) and wild mushrooms in the fall, hunting deer and turkey in the winter, the arrival of wild greens (cochanny, poke, wild onions) in the spring, and the availability of huckleberries and crawdads in the summer months.[1] In short, subsistence—as an approach to interacting with the land, with each other, and with nonhuman persons—persists in Cherokee communities, despite a relatively high level of participation in wage labor and the market economy.

Subsistence activities aid in the transmission of vital cultural knowledge when carried out collectively, and thus the cumulative effects of encroachment, fences, fire suppression, man-made lakes, and environmental degradation have had profound effects on Cherokee cultural reproduction due to the resulting restrictions they place on resource access and availability. Once a widespread activity among Cherokee families in the late summer, huckleberry gathering has significantly declined over the years due to limited access, inundated gathering areas (by both water and underbrush), and decreased mobility through the woods. Although huckleberry gathering is still practiced by some, many Cherokees would rather not battle the scrub, ticks, chiggers, snakes, and angry landowners / forest rangers in order to obtain them. What is lost is an important opportunity for intergenerational bonding, cultural transmission, environmental education, and identity-building that was once a part of the Cherokee seasonal round. Due to increasingly low yields, the annual huckleberry festival in the town of Jay (Delaware County) frequently must import its huckleberries from Arkansas instead of gathering them locally. The irony is not lost on many elders today, who know that the berries were once abundant (as recorded in the descriptions provided by J. D. Whitmire in chapter 2 and Ross Bowlin in chapter 3). Thus enabling subsistence as a vital component of cultural continuity requires healthy ecosystems and increased access to them.

Further, subsistence activities comprise economic systems in their own right that have been marginalized by capitalist incorporation and development. Sámi scholar Rauna Kuokkanen (2011) argues for critical attention to the complexity of indigenous subsistence economies and their foundational role in indigenous philosophies and systems of governance. Through a discussion of sustainability and reciprocity as key principles of indigenous economies that "reflect land-based worldviews founded in active recognition of kinship relations that extend beyond the human domain," Kuokkanen distills her analysis to the concept of the *social economy* (219). She argues that centering within indigenous governance models an economy embedded in social relations "would foreground not only indigenous economic systems and their significance in their entirety but also social institutions as the basis of forming contemporary political organization and governance" (233). Thus centering the social economy in indigenous governance today effectively centers elements of traditional governance that in many cases have been overshadowed, such as the roles and authority of women, inter- and nonhuman relationships, and landscape health. This stands in contrast to a focus on capitalistic economic development, which tends to be the center of corporate forms of governance that are prevalent throughout contemporary American Indian and First Nations polities. Subsistence economies, Kuokkanen writes, "offer an alternative perspective and critique to the self-destructive growth logic of capitalism" (231). Although Kuokkanen does not entirely discredit economic development projects as means to improve indigenous well-being and quality of life (pointing out that most indigenous economies are indeed "mixed" economies, much like that of Oklahoma Cherokees), she advocates for attention to how the concepts and values embedded in subsistence ways of life might guide discussions on indigenous governance and policy.

Kuokkanen's social economy framework for indigenous governance studies opens up more conceptual space for discussing the relationship-based approach as a process that attends to the ecology of relations in its broadest sense. By this, I mean both the "kinship ecology" that expresses human–nonhuman interrelatedness (Salmón 2012) and the importance of managing interhuman relations within the community. Anishinaabe legal scholar John Borrows (2002, 46) frames this relational web in terms of the development of indigenous law: "Aboriginal peoples developed spiritual, political, and social conventions to guide their relationships with each other and with the natural world. These customs and conventions became the foundation for many complex systems of government and law." The adoption of corporate systems of governance by indigenous nations has upset many of these customs and conventions in favor of efficiency and has detrimentally affected the way people view the political process and thus how governmental actors and tribal citizens interact. With this in mind, the next sections will explore the explicit interhuman dimensions of the relationship-based approach, specifically pertaining to the way the

Cherokee Nation governmental bureaucracy has related to rural Cherokee communities and how the elders' group provides a useful intervention. Rather than a politics of refusal, central to my narrative is how the elders' group has engaged dialectically with state actors and in the process has influenced state practice.

Structure and Process in Cherokee Governance

Cherokee history from the early nineteenth century shows that the formation of a centralized Cherokee state was a difficult and sometimes violent process. This process entailed asking formerly autonomous Cherokee towns to sacrifice some of their autonomy in order to present a unified resistance to colonial forces. Rebuilding the Cherokee Nation in the mid-twentieth century involved another call for unity. In 1967, Ralph Keen, a Cherokee who had been working as assistant director of the Bureau of Indian Services for the University of Utah, was called back home by Principal Chief W. W. Keeler to serve as the general business manager of the Cherokee Nation. On a technical level, this job entailed managing the transfer of Bureau of Indian Affairs (BIA) funds to a tribal account, but it also included serving as a liaison to Cherokee communities. In all accounts, it is clear that Keen understood Cherokee community dynamics and how to meaningfully engage them in the process of rebuilding the tribal government. On May 6 of that year, Keen spoke the following words to a crowd at a prominent ceremonial ground near Vian, Oklahoma:

> It's always discouraged me that we have so many Cherokee Indian people and yet they don't act as one group. They act as 100 different communities. I hope that in the near future sometime that all Cherokee people will work together. I think this is possible . . . because for the first time [since Oklahoma statehood] we have been allowed to work at it. That's why I'm here. I'm here to somehow or another build an organization called the Cherokee Nation of Oklahoma. And you know there used to be a Cherokee Nation before statehood. Until that time the Cherokees were doing well for themselves. When congress took away from us the right to govern our own is when we started having hard times. . . . Chief Keeler has worked for a long, long time to get congress to approve us running our own business. He finally did and that was when he

hired me. I don't know how to get all of this done. But I do know the first thing we have to do is get ourselves organized.

Calls for national unity in Cherokee society have repeatedly presented themselves in times of crisis, which unfortunately have defined much of Cherokee history in the last two centuries. But in the forty years since Keen's speech, major acts of federal intervention (like forced removal or allotment) have ceased, and the federal Indian policy of self-determination has given Cherokees the chance to focus inward. After once again rebuilding a governmental infrastructure and reestablishing a strong tribal political presence, Cherokees are returning to a political aesthetic of community autonomy. This "aesthetic," although not entirely grounded in practice (which I will discuss further), situates cohesive Cherokee communities as more central players in the political arena of the Cherokee Nation. While maintaining the central government as an administrative entity, there is a general movement toward reinstilling a strong sense of community identity as well as promoting community control over local affairs. This dialectical process is being influenced by both Cherokee communities themselves and Cherokee Nation governmental actors as they engage each other in the course of community development projects. Such projects are at the core of an overarching strategy that looks to tribal history for inspiration.

Dojuwa Siquanidv, or Redbird Smith, was an important figure in the history of Cherokee nationalism. A leader in a time of great turmoil, he devoted himself to the revitalization of religious traditions while simultaneously engaging with politics. The following quote shows his own perspective on the teachings he received throughout his life—namely, the place and purpose of Cherokees in relation to the rest of humankind:

> I have always believed that the Great Creator had a great design
> for my people, the Cherokees. I have been taught that from my
> childhood up and now in my mature manhood I recognize it as a
> great truth. Our forces have been dissipated by the external forces,
> perhaps it has been just a training, but we must now get together as
> a race and render our contribution to mankind. We are endowed
> with intelligence, we are industrious, we are loyal and we are
> spiritual but we are overlooking the Cherokee mission on earth,
> for no man or race is endowed with these qualifications without

a designed purpose. . . . Our pride in our ancestral heritage is our
great incentive for handing something worthwhile to our posterity.
It is this pride in ancestry that makes men strong and loyal for their
principal in life. It is this same pride that makes men give up their
all for their Government. (Gregory and Strickland 1967, 481)

Dojuwa's statement articulates a belief that is prevalent throughout
many other indigenous peoples whose name for themselves translates into
"the real people" or "the principal people." Although some might interpret
this belief as a sign of chauvinism, the general concept behind it is one
of responsibility—a responsibility to maintain continuity as a people by
living under the "rule of law" that was given to them by the Creator (Wahrhaftig and Lukens-Wahrhaftig 1977, 231). Dojuwa's concept of a "designed
purpose" further indicates a responsibility toward humankind—to use
Cherokee attributes, traditions, and values in order to help make the
world a better place.

His final statement is less clear and somewhat cryptic. If the date for
this quotation is correct (as I could not find a proper record), Redbird
Smith was writing in the twilight of his life. (He died in November 1918.)
He had seen in others and had witnessed his own disillusionment with
politics and government during the Allotment Era. In 1906, the Nighthawk Keetoowah Society separated itself from the body politic of the
Cherokee Nation. The act symbolized a formal declaration of independence from any other faction of Cherokee society, and the Nighthawk
Keetoowahs proceeded to devote all their energy toward their religious
duties (Thomas 1953, 173). Thus we cannot be sure to which government
Redbird Smith was referring—was it the exclusively religious "government" of the Nighthawk Society (of which he was "chief"), or was Smith
writing with reference to the old Cherokee Nation that had thrived
before allotment, with the hope that future generations might enable its
resurgence? Regardless of his intention, the "pride that makes men [and
women] give up their all for their Government" reveals a sense of nationalism that has been revitalized in Cherokee society today.

During the course of my fieldwork—more than ninety years from
when Redbird Smith wrote these words—his great-grandson, Chad-
wick "Corntassel" Smith, occupied the position of Principal Chief of the
Cherokee Nation, and he used this same quotation to promote contemporary nation-building. As principal chief, Smith composed a forty-page

document titled *Declaration of Designed Purpose: Yesterday, Today, and Tomorrow* to provide Cherokee citizens and employees with a brief history of Cherokee politics, a description of the contemporary governmental structure, and "the vision, mission, and guiding principles to lead the Cherokee Nation for the next century." The document is praiseworthy in its scope and goals and is intended to provide a context for envisioning a strong nation, as well as to familiarize non-Native employees with Cherokee Nation history and the foundations of tribal sovereignty.

Formulated in part by an appointed leadership team after a series of "direction-setting" meetings, Smith's vision for the Cherokee Nation is clear and specific: (1) "The Cherokee people shall enjoy and exercise an enriching cultural identity and way of life, which includes a thriving command of our language, cultural history, art, traditions, wisdom, and lifeways"; (2) "Cherokees and their government shall become economically self-reliant and sufficient to the extent that the Cherokee Nation is not required to accept federal funds to meet the needs of its people and every Cherokee has the opportunity to pursue the career of his or her choice"; and (3) "The government of the Cherokee Nation shall become, and maintain itself as, a strong sovereign government that protects the Cherokee people." The term *gadugi*, which once referred to need-based economic cooperatives (Fogelson and Kutsche 1961), is invoked to convey the mission of the Cherokee Nation, expressed as "working together as individuals, families, and communities for a quality of life for this and future generations by promoting confidence, the tribal culture, and an effective sovereign government." The text also calls on the Cherokee "spirit" (inherent in Redbird Smith's concept of "designed purpose") as a guiding principle and emphasizes that Cherokee values and culture should be upheld and promoted among Cherokee Nation staff and employees. The broad idea is to integrate traditional sociocultural aesthetics and forms into the tribal bureaucracy. During Smith's tenure as principal chief (1999–2011), the *Declaration* was one example of his administration's platform of cultural and linguistic revitalization.

In addition to the *Declaration*, Principal Chief Smith's administration listed three priorities that made up a national strategy: jobs, language, and community. According to this platform, all Cherokee Nation programs and departments were compelled to contribute to each priority. The strategy was intended as a road map for rebuilding a nation, and it addressed three interconnected aspects of Cherokee cultural continuity.

For one, the recent past has shown an increasing amount of out-migration by young families, who relocate to urban centers in search of better economic opportunities. Creating jobs for tribal citizens provides young families with the opportunity to remain at home in the nation. Second, like many indigenous languages, the Cherokee language is endangered. As elders repeatedly stress, the value in its perpetuation lies in its direct link to Cherokee traditions and knowledge. Last, promoting healthy and sustainable communities ensures that Cherokees continue to have a strong sense of identity based on kinship ties and social obligations. Strong communities also provide roots for those who do decide to leave the nation and may desire to return in the future. In short, the strategy was the Smith administration's approach to fostering the perpetuation of the Cherokee Nation as a people.

In 2008, "Strategic Work Teams" were formed in order to develop ways to implement each priority through long-term planning. The Community Strategic Work Team (CSWT)—comprising mostly community-based tribal employees—formulated a series of goals, guidelines, and statements that articulate an ideal relationship between the Cherokee Nation government and Cherokee communities. The vision composed by the CSWT reads, "Communities shall enjoy and exercise a reciprocal relationship with the Nation that advances the accomplishment of community driven goals. It is through the accomplishment of these goals and *gadugi* that our communities will be safe, stable, and cohesive." A "reciprocal relationship" is defined as one wherein Cherokee government and communities offer their available resources (e.g., government resources may include funding and technical assistance; community resources may include leadership and volunteer work) to strengthen communities and, in doing so, to strengthen tribal sovereignty. Thus the CSWT plan emphasizes the establishment of partnerships between Cherokee government and communities in an effort to recognize local authority and leadership (e.g., elders and community-endorsed leaders) and to center community concerns and goals. Overall, the strategy calls for meaningful *engagement* from all parties.

These visions, goals, and strategies represent a significant repositioning of governance priorities in the Cherokee Nation; they demonstrate a clear transition from outward to inward thinking. Some have termed this movement a "cultural renaissance" in the tribal complex. Indeed, Cherokee culture, language, and traditional values have never been stressed to this extent in the operations of the tribal government since before Oklahoma statehood. Due to this radical shift, it is not surprising, then, that the implementation of these goals and visions has encountered obstacles. The current tribal bureaucracy and governmental structure were created for very different purposes under very different circumstances. Most of the tribal bureaucracy was directly transferred from the BIA, and the unicameral corporate model of government was intended to be a temporary solution for filling a sixty-year gap in tribal self-governance. Thus the political structures and bureaucratic processes that the Cherokee Nation operates under today have inhibited the changes that the Smith administration sought to make. In other words, whereas the Cherokee Nation government has attempted to move its operations toward a community- and culturally centered approach, it lacks the ability to accommodate the ideas contained in that vision—hence the "political *aesthetic*" I mentioned earlier, which does not equate to actual practice.

For example, the preliminary proposal by the CSWT to higher-level Cherokee Nation bureaucrats fell short of many participants' expectations. The proposal, based on the vision and goals described before, was presented to Cherokee Nation "Group Leaders"—individuals among the executive branch who directly report to the principal chief on matters pertaining to each of the sixteen "groups" that make up the "Team Organizational Structure" of the Cherokee Nation. With some exceptions, many of the Group Leaders were not willing to get on board with the CSWT's proposal for engaging and empowering communities, despite the fact that the plans had been catered to the Group Leaders using specialized technical language and diagrams commonly seen in strategic business plans. This reaction was couched in the Group Leaders' bias toward specialized knowledge and their reluctance to recognize other forms of expertise that are not generated by degree programs. According to one of the CSWT members who attended the meeting, many Group Leaders implied that they "know what's best for the communities" based on their knowledge obtained from college degrees.

Theoretically speaking, this dynamic is predictable. Max Weber's (1946a, 196–244) foundational writings on bureaucracy illuminate these tendencies—namely, the development of office hierarchy and the emergence of the "objective expert." Weber writes, "The principles of office hierarchy and of levels of graded authority mean a firmly ordered system of super- and subordination in which there is a supervision of the lower

offices by the higher ones. . . . Office management, at least all specialized office management . . . usually presupposes thorough and expert
training. . . . The possession of educational certificates . . . are [sic] usually
linked with qualification for office" (197–200). Later, he describes how
bureaucracy dehumanizes official tasks and policies by "eliminating from
official business all love, hatred, and all purely personal, irrational and
emotional elements which escape calculation" (216). By expecting workers and officials to disregard these elements of social life while engaged
in work at the office, bureaucratic authority is able to supplant that of
older social structures: "The more complicated and specialized modern
culture becomes, the more its external supporting apparatus demands the
personally detached and strictly 'objective' *expert*, in lieu of the master of
older social structures, who was moved by personal sympathy and favor,
by grace and gratitude. Bureaucracy offers the attitudes demanded by the
external apparatus of modern culture in the most favorable combination"
(ibid.). In the case of the CSWT presentation, the Group Leaders possessed both the structural authority (from the system of office hierarchy)
and the symbolic authority (from college degrees) to reject the CSWT's
proposals—even when the majority of Group Leaders, quite frankly, were
not familiar with Cherokee community life.

On another level, while the CSWT proposals contained well-
thought-out, sincere ideas for empowering communities, there was still
something missing—namely, the communities themselves. Although
members of the CSWT were mostly "community people" (i.e., reared
in a Cherokee community), the proposals were nevertheless formulated
from the top down. Individuals who were a part of the CSWT were also
tribal "officials" who, according to Weber, enjoy "a distinct *social esteem*"
by nature of their positions (199). This leads us to consider the lack of
meaningful community representation within the Cherokee Nation
government—a product of the corporate structure that inhibits any true
delegation of authority to communities.

As I discussed in chapter 3, the corporate model of tribal government
developed by Principal Chiefs Keeler and Swimmer originated out of
their backgrounds as businessmen. At the time, they believed this model
was the most appropriate in order to provide immediate services to tribal members and to quickly rebuild an institution that had been virtually
defunct for more than sixty years. Yet, as many tribal citizens expressed in
the 1999 constitutional convention, the Cherokee Nation has outgrown

the corporate model of government based on its "increased governmental responsibilities and the competing demands of a larger and more diverse citizenry" (Lemont 2006, 300). Additionally, Eric Lemont notes that unicameral tribal councils "were never intended to reflect and balance sociocultural groupings within tribes, such as family allegiances, clans, or bands. Nor were they intended to allow for the efficient operation of sovereign tribal governments. As in Swimmer's 1976 constitution, the motivation for unicameral councils was to facilitate the receipt and disbursement of federal funds through a corporate structure" (301). Chippewa sociologist Duane Champagne further notes that a legislative system comprising a single body of elected tribal councilors assumes that a society views itself as a collection of individual voters. This view, embedded in Euro-American ideals of individual rights and democracy, ignores "local community powers, [and promotes] conflict between the elected government and social and political forces that are not formally represented within the tribal government" (Champagne 2006, 19–22).

One situation during my fieldwork demonstrates the distance that many tribal citizens perceive between their communities and the tribal government. In the late summer of 2006, I attended a community meeting in Bell, Oklahoma—located in predominantly rural (and predominantly Cherokee) Adair County. During this specific meeting, the tribal councilors who represented the region had arranged to put on a "hog fry" for the occasion.[2] The meeting took place in the large community building, and many folks showed up for the event. After the two tribal councilmen addressed the crowd, people began to raise concerns about the councilmen's lack of attention to local affairs. In a surprisingly confrontational tone (uncharacteristic of typical Cherokee signs of disapproval, especially in the context of a large gathering), one Cherokee Nation citizen—a resident of one of the poorest Cherokee communities in northeastern Oklahoma—stood up and declared to the councilmen, "We don't even know you." In response, one councilman proceeded to give out his cell phone number to the crowd, while the other claimed in defense that he had visited the community a few times. This tense situation encapsulates the feelings of many tribal citizens throughout the Cherokee Nation, which stem from a lack of control over, and knowledge of, tribal governmental affairs.

As such, the Cherokee Nation government today represents solely a central authority and not something that communities feel they can meaningfully influence or change. Duane Champagne (2004) notes that what made the 1827 and 1839 Cherokee Nation constitutional governments so successful were the ways in which their founders handled centralization. Through bicameralism, traditional and localized leaders (who were mostly village-endorsed elders) were a concrete source of authority among the tribal government, manifested in the National Council. This structure originated as a conservative check to the National Committee and gave autonomous Cherokee townships direct access to political power. The system of community representatives created in 1968 as a response to community activism (the Original Cherokee Community Organization [OCCO]) was one attempt to recognize rural Cherokee communities. According to Wahrhaftig (1978, 504–5), the representatives took hold of this system and used it as a venue for asserting community voices. With the new constitution in 1976, the unicameral tribal council replaced the community representatives. In the current political configuration, even though tribal council members may be from Cherokee communities, with only seventeen seats, there are simply not enough council members to provide adequate representation for communities in the central government. (Cherokee communities currently number somewhere between sixty and seventy.) As Vine Deloria Jr. and Clifford Lytle (1984, 247) attest,

> Indian tribes in their original setting never attempted to govern a large number of people. . . . Indians realized that it was not good government to have leaders and representatives who did not have some kind of personal acquaintance with the people they led. . . . This close correlation between the people and the leadership positions in the tribe ensured that the council represented all points of view that were regarded as important within the community. Tribal governments should consider substantially expanding their council membership to ensure that a more intimate ratio of people to elected officials exists.

But it is more than just a matter of numbers. The current governmental model and bureaucratic system have eliminated the role of tribal elders (in the Weberian sense, the "old masters"). The absence of the traditional authority and wisdom of elders creates another source of tension that tends to strain relationships and distance communities from the tribal government.

The change necessary to ameliorate these conditions is not a radical one for the Cherokee Nation. Along with Champagne (2004), I argue for the resurrection of the bicameral legislature as one way to address the structural limitations of the current Cherokee Nation governmental system. Champagne (2004, 57) proposes that, as in the historical model, "the [current] tribal council can serve as a lower house [i.e., the National Committee], while an upper house [i.e., the National Council] can be constructed from elders or major confederated groups [communities] who exercise influence and authority already within the [tribal] community." It would reasonably follow that the upper house would be apportioned by the number of Cherokee communities per district, while the lower house would be apportioned by a fixed number per district. Cherokee citizen John Keen (son of Ralph Keen) made a very similar proposal during the 1999 constitutional convention (see Lemont 2006, 301–2); however, as I stated in chapter 3, the motion was ultimately rejected due to the monetary cost it would potentially entail. Given the present context, I argue for seriously reconsidering this proposal during a future constitutional convention. (At the time of writing, the next convention is due to be presented to Cherokee citizens as a voting issue in 2015.)

This structural change would be well supplemented by attending to issues of process, or how things "get done" at the tribal complex. The corporate model of government has not only limited community representation but also profoundly influenced institutional procedures and planning. Patrick Sullivan (2006), in a critique of the influential Harvard Project on Indian Economic Development in the context of Australian Aboriginal communities, has noted that often the approach to developing tribal "good governance" is founded in standard business management practices. Such an approach confounds governance as *political life* with governance as *bureaucratic management.* The origins of this approach lay in liberal theories of economic development for Indian communities, which encourage "free flows of capital into Indigenous communities, utilising the Indigenous labor resources, linking communities to market networks and contesting communalism" (8). As such, "good governance" is more about providing stable and efficient institutions that create a low-risk environment for outside investors rather than building a political system that manages the distribution of authority throughout a national community (27).

The operational character of the Cherokee Nation bureaucracy reflects this economic approach to tribal governance. The employee orientation program of the Cherokee Nation, titled the "Organizational/Employee Development and Communications Passport Program," purports to "build Cherokee Nation employees" through a series of workplace training sessions. In one of these sessions, new Cherokee Nation employees are taught to treat anyone who walks into the tribal complex as a "potential customer." Smith's *Declaration of Designed Purpose*, despite its strengths as a nation-building document, reveals upon closer analysis similar business-oriented characteristics. The eight-point direction-setting statement includes "strategic initiatives" (to develop "organizational team structure"), "desired outcomes" (to "achieve operational performance"), and "goals and objectives" (since "goals should be 'SMART'—Specific, Measurable, Achievable, Related to the Mission, and Time-bound"). In this regard, the *Declaration* resembles more of a business plan than a national manifesto.[3] Additionally, in order to implement the vision, mission, and strategies of the *Declaration*, at the time of my fieldwork, the tribal bureaucracy employed the "balanced scorecard" system, designed by Harvard Business School professor Robert Kaplan and Dr. David Norton, president of the Palladium Group (a consultancy firm)—the efficacy and academic foundations of which have been called into question recently (Nørreklit 2003).[4]

Because of the continued influence of corporate models on governmental operations, the Cherokee Nation government has found itself in the midst of an institutional identity crisis. The operational design has moved too far in the direction of corporate strategy without paying attention to foundational aspects of governance (expressed as "political life" by Sullivan). This has created a situation in which "nation-building" strategies must be funneled through models designed for generating profits, increasing worker efficiency, and ensuring loyal customers, which, although they are potentially positive goals for some areas of tribal management, are incongruous with the goals of strengthening communities, enriching cultural identity, and maintaining sovereignty. The promotion of abstract cultural values in the tribal government (as expressed in the *Declaration of Designed Purpose*) may recenter institutional priorities, but they are only symbolic until actual *processes* are modified to account for these values. While I acknowledge that tribal economic pursuits are necessary for establishing self-sufficiency, I argue that nation-building could be better accomplished by decentering top-down approaches and strategies grounded in economic principles in exchange for redistributing authority and building relationships between the central government and communities.

Sullivan (2006, 27, 30) frames this process in terms of creating "effective channels of communication with the wider governance environment of a community" and "crafting effective consultation, information sharing, and permission getting processes." Creating such channels of communication, he stresses, is a *continual* process:

> Consultation with the wider community needs to be continual and part of daily life. It needs to happen wherever people find it congenial. For organisations this may be in council meetings, for families it will be in family gatherings, for youth groups it may be around the basketball court or similar. Information-sharing should also take place during the active use and management of the land, the daily work of functional organisations. There must also be recognition that getting informed consent is always a continual process. It is not a one-off sign-off. Conditions may change, new information may come in, new understandings may be reached in the light of experience, and different interests may arise as individuals develop and the composition of groups changes over time. An important part of ongoing permission-getting is an agreed monitoring process, since changes to procedures need to take place in light of previous success or failure with implementing decisions previously arrived at. (30)

Based on his work with Australian aboriginal communities, Sullivan rejects attention to structure in favor of looking solely at process, thereby moving away from the problem of obtaining sufficient community representation within a tribal organization. Reacting to Cornell and Kalt's (1998) concept of "cultural match" (as advocated by the Harvard Project), Sullivan's (2006, 12) main stance is that *culture*, as an organic, living entity that is expressed within and among a group of people, should be left where it belongs: in the community, not reductively codified in a structure that inhibits its free expression. However, Sullivan writes based on a situation in which foreign institutions are being imposed on indigenous societies. While his critique is important for understanding the unexamined assumptions and power relations in economic development models, the Cherokee Nation case here is slightly different. For one, attention to structure is relevant with regard to Cherokee governance because structures have served a much larger historical role and have thus been made culturally relevant on the Cherokees' own terms. Arguing for a bicameral legislature is not so much trying to fit abstract culture into a model of government; it is more a recognition that the model works well with the configuration of Cherokee society (see Champagne 1992). Further, the proposal is not to return to some far-off precontact traditional structure. On the contrary, the system worked for the Cherokee Nation in the very recent past. Where efforts to "incorporate" culture are evident, they should be viewed in the framework of Sullivan's critique; however, the ability of indigenous people to transform "foreign" institutions remains a promising prospect. In short, I argue that both structure and process are important in the Cherokee case: creating adequate space for community representation while engaging communities through relationship-building.

Nevertheless, as an addition to Sullivan's process-centered approach, I suggest that what I term "articulatory projects" can function as effective means of consultation and relationship-building. These projects, as in the case of the elders' advisory group, accomplish the same goals as those sought by top-down business-oriented strategies, but by very different means. Borrowing from Chantal Mouffe's (1979, 193) notion of "articulating principle," which describes the unification of a diverse group of people around a specific political project, articulatory projects seek to unite the realms of central government and autonomous community around specific topics or objectives. Such topics, as in the elders' group's discussion of traditional plant knowledge, serve as focal points from which larger topics are raised and addressed in the context of meaningful dialogue. I draw on one example from my fieldwork to illustrate my point.

Gathering Rights and the Politics of Resource Access on Tribal Land

As I discussed earlier, the subject of issuing permits for gathering on tribal lands has been raised among the elders' advisory group in response to many accounts of overharvesting or harvesting disrespectfully. The tribal councilors' rejection of this proposal on the basis of citizen equality under Cherokee Nation law once again highlights what Ronald Niezen (2003) has termed the "Weberian dilemma" of indigenous governance. With regard to the employment of bureaucratic governance structures by indigenous nations, Niezen writes, "What do international bureaucracies, bastions of state interests and legatees of Enlightenment rationalism, have to offer people struggling, seemingly against the current of modernity, to maintain honor and family obligations, nature spirituality, subsistence economies, and the authority of elders in governance?" (140–41). Although I stress that the councilors' rejection was on an informal and preliminary basis, the point is no less salient: The current structure of the Cherokee Nation government, based as it is on rationality, citizen equality, and bureaucratic order, inhibits the influence of "traditional" sources of authority. Nevertheless, more central to my objectives herein is how indigenous communities have developed ways to deal with this dilemma. The dialectical relationship between the Natural Resources Department (NRD) and the elders' advisory group represents how indigenous communities are negotiating it without succumbing to a zero-sum, either/or outcome.

An influential factor of the tribal councilors' reaction was that, independent of the elders' group's request to establish a system of gathering *permits*, councilors had been receiving comments from their constituents regarding the elucidation of the gathering *rights* of Cherokee Nation citizens on tribal lands. Although both topics concern the act of gathering, it is clear that they represent two different positions: the *regulation* of gathering activities versus the recognition of the *right to* gather. As I discussed in chapter 3, the two sides of the issue demonstrate the precarious situation that NRD personnel must navigate as land managers. Whereas many Cherokees see gathering as their right guaranteed by treaty, the Allotment Era severely diminished the Cherokee Nation land base, resulting in a very limited amount of space to gather compared to the Cherokee Nation's original landholdings. Further, because the knowledge of how to properly and respectfully harvest natural materials has diminished over time, the activity potentially threatens the limited resources on tribal lands. Last, most plots of tribal lands are isolated and are only accessible by trespassing on private property. In the case that a tract of tribal land is landlocked, the "right" to gather is only symbolic. Due to these factors, Pat Gwin (who had become the NRD Director), when requested by the tribal council to consider formulating a "gathering code" for the Cherokee Nation, came up with a list of seven questions that illuminated the problematic nature of such a request:

1. What species would people be allowed to gather? Will there be a list of restricted or endangered species?
2. Will gathering be allowed for commercial purposes?

3. Will "nondestructive" activities be exempt from regulation (e.g., gathering huckleberries or mushrooms)?
4. Will these rights extend to tribal citizens only, or are spouses and adopted children included?
5. Should the NRD help identify and locate rare species? Or should the NRD limit access to increasingly rare species?
6. Will the code prioritize certain uses (e.g., crafts, medicine, food)?
7. Will gathering be allowed by ATVs or other vehicles, or walk-in only?

In the presentation of these questions to the elders' advisory group, it was clear that both the NRD and the elders shared an end goal: to proceed cautiously and find some way to regulate gathering activities on tribal lands. One member of the elders' group recommended that people should have to get the permission of the group before harvesting. Another agreed and noted that many people are gathering plants in order to sell them and that they gather large quantities at a time. He said the only way to control this situation would be to use the authority of the elders' group. He proposed closing off gathering access to the general tribal citizenry. If someone is in need of a certain plant, a member of the group would have to go and get it for him or her. Otherwise, people would overharvest, and there would be none left.

Another group member offered a more moderate outlook based on his own observations. In his experience, the majority of Cherokees who harvest plants are seeking the materials to make traditional crafts, and it is the younger part of this population that has been known to disregard sustainable harvesting practices. Therefore, instead of restricting all types of gathering on all tribal lands, reserves of land could be classified according to the materials gathered there. In other words, the NRD could designate certain tracts for craftspeople and allow them access to those areas freely, with the hopes that individuals will take heed of the elders' group's instructions on sustainable harvesting practices and recognize the "common pool" nature of the resources. Interestingly, someone proposed putting up billboard signs on how to harvest properly in order to raise public awareness of the issue.

Returning to the subject of permits, Pat wondered that if the tribal council somehow approved them, would such permits be written (with expiration dates, registration numbers, etc.), or would they be based on just verbal approvals? What would the approval process entail? Would there be written or verbal tests that "qualified" certain people over others? Exactly what role would the elders' group play in this process? Crosslin commented that due to the scarcity of resources these days,

> the controls are going to be put on us [Cherokees] and we're going to have to cope with that. We [in this group] are going to have to start scrutinizing people. We're going to have to take a look at people and see if they are really spiritual or not. We have to learn how to evaluate what people are saying and doing and whether they are following man-made rules, or Creator-made rules. We should be able to tell if they aren't coming from the right place spiritually. [He expressed that this would be one way to tell if people are harvesting the resources in the right way.] We need a lot of changes. Our people have gone too far the other way. We gathered here are small needles in the haystack trying to bring back important plants. And we're going to run into trouble if we don't protect ourselves. But if those that would try to break us apart could learn the original teachings—if they can learn the truth—then they will respect what we are doing.

Crosslin was anticipating the criticism that the group might receive for placing restrictions on Cherokee gathering rights, and he recommended that the group members ceremonially "go to water" together to purify and protect themselves against any outside negative intentions. This act of taking precautions in case of potential criticism and attack shows how seriously the group takes their potential to influence decisions that affect the larger community. His invocation of the "original teachings" and "Creator-made rules" signals that the group seeks to operate from a higher spiritual plane in order to legitimate potentially bold acts (e.g., speaking openly about plant medicine and restricting access to resources in order to ensure their health). Crosslin also suggested a screening process that differed dramatically from standard permitting procedures. Although he was in favor of establishing a permitting system, he advised that the approval process include a "spiritual" element.

The issue of gathering rights and regulations remains unresolved, but the dialogue between the NRD and the elders shows how their concerns converge and reinforce one another, even while they approach the issue from different angles. The Cherokee state, represented by Pat's questions, demands legibility about who can collect what, where, how, and under what kinds of oversight. On the other hand, the elders see a need to restrict permission to people who are qualified, so to speak, but they also see the problems inherent in the formalistic and bureaucratic method for this proposed by the state (in the form of permits). While Crosslin admitted that Cherokees need to make certain concessions in order to address the challenges of the times (and did not deny the effectiveness of a permit system), he also offered an additional nonbureaucratic method for "scrutinizing" people who wish to exercise their gathering rights. And it is notable that Pat, as he later expressed to me, thought that the group's stance would lend legitimacy to his position when faced by the tribal council. He expressed relief in knowing that his deference to the elders' group had transferred the weight of the issue to a more capable and qualified decision-making entity.

These dynamics illustrate how through dialectical engagement the complex challenges of Cherokee state transformation are being addressed; they show why we cannot take for granted the Weberian dilemma as an unresolvable problem. The alliance between the NRD and the group of elders accomplishes the same desired ends as the previously proposed top-down business models: It brings together bureaucratic and traditional approaches to governance and connects community concerns with the central government. But the means by which it arrives at that point are notably different. Through a process-oriented approach that entails consultation and opening channels of communication, the initiative builds relationships and trust. And although the group coalesced around the subject of traditional plant knowledge, the elders use the forum to voice related concerns—exemplified in their discussion of gathering rights and regulations, as well as the broader discussions of Cherokee governance that follow.

Unity and the Spirit: Traditional Ideals of Cherokee Governance

Throughout its development, the elders' group has become a forum for discussing ideals of Cherokee governance and group organization. From its inception, the group has sought the counsel of their elder and spiritual adviser Crosslin Smith on these matters so as to ensure the success of the overall initiative. My close involvement in the group as convener and notetaker has given me insights into this topic that inform my overall narrative of Cherokee state transformation. Above all, Crosslin has stressed two concepts to which the group must adhere in their endeavors: unity and "the spirit." The concepts are best described in his own words in relation to the name of the group, *Galvquodi Igatiha*, or "divine equality":

> Equality is in the spirit. No one has a stronger spirit than another. The difference is in what degree of loyalty exists for that spirit. And if the group is fully loyal, then they are special people—that's what we want. Supposedly that's what the old ones used to work toward in the clan medicine men—they looked for the best people. If you had a full house of these people, then you had a power structure. . . . The unity of the group is its strength. It's hard to find people these days who are pulling together, but that's what we need. There will be opposition out there. But one way to avoid that is to stick together—let's get this done. If those who oppose us get you to talk against someone in this group just once, then they've done their damage. This program must start with the understanding that what we do is for everyone. When we can unite under these old teachings, we can start to really accomplish our goals. We will truly be together, not by material or physical stuff, but by the spirit. . . . It is said that if two people are in complete accord with one another, that is divine power. With three people in accord, this power is enhanced. And a whole group in accord in this way can affect circumstances far beyond themselves. If they are in accord, then you can really generate power like that. There is no limit to that power.

This statement reveals the aspirations that Crosslin has for the group. It has become clear to me that Crosslin views this group as a part of the legacy he wishes to leave behind. Throughout the group's existence, Crosslin has encouraged slow deliberation and emphasized that all group members should grasp the concepts of unity and the spirit before proceeding. Other group members have sometimes expressed frustration with how this process is inhibiting the work of preserving traditional plant knowledge, but Crosslin has gently insisted that laying a strong spiritual foundation is essential. His reasoning comes from his own extensive experience and observations of Cherokee institutions, including the OCCO.

Many in the elders' group remember the Original Cherokee Community Organization, through either personal experience or hearing stories from family members. This organization has been brought up in our meetings as a point of comparison. In fact, for this reason, the introduction to the declaration of the elders' group (see the Appendix) has similar wording to that of the OCCO. Yet Crosslin, who worked closely with Ralph Keen (quoted in the beginning of this chapter) during Principal Chief Keeler's efforts to reinvigorate the Cherokee Nation government, observed the actions of the OCCO in the 1960s and asserts that the organization's dissolution was caused by their lack of unity in the spiritual sense that he now advocates. "They weren't together," he said. Making this connection between the elders' group and the OCCO is important because, although Crosslin saw the actions of the OCCO as beneficial to Cherokee people, he is cautious about the elders' group imitating its style due to its members' failure to fully unite in a spiritual sense.

Yet despite Crosslin's desire to distance the elders' group from the OCCO on this foundational basis, there are useful parallels between the two that yield insights into what constitutes traditional Cherokee forms of governance and organization. Albert Wahrhaftig (1975a), and later another social scientist, Kenneth Fink (1979), analyzed the OCCO as a "Cherokee institution." Their studies on the OCCO and other Cherokee assemblages reveal some concrete traits of Cherokee social organizations that I will discuss, augmented with my own observations from the elders' group.

Cherokee institutions, like Cherokee community life, are firmly based in interpersonal relationships.[5] While I was organizing the first elders' group meeting, often what sparked the most interest in those whom I invited was the mention of who else planned to attend. Knowing those involved and who they could expect to see at the meeting clued people in to what type of meeting it would be. The high importance placed on relationships reflects how Cherokees "go to extremes to avoid giving offense to others" (Wahrhaftig 1975a, 138). Thus, in organizing the meeting, it was equally important for me to think about how all the attendees would get along. Although this might seem an overly selective and therefore biased approach, it was nevertheless a vital part of planning the meeting. Inviting individuals who might clash with each other would have been counterproductive and irresponsible on my part and would have unduly put all those attending in an uncomfortable position, which is another reason people were generally curious as to who would be there.[6]

The group dynamic continued to rely on relationships to determine individual roles, although at first these roles were unspoken and related to how (and how much) an individual spoke. The anecdote I gave in the introduction demonstrates this dynamic: At first, Charlie Soap assumed a speaking position and guided the discussion; however, upon the arrival of Crosslin, his demeanor changed completely out of respect for his elder (and also a specialist on the subject of medicine). Fink notes that "roles" within Cherokee institutions are expressed only in a very limited sense. Writing on the early formation of the OCCO, he says, "Instead of thinking of a task and then designing roles to fit the task, individuals would emerge who were interested in and who could competently handle a task" (Fink 1979, 464). Leaders assume their positions more in terms of serving the larger whole through their respective skill sets rather than as coercive "bosses." Generally, people must feel like they all "have a hand" in how things are being done (Wahrhaftig 1975a, 145), although this is not to say that individuals will not defer to those who are more knowledgeable (usually elders) with regard to reaching consensus for the benefit of the group.

As the generally preferred method of decision making, consensus is another topic that demonstrates the pervasive tension in Cherokee society between unity and autonomy. Because Cherokees value interpersonal relationships and "go to extremes" to maintain them in a harmonious way, Cherokees have developed a high respect for individual autonomy. This is expressed in the disapproval of any type of coercive authority in Cherokee institutions or among the community. In the case that consensus cannot be reached, after the dissenting position has been made clear, a person's disapproval is expressed through nonparticipation, or withdrawal—the idea is to simply desist, thus avoiding overt hostility but nevertheless making a point (Wahrhaftig 1975a, 137–38). Because withdrawal often leads to factionalism, in order to avoid this situation, usually the matter is dropped if consensus cannot be reached. Unity, therefore, is a highly valued principle in the context of Cherokee social organization. It not only expresses solidarity but attests to the strong foundation of a collective decision as a product of slow, thoughtful deliberation.

The principle of building a strong foundation through thoughtful deliberation is another key component of Cherokee institutions. This characteristic was displayed in the historical formation of the Cherokee state in the early nineteenth century, and it continues to this day. Ganohalegi expressed the concept to me using an analogy of a train— "it takes a long time and a lot of energy to get it moving, but once it's got up to speed, its momentum is strong and it's hard to stop." Further,

Fink (1979, 463) writes that, to Cherokees, a strong foundation "will not easily factionalize because it will be based on consensus. . . . 'Building a strong foundation' takes time . . . time to discuss, to analyze and to decide what actions will be necessary to allow Cherokees to return to the God given design outlined in the 'White Path.' Thus with sufficient time not only will the organization achieve consensus, it will also have the sacred sanction necessary for it to be considered an 'Indian way of doing things.'"

Because of the profound significance of unity to Cherokees, it is no wonder that the "sacred sanction" that Fink mentions is expressed in conjunction with consensus. In the early 1980s, Archie Sam, the late Natchez-Cherokee elder and spiritual leader, gave an eloquent description of the sanctity of unity. Speaking of the ceremonial stomp dance, he said, "From the start you must have people who are united in body and mind, people who are going through the rituals as one person totally united. If this is so, then the sacred fire picks up and sends out waves like a radio station. If everyone is putting out the same waves, then the outpouring through the fire and smoke is sure to reach God. Unity is a fantastic power. Nothing needs to be spoken when this is so. God feels it and responds. No audible prayer can be as strong" (Mails 1992, 326). Crosslin's words resonate with those of Archie Sam. They speak to the value of coming together in spite of any petty political or social divisions. Thus, whereas factionalism is a dangerous impediment to the creation of successful tribal institutions, Cherokees have developed a sense of reverence for its polar opposite. Nevertheless, this definition of unity still respects autonomy (of the individual or community) by the way things get done (deliberation and consensus). To Cherokees, unity is a delicate balance.

My discussion speaks to three defining characteristics of Cherokee institutions: (1) careful attention to interpersonal relationships and individual autonomy, (2) preference for consensus through slow and careful deliberation, and (3) foundations built on a sacred sense of unity. These traits stand in marked contrast to standard bureaucratic procedure. As Weber (1946a) has described in his ideal-typical model of bureaucracy, the institution operates "without regard for persons" (199, 208, 215–16), within a hierarchical structure of authority and decision making (197), and with heavy attention to efficiency (214–15). Although actual practice may not always follow this model, Weber's analysis illuminates that the tendencies of bureaucratic institutions are to conform to these traits.

Given that bureaucratic and traditional Cherokee institutions—in their ideal types—are virtually incommensurable, what makes the ethnobotany initiative significant is the *alliance* between the two, resulting in an articulatory project.

Meetings have become the format for the elders' group's efforts, and in these beginning stages, they have been necessary venues for the deliberation of the group's mission and goals. Yet the meetings also encapsulate the new formation that has been created out of the alliance between a Cherokee Nation bureaucratic agency and a small group of elders. During these meetings, presentations are made, items are discussed, and strategies are devised. Taken out of context, this last sentence would reflect the activities of a regular business-oriented bureaucratic meeting at the tribal complex. However, the elders' meetings are conducted "out in the communities" (i.e., in a rural area of the eastern part of the Cherokee Nation), often outdoors, and usually seated around a fire. Further, the elders are given free reign over the discussion. Presentations and an "agenda" (more of a list of proposed talking points) do provide a loose structure to the meetings, but not enough to detract from the informal flow of conversation and frequent storytelling that characterize them. Food is also ubiquitous during the meetings, and although the NRD has a small budget for taking care of this, often group members bring a dish to share "potluck" style. As such, meetings not only serve to "take care of business"; they are also cherished opportunities to maintain and renew relationships. Many have expressed how the meetings remind them of what people did years ago when meetings of this sort were more commonplace. As Ganohalegi said, "People used to visit one another." Small gatherings among peers to discuss important topics outside of family and work obligations once had a firm place in the Cherokee social world, and many feel like the group meetings are reinvigorating this.

Yet the group is not without challenges. Some of the first topics to be discussed concerned its relationship to the Cherokee Nation government— specifically how to maintain group autonomy and permanency. For instance, there was caution when discussing funding this initiative through a Cherokee Nation program or department. This was expressed by Crosslin, who said, "Anytime an Indian program in this Nation comes up, [the powers that be] act totalitarian and shut down what the Indian group has proposed." Crosslin's statement echoes my earlier assessment of office hierarchy and institutional condescension among higher-level Cherokee Nation officials. Similar comments made it clear that the larger tribal political apparatus could not be trusted to handle sensitive cultural knowledge with the appropriate respect and protocol. Reasons for this stem from the tendency of program administrators to attach strings to tribal funding—in which case the group would lose its autonomy and the ability to determine its own course of action. This concern is also based on the perception that many government officials would not recognize the significance of this project and the reasons it must be treated in a delicate and deliberate manner.

But despite the reservations the group had with tribal funding, the option was not completely cast away. Indeed, Cherokee Nation funding that is free of federal oversight and influence seems like the most logical source of funding for this project so as to keep sensitive knowledge within the tribe. During our fourth meeting, group members devised strategies to account for the incompatibilities between their group and the tribal government. One such strategy was proposing a tribal council resolution, outlining the group's purpose and goals and requesting a commitment from tribal funds. Ironically, this strategy uses the tribal government's formal process—but it does so in order to solidify the group's autonomy and thus establish an alternative method of decision making. This demonstrates a central point: that when faced with obstacles that ran contrary to a traditional way of doing things, the group reacted by innovating, thus creating something new while maintaining a foundation of traditional values. Instead of rejecting the Cherokee Nation governmental structure, the elders' group proposed going *through* it in order to create space for a different set of principles. Such transformative processes will be critical points of study in the near future, as Cherokees create new forms of governance that bridge the gap between government and community.

Other challenges have to do with reconciling traditional forms of operation with changing circumstances. For one, the tradition of slow deliberation is difficult to justify amid the urgency of rapid knowledge loss. This point was deeply felt when, after just one year of the group's existence, one of the group elders passed away. Another challenge is the adoption of formalized mechanisms for group organization so as to properly identify the group (e.g., the group's declaration—see the Appendix) and to ensure certain provisions in dealing with membership, meetings, and so on (e.g., bylaws). Although such formalized mechanisms facilitate certain tasks and dealings with the Cherokee Nation government, they potentially create a structure too rigid for the free flow of knowledge and ideas between group members that currently characterizes group dynamics.

Nevertheless, spurred by the plant booklet incident discussed in chapter 4, the group moved to elect a seven-member board of directors and subsequently adopted numerous documents to submit to the Cherokee Nation tribal council and executive office, including a set of bylaws; a draft council resolution; a draft executive order; a descriptive document on the group's formation, history, and long- and short-term goals; and a draft memorandum of agreement for the establishment of "tribal conservation areas" to be managed through the joint relationship between the group and the NRD. Additional positions of secretary and spokesperson were created, with the secretary being a member of the board who keeps the group's minutes and the spokesperson an employee of the Cherokee Nation who acts as a liaison between the group and the tribal government. While the original goal was to incorporate under the Cherokee Nation, the group decided to seek 501(c)3 nonprofit status but to maintain a definitive link to the Cherokee Nation through the "liaison department," which keeps the books of the group and provides institutional support. At the time of writing, the incorporation documents are undergoing final revisions and approval by the group, with the hopes to begin seeking grant funding for its conservation and educational projects in summer 2015. A unique attribute of the group is that there are no chairpersons or any other officers other than the secretary that might impose hierarchical influence on group members.

There are other challenges that I will leave to be discussed among the group as internal issues. After all, it is hard to write definitively about something that is still in the process of formation. The key to addressing these challenges is the ability to innovate when necessary. If the group is able to maintain its autonomy and permanency, I am confident that its current makeup will be able to find ways to overcome any obstacles. But there are larger implications of the group that transcend its temporality. Its existence thus far speaks to the efforts on both sides of the government–community divide to bridge the gap created by state-building. It represents how this process might work by diverging from business plans and standard bureaucratic procedure and bringing initiatives into the communities— thus providing a very different setting and recognizing a very different style and source of authority. The model of the group itself could serve as a prototype for similar articulatory projects that coalesce around other pressing issues. As the past chapters have shown through the movements led by White Path, Oochalata, and the OCCO, these projects are not necessarily about the singular topic that they may use as a focal point. Rather,

I have hoped to show that such projects, when carried out according to the appropriate social and cultural protocols, create valuable channels of communication that connect community concerns and knowledge to tribal governmental policy.

Conclusion

The discursive space that the elders' group has opened within the Cherokee Nation polity represents the kind of "cultural revolution" that Corrigan and Sayer (1985) describe as a key process of state formation, wherein the ways the world is made sense of are transformed. However, the cultural revolution that the elders' group is prompting has a different agenda than that of English state formation. While the elders engage with state forms and processes, they are also asking *the state* to make sense of the world in "new" (i.e., traditional) ways through addressing the relationship-based approach to environmental governance, which, as this chapter has shown, has as much to do with interpersonal relationships as it does with relationships with the nonhuman world. And rather than just incorporating an abstract notion of "culture" into the tribal bureaucracy, the process of addressing the relationship-based approach entails reconfiguring state practices and acknowledging alternative sources of authority. As an articulatory project, the elders' group is actively defying the perceived opposition of "state" and "culture" by bringing them together in practice, where people can learn and develop alternative approaches that elude the conceptual and ethical legacies of U.S. colonial settler-state history. Furthermore, as the elders' group engages the Cherokee state and challenges the way "it" makes sense of the world, state actors simultaneously contribute their knowledge of and experience in the process of tribal natural resource management. These dialectical engagements result in the convergence of the resource- and relationship-based approaches in Cherokee environmental governance, and rather than the breakdown of the state, the product is a modified, uniquely indigenous one.

Kuokkanen's social economy framework for indigenous governance bears much in common with the relationship-based approach, even if my emphasis on indigenous state transformation may ultimately depart from her implications. And while Oklahoma Cherokees and the northern Canadian First Nation communities of which Kuokkanen writes may differ in their degree of reliance on subsistence practices, the values that underlie them are nonetheless equally present and significant. Kuokkanen stresses the values of communalism, reciprocity, and sustainability, and the elders' group clearly articulates these values through the concept of *honoring the spirit of the land* and in their Cherokee name, *Galvquodi Igatiha*, which expresses equality and group unity. Also similar to Kuokkanen, my analysis of the elders' group critiques the corporate form of governance, specifically its tendency to devalue social institutions in favor of efficiency and formal procedure. Through their emphasis on interpersonal relationships, deliberation, and a sacred sense of unity, the elders assert an alternative approach to governance that demands a radical shift in current practice. Thus I argue that centering the interhuman and interspecies relationships that make up the social economy framework in the Cherokee Nation will entail aligning the way we view governance with both historical formations (structural reform) and ways of operating that facilitate political participation (attention to process). On a more basic level, the perspective of the elders' group begs the question: What would the Cherokee Nation's national strategy look like if we included "Environment" or "Land" alongside "Jobs, Language, and Community"?

Vine Deloria Jr. and Clifford Lytle once identified the crux of American Indian economic development as a matter of upholding a "natural economy":

> The fundamental question of economic stability on the reservations revolves about the dilemma of whether the land is to be exploited, and therefore simply another corporate form of property, or to be a homeland, in which case it assumes a mystical focal point for other activities that support the economic stability of the reservation society.... The critical factor in achieving economic stability seems to be in encouraging tribal officials to develop programs that are perceived by the people as natural extensions of the things they are already doing. A natural economy maximizes the use of the land in as constructive a manner as possible, almost becoming a modern version of hunting and gathering in the sense that people have the assurance that this kind of activity will always be available to them. (Deloria and Lytle 1984, 258–59)

More than thirty years later, American Indian nations find themselves confronting the same issues, but with more urgency. The elders' group is one example of a voice that asserts from within tribal policy circles a relationship-based approach to governance. I have argued that due to their engagement with the state, compounded with the unique environmental challenges we must confront today, the elders' group represents a new chapter in Cherokee environmental governance. But while this may be so, we are only at the beginning. It is up to current and future generations of Cherokees to forge ahead and enable its full expression.

· CONCLUSION ·

Sovereign Landscapes

Spiritual, Material, and Political Relationships to Land

WE GATHERED AT CROSSLIN and Glenna's house for the elders' group's
tenth meeting in June 2012. Crosslin had requested that they host the
meeting there so that he could perform a ceremonial blessing for the group
through what he calls a "water treatment." Cherokees have been going to
water since time immemorial for purification and renewal (see Kilpatrick
1991), but nowadays Crosslin brings the water to them. That morning, I
had done as he had asked and filled a clean trough with well water, posi-
tioning it facing east just outside of his house. Before the blessing, Crosslin
offered some thoughts to the group that lent both advice and profound
encouragement:

> This group is the best thing that has been started in our culture,
> with our people. We will succeed in our endeavors. . . . I see grand
> things with this group in the future: greenhouses, machinery,
> sections in hospitals for our traditional practitioners, and so on.
> When will the group be ready for this? At some point you'll have
> to get off the ground with this thing. [The Cherokee Nation] will
> grant you land, and you'll have to know what to do with it. And
> of course, you'll have to start educating the young people. If you
> have a storehouse or greenhouse, not everyone will know how to
> use the herbs. Most people don't know one plant from another,
> and it's the same with trees. You will need someone who can say
> "this is used for that," and so on. Nowadays, the folks I work with
> are entirely dependent upon me for this. In time, we'll have to
> get the younger people to learn, and not just anyone, but those
> with a recognizable innate ability. And they must also have some
> maturity about them. This is a difficult combination to find. . . .
> You will also need to develop evaluative knowledge regarding

· 171 ·

what types of outside comments or actions to overlook and what
to pay attention to. Jealousy is prevalent these days. But we need
not be influenced by negative things that come toward us—don't
entertain them. Let them pass like water off a duck's back. The
unity of the group is its strength.

Crosslin had once again stressed the importance of group unity, along
with the need to educate youth as a foundational goal. His vision of
machinery may seem odd at first glance, but the idea references his hopes
for a center for Cherokee environmental education that would entail a
new building and manicured trails to highlight significant plants. He has
also proposed a traditional medicine institute, which would mirror the
design of homeopathic schools and would offer a curriculum of Cherokee medicinal knowledge and healing approaches to Native American
medical students. In his opinion, Cherokees are late to develop such an
institute—"if anyone should be doing it, it's us." With regard to the land
grants he mentioned, the group has prioritized the establishment of "tribal
conservation areas" through an agreement with the Cherokee Nation that
would bestow the elders' group with stewardship responsibilities. Crosslin's statement shows how he sees the group at the intersection of cultural
revitalization, education, and tribal environmental policy. And above all
is Crosslin's faith in the special significance of the group, indicated by his
opening words. For someone of his stature, knowledge, and experience,
this is a remarkable assertion. To the group, it is humbling, but it's also a
call to take up the responsibilities that Crosslin identified.

This book has been an attempt to explain why, as Crosslin asserted,
the elders' group represents a momentous formation in the Cherokee
Nation. During the course of almost three hundred years, Cherokees
have developed intricate relationships to place removed from their original homelands, and these relationships have taken on spiritual, material,
and political forms. Coming to know the western lands in these ways has
involved transferring knowledge and practices from the homelands, gaining new knowledge through experience and divination, and confronting
the seemingly unrelenting forces of settler colonialism—all of which have
shaped and reshaped, produced and reproduced physical landscapes.
Cherokees today are coming to terms with this history and its present-
day manifestations by imagining and creating ways to counteract the
forces of settler colonialism that have disrupted their relationships to

the nonhuman world. And while responses to colonialism have often involved mimicking colonial forms and subsequently articulating Cherokee versions of them, today Cherokee communities, elders, and land managers are engaging in dialogues that question the extent to which these forms have become out of balance. As Cherokees begin to assert a relationship-based approach to environmental governance, one that acknowledges the agency of nonhuman beings and traditional sources of authority, they create the conditions for fostering a way of life that values respect over control, and physical and spiritual sustenance over profit margins—they produce *sovereign landscapes.*

This process is a snapshot of indigenous state transformation, and this book has illuminated how Cherokees are reversing past theoretical frameworks by requiring that the state itself reconfigure the way in which it makes sense of the world. Whereas the Cherokee Nation has in the recent past regained considerable control over its own affairs through the use of state forms, it is now in the position to articulate a type of governance that represents concepts, values, and processes that have more often been associated with antistate practice. The significance of this new chapter in environmental governance is in its ability to accommodate both the practicalities of a resource-based approach within a settler-colonial context and the necessity of a relationship-based approach for achieving cultural, spiritual, and environmental health as expressed in indigenous values toward the nonhuman world. The relationship-based approach also lends vital legitimacy to the Cherokee state in its dealings with communities and traditional sites of authority. Although I have argued that acts of reform are necessary to account fully for traditional Cherokee ideals of governance, the dialectical process embodied by the assertion of the relationship-based approach accomplishes much toward addressing the holes in current Cherokee Nation governmental policy.

This has implications for Indian Country and indigenous peoples throughout the globe. The relationship between legitimacy and sovereignty has been central to recent critiques of indigenous governance. Here I return to the work of Mohawk scholar Taiaiake Alfred and Cherokee scholar Jeff Corntassel, who write, "Large-scale Indigenous efforts to confront state power by mimicking state institutions (via land claims and self-government processes) only deepens these divisions [among Indigenous people]. . . . To a large extent, institutional approaches to making meaningful change in the lives of Indigenous people have not lead to what we understand as decolonization and regeneration; rather they have further embedded Indigenous people in the colonial institutions they set out to challenge. This paradoxical outcome of struggle is because of the logical inconsistencies at the core of the institutional approaches" (Alfred and Corntassel 2005, 603, 611–12). To Alfred and Corntassel, "institutional approaches," in their commensurate dialogue with state power, remove indigenous governance from indigenous communities. Such institutions thus lose their legitimacy among indigenous communities and become merely extensions of the dominant state. The authors propose that the concepts of "peoplehood" and "Fourth World" provide alternatives to the institutional approach, where peoplehood entails centering respectful relationships in the resurgence of indigenous nationhood, and Fourth World locates the sites of such resurgences on indigenous lands and among indigenous systems of law (609–10). The concepts themselves are compelling, but their proposal, founded on the regeneration of "authentic Indigenous existences" (610), categorically rejects processes of indigenous political innovation and the ability of indigenous communities and individuals to transform imposed political institutions.

In my reading, the concept of peoplehood that they cite (Holm, Pearson, and Chavis 2003) does not support this conclusion. Tom Holm (Cherokee/Creek), J. Diane Pearson, and Ben Chavis (Lumbee) describe peoplehood as a matrix of four interlocking factors: language, sacred history, ceremonial cycle, and place/territory. In sum, they intend for the "peoplehood matrix" to function as a dynamic model that can help to explain the persistent and unique human groupings exemplified by many indigenous peoples. They arrive at the conclusion that peoplehood is the foundation of indigenous nationalism and sovereignty: "[Peoplehood] predates and is a prerequisite for all other forms of sociopolitical organization. . . . Sovereignty, therefore, is inherent in being a distinct people" (17). As Holm (2005, xv) later writes with regard to U.S. Indian policy in the Progressive Era, "Peoplehood was ultimately the reason underlying Native cultural resiliency. Indians managed, despite every effort on the part of the federal government, to maintain their identities as sovereign sociopolitical entities."

Holm's explanation of peoplehood as a foundational concept that undergirds indigenous cultural resiliency shows its utility for assessing contemporary indigenous political realities—it accounts for both the "institutional approach" and what one might call the "relational approach" to indigenous governance. In other words, the peoplehood model upholds indigenous institutions while emphasizing the need for dialogues over land/environment, spirituality, language, and traditional teachings. Peoplehood, then, is a model through which to view and explain indigenous action. As Holm, Pearson, and Chavis (2003, 18) state, "Native American peoples have taken foreign ideas, institutions, and material goods, filtered them through the matrix of peoplehood, and given them meaning within their own cultures and societies." In this respect, we might view the dialectics of indigenous state transformation as the act of filtering state structures through the matrix of peoplehood.

I do not deny the potential contributions of indigenous political formations that reject state forms. The visions of Alfred and Corntassel in this regard show promise and relevance to some indigenous situations. Furthermore, many of their "mantras" for achieving decolonization—including "land is life" and "language is power" (613)—clearly coincide with my own conclusions. But instead of dismissing indigenous governments that employ state forms, it is important to study their internal deliberations and in the process ask, how do they engage with their citizens and communities as these forms expand? And further, what social and cultural mechanisms exist for tribal citizens and communities to hold such structures accountable to their needs and to their identity as a people? We need more attention to local cases that take these questions into account. *Pace* Alfred (1999), we need indigenous *ethnographies* as much as we need indigenous *manifestos*.

In his more recent single-authored work, Corntassel (2008, 2012) has proposed the notion of "sustainable self-determination" as a term to describe processes that enable "the freedom to practice indigenous livelihoods, maintain food security, and apply natural laws on indigenous homelands in a sustainable manner" (2008, 118). I resonate with this concept and with his argument for shifting attention away from a rights-based framework in favor of a responsibilities-based one, but I add complexity to his discussion on how to achieve these goals. Ultimately, Corntassel—like Alfred—specifically refuses "statist" approaches to sustainable self-determination (121, 124). I argue that indigenous state transformation is in fact a vehicle for arriving at a similar destination. While this shouldn't preclude a critique of indigenous "statist" institutions via intense scrutiny, we cast away our existing political structures at our own peril.

I am as disillusioned as anyone about the decisions that some of our tribal governments make, particularly those that are heavily influenced by capitalist ideology, settler-state hegemony, racism, and structures of heteropatriarchy. However, I don't think the answer is to dismantle our governments but rather to give them direction based on the type of dialectics that I have identified in this book. It should be clear, then, that my critique is not aimed at the state form but more precisely the corporate form of governance and how it poorly accounts for the degree and quality of representation required by Cherokee governance values. I agree with Alfred (1999, 5) on the importance of indigenous values of harmony, autonomy, and respect, but dismantling indigenous statist institutions is not the only way to achieve the recovery and preservation of these principles—there can be indigenous states that do things indigenously. Key to this process is the knowledge and foresight that when we adopt these kinds of forms, we need to think critically about what they do and how we can transform them.

We are not confined to the model of the territorial state, although increasing landholdings within our traditional territories and establishing a strong degree of environmental sovereignty within them is a significant goal. The difference, of course, lies in how one conceives of that territory—is it a home for humans and their nonhuman relatives that must be responsibly stewarded, or is it solely a space that holds resources to be exploited? And further, for indigenous nations that have been forcibly relocated to other lands, to what extent does reterritorialization impinge on previous inhabitants who called (and still call) those lands home? Among traditionalist circles in the Cherokee Nation, a sense of humility permeates discussions of land stewardship, as exemplified in Crosslin's teaching to "honor the spirit of the land." In November 2013, Crosslin was asked to perform a blessing during the release of two rehabilitated bald eagles on Cherokee Nation land, during which he explicitly spoke of the Caddo homelands on which the group stood. After the successful release of the eagles, a man from the crowd approached Crosslin, identified himself as a Caddo Indian, and conveyed to him his appreciation for the acknowledgement of his people's traditional territory. This scenario illuminates a consciousness of displaced indigeneity and adds depth and complexity to the phrase "sovereign landscapes." As the Cherokee Nation strives for autonomy, self-determination, and the reclamation of lost lands, we are compelled to acknowledge that no place can be completely bound by political borders.

Toward an Integrative Political Ecology / Indigenous Studies Framework

I began this book with three stated goals, one of which was to propose linkages between the fields of American Indian studies and political ecology and to show how both fields gain greater analytical depth when brought together. In short, a political ecology view of American Indian studies offers insights into some of the critical issues in Indian Country that surround environmental governance and land control. An American Indian studies view of political ecology brings to bear unique articulations of environmental sovereignty that are couched in reaction to settler colonialism and tempered by relational approaches to land and nonhumans. At the very least, linking the two creates a framework that rejects the "ecological Indian" debate as a starting point for discussing environmental issues in Indian Country. At most, the two fields mutually benefit from new research directions and approaches.

To be sure, this is not an altogether new area of inquiry. Many scholars have explored political-ecological dimensions within their work with Native communities, and so, even if they do not explicitly seek to engage the two fields, numerous studies have established important benchmarks that can point to future directions. Paul Nadasdy's work with the Kluane First Nation has interrogated the trend of looking to indigenous peoples for ecological knowledge without accounting for structural inequities and the institutionalized privileging of Western worldviews (Nadasdy 2003). This has critical implications for settler-state natural resources programs that with good intentions seek to "incorporate" traditional ecological knowledge but in the end distort indigenous perspectives and extend state power into Native communities (Nadasdy 1999). Dana Powell and Andrew Curley (Diné) present a constructive analysis of intratribal environmental politics on the Navajo reservation that explicitly avoids the reduction of political debate to simplistic notions of infighting, factionalism, and corruption and instead engages the local and extralocal influences on tribal policy, energy development, and grassroots environmental activism (Powell and Curley 2009).

Studies in tribal environmental law also provide useful approaches. The U.S. Environmental Protection Agency's (EPA's) "Treatment as State" (TAS) policy allows American Indian nations to establish their own water quality standards over surface waters within tribal boundaries if they are in compliance with EPA guidelines and science. In the case of *Albuquerque v. Browner*, this policy enabled the Isleta Pueblo to promulgate higher water quality standards than the upstream City of Albuquerque and ultimately mandated the city's compliance. In their exploration of the TAS policy, Anna Fleder and Darren Ranco (Penobscot) ask whether this status advances tribal sovereignty—in the ability of tribes to extend environmental standards beyond their land bases—or inherently confines tribes to federal scientific and bureaucratic standards (Fleder and Ranco 2004). The latter two studies skillfully acknowledge the centrality of indigenous sovereignty, even while calling into question some of its inevitable flaws. All these studies provide nuanced looks at the intricacies of settler–indigenous relations and illuminate how for American Indian and First Nations peoples, the political is inherently environmental. Several other areas offer important contributions, including studies on tribal land conservation (Wood and Welcker 2008; Middleton 2011), tribal renewable energy development (Powell 2006; Kronk 2010), environmental risk assessment and justice in Indian Country (Harris and Harper 1997; Wolfley 1999; Holifield 2012), and indigenous climate change action and activism (Grossman and Parker 2012).

Indigenous involvement in climate change issues highlights the global implications of indigenous environmental governance. Alan Parker (Chippewa/Cree) and Zoltán Grossman have documented the development of the United League of Indigenous Nations (ULIN) and its explicit stance against the climate crisis (Parker and Grossman 2012). At the time of its formation in 2007, the ULIN consisted of representatives from eleven indigenous nations, including American Indian / First Nations representatives from North America, Maori representatives from Aotearoa / New Zealand, and representatives from Aboriginal Australian nations. The organization formed during treaty negotiations between the original delegates, and as of 2011, the Indigenous Nations Treaty has been ratified by more than eighty-four indigenous nations (Parker and Grossman 2012, 18). Despite this significant representation in the ULIN, in his essay "Recommendations to Native Government Leadership," Parker (2012, 192) points out the complete lack of representation from tribal governments in the United Nations Framework Convention on Climate Change and urges active participation. Parker asserts that indigenous nations must "have a voice and presence at the international level."

I propose that indigenous state transformation, in its foundational process of connecting land-based epistemologies with political sovereignty, helps us to understand the possibilities for influencing global change as indigenous peoples. Key to the ability to incorporate successfully a relationship-based approach into national and global forums is the ability to hash it out at home, and we have seen in the Cherokee Nation through time how this process is a central element in the convergence of grassroots and tribal (national) politics in practice. Its most recent manifestation—although certainly not the only one—is the elders' group, which seeks to provide guidance to its nation based on principles of unity, "divine equality," and respect for all life. These notions, although grounded in Cherokee cultural knowledge and perspectives, clearly have universal application. In his book *Environmental Governance: The Global Challenge*, Lamont C. Hempel (1996, 219) writes,

> Deliberative democracy is a form of popular government in which citizens are directly engaged in the challenge of self-rule through their participation in educative public debates about policy issues and processes. The essential feature is open engagement in a contest of ideas in order to make informed choices about policy or about representatives who are delegated to make policy. All true democracies are deliberative to some extent, but the goal of popular deliberation has often given way to situations in which nearly all of the deliberating is done remotely by representatives, both elected and unelected.

Hempel notes that large states with large populations have decreased the possibilities for face-to-face deliberation, which makes deliberative democracy difficult to implement today. Instead of resignation, however, Hempel discusses promising methods for achieving large-scale deliberation (see 220–22) and ultimately argues for "the need to connect local policy-making processes that are conducive to deliberative democracy with environmental strategies that must sometimes be global, or at least regional, to be effective. Communities that foster face-to-face interaction, informed by a sense of place and bioregional knowledge, are essential ingredients in the formation of an environmental ethic that can simultaneously guide policy making at the local, regional, and global levels. . . . the reestablishment of civic community is one of the most fundamental prerequisites for developing a healthy system of environmental governance" (222).[1] The traits of the elder's group that I discussed in chapter 5—attention to relationships, deliberation, and a sacred sense of unity—answer Hempel's call to reestablish civic community on the local level in order to influence global decisions and processes (for which he engages the term "glocalism"). And where Hempel writes of a "loss of connection . . . that undermines traditional values of land stewardship, communal pride of place, and a sense of interconnectedness with nature," the elders' group offers a vital perspective couched in the continuity of an indigenous philosophy and politically integrated via the relationship-based approach to indigenous environmental governance.[2]

Yuchi/Muscogee scholar Daniel R. Wildcat (2009, 11–12) similarly offers a treatise on "how humankind might reexamine lifeways that, although hardly without failures and mistakes, suggest in practical terms how we might adopt life-enhancing cultures situated in a symbiotic relationship with nature." He stresses that a realist perspective is necessary—one that addresses "practical questions about the means and consequences of extending the political and moral sphere of our 'human condition' to life beyond our human selves" (103). His recommendations are unabashedly local: "people- and place-specific investigations" of dwellings (indigenous-inspired architecture), food (indigenous agriculture and food sovereignty), and assessment based on indigenous environmental knowledges, values, and philosophies of intergenerational equity (115–31). Maria Carmen Lemos and Arun Agrawal (2006, 319) have likewise identified the need for challenging "contempocentrism" in favor of "long term sustainability and a concern for nature." What all this suggests is that at the heart of the global ecological crisis is a worldview problem. As Wildcat and many other indigenous scholars and activists have identified, it is a matter of viewing the world through a lens of "relatives" versus "resources" (Wildcat 2009, 64; see also LaDuke 1999; Salmon 2012). I have proposed that, in accounting for indigenous systems of resource management, we must necessarily view this as a spectrum and in contexts of settler colonialism and political economy, but the message is no less clear: that indigenous philosophies stress a relatedness to other-than-human beings that fundamentally shapes the ethics of human life.[3]

Human ecologist Fikret Berkes (1999, 163, 167) writes, "Perhaps the most fundamental lesson of traditional ecological knowledge is that worldviews and beliefs do matter" and, in turn, that struggles over indigenous traditional knowledge in settler environmental policy always come back to the central issue of resource management power. This is where political ecology can help. Through an engagement with American Indian studies—and therefore with the analytical concepts of land, sovereignty, and settler colonialism within this field—political ecologists can help to promote and foster the maintenance of American Indian relationships with the land and nonhumans through self-determination. As Paul Robbins (2004, 12) suggests of the field as a whole, First World political ecology can seek to present counternarratives that work against liberal arguments that denigrate American Indian treaty rights to subsistence-based harvesting practices as "special rights" (see Silvern 1999, 2000, 2002a) and counternarratives that confront positivist views of environmental policy and management that seek to discredit American Indian political claims as merely "cultural perspectives" or spiritualistic appeals (Berkes 1999, 167). Ultimately, political ecology can help to work toward what Lloyd Burton (2002, 27) has identified as "cultural co-evolution," in which American Indian knowledges and systems of governance assume a normative place in settler society as "wisdom born of experience of thousands of years of inhabiting this environment, which the dominant culture simply does not possess because it does not share that experience."

Indigenous state transformation—through its dialectical processes and multifaceted approach to environmental governance—has something to teach the world. Its simultaneous participation in and critique of the state system thrusts indigenous nations onto the global stage and asserts an unavoidable voice. This book presses the world to learn from this process in the Cherokee Nation and other indigenous nations. More immediately, it is a call for my Cherokee Nation to swiftly and to the fullest extent employ the relationship-based approach as a guiding principle for tribal development in order to enable a better life for our future generations— indeed, for the future generations of all people.

The Imperative of Relationship

Prior to the late eighteenth century, Cherokee governance and the non-human world were practically inseparable. The seven matrilineal clans—wolf, bird, bear, lion, deer, wild potato, and hawk—were at the center of village decision making, and Cherokees related to one another through these kinship structures that recognized the teachings of the nonhuman world at their very foundation.[4] Today, "the environment" and the practical reality of tribal "natural resource management" exist as a result of five hundred years of settler colonialism and two hundred years of industrial development. And while American Indians have been subjects of the former, and their lands the object of the latter, the Cherokee elders' group and others like it throughout Indian Country seek to instill within their systems of governance the imperative of relationship that has been carried forward through generations.[5]

This book has shown the successes and possibilities of such a project, as well as some of its obstacles. At the time when I carried out most of my extensive fieldwork (2004–9), the Cherokee Nation Natural Resources Department (NRD) prided itself on the "cultural forestry" programs that I discuss in chapter 3. But the tide of tribal administration has since changed, and today the NRD has become an entity strictly for the management of economic, resource-based activities. While I view this as a step backward for the NRD, the change has enabled its former director to devote more time as the liaison to the elders' group and to the maintenance of the Cherokee seed bank and heirloom crop program. Indeed, in many ways this has opened up possibilities for the elders' group due to the increased visibility of his position (as he now directs the Office of Administration Support, which reports directly to the Cherokee Nation Secretary of State). Time and leadership will tell whether the NRD will go back to incorporating a relationship-based approach into its activities, but the elders' group nevertheless continues to represent this approach and to inform tribal policy and decision making.

In October 2013, the group met on the same tract of land where Crosslin performed the blessing for the two rehabilitated bald eagles. The group has identified this eight-hundred-acre tract as a starting point for its conservation and cultural revitalization efforts, and plans are under way to officially lease this piece of tribal land to the group, along with stewardship responsibilities. We were blessed that day by the welcome interruption of the calls of four eagles circling above. As we all looked to the sky, I couldn't help but feel—perhaps along with others in the group—that this work was being intently watched. How might we hear the deliberations of our nonhuman relatives? And in our ever-fumbling, ever-human attempts to set things right again, how long must they wait?

Acknowledgments

I EXTEND MY DEEP GRATITUDE to the many Cherokee individuals and communities that opened their doors to me and welcomed me as family. Above all, Crosslin and Glenna Smith have given me their support, friendship, and counsel, and I am humbled that they have embraced me as a grandson. I hope this book lives up to their confidence in the project and in me. I also thank their family, Cathy and Junior especially, for their warmth and hospitality. It has been a great honor to work with the *Galv-quodi Igatiha* elders' advisory group, of which Crosslin and Glenna are members. Had the group not put their minds together and sustained their energy and faith behind the work they do, this book would surely be at a loss, as would the Cherokee Nation. Many in the elders' group requested that I acknowledge them by their Cherokee name only. My thanks go to Unanetlv Delatiyv, Ganohalegi, Ulisgani, Hastings Shade (Tsigesv), John Ross, Bonnie Kirk, Anna Sixkiller, Phyllis Edwards, Nancy Scott, and Ed Fields. Pat Gwin has become a true friend and indispensable partner in this very important work. Mark Dunham and Nancy Rackliffe have also devoted their time and energy to the group. *Doyu itsvyalihelitseha.*

This book began as a dissertation, and thanks to key individuals, I had the opportunity to develop the foundation of the project before entering graduate school. Nancy John (Creek/Choctaw), director of the Cherokee Nation Office of Environmental Programs, detoured from her ever-full agenda to notice a persistent young researcher and subsequently pulled all the strings necessary to arrange for my employment with the Cherokee Nation during each of my trips to the field. Thank you for your unending support and advocacy. I also owe many thanks to Jeannine Hale, former administrator of Cherokee Nation environmental programs, for her strong support of my work and for her own work with environmental issues during her time at the Cherokee Nation. Thanks also to Angela Drewes, who served as the Cherokee Nation Management Resources Group Leader during much of my fieldwork, and to all the interns and staff members of the Cherokee Nation Office of Environmental Programs and Cherokee Nation Natural Resources Department for their help along the way.

Dr. Richard Allen, Cherokee Nation policy analyst, never ceased to offer his time for discussions and his thoughts on my research, and he has become a dear friend and mentor in the process. The staff of the Cherokee Nation Community Services Office during my fieldwork also provided friendship and valuable thoughts and reactions to my work—namely, John Ross, Nancy Scott, Sam Ed Bush Jr., and Charlie and Doris Shell. The support and encouragement of Community Services Group Leader Charlie Soap was especially uplifting. Marvin Jones, former director of Cherokee Nation Self-Help Programs, is as fine a Cherokee intellectual as I have ever met, and I thank him for his insights on my work. Myra Robertson, director of Blue Sky Water Society, Inc., and an officer for Cherokees Helping Initiate Progress (CHIP), has been a friend and a source of guidance throughout my work, as has her brother Sam Ed Bush Jr. Many other folks at Cherokee Nation have contributed in various ways to the development of my research, most notably Bobby Gail Smith, Cora Flute, Ryan and Dawnena Mackey, J. P. Johnson, Donna Gourd, David Justice, David Cornsilk, and the fine folks in the Department of Education. Thank you.

When I was just beginning my work in Tahlequah, the staff of the Cherokee Heritage Center in Park Hill befriended me and offered suggestions and contacts for the project. Thanks to Tonia Weavil, Becky Adair, Gene Norris, Roy Hamilton, Josiah, Robert Lewis, and Perry and Kathy Vanbuskirk for their help and friendship.

Instructors Harry Oosahwee and Wyman Kirk of the Northeastern State University Cherokee Language Program welcomed me into their offices as a student of the Cherokee language. Wyman graciously donated time and materials for my unofficial independent study of the language in fall 2008. As a fellow academic and Cherokee ethnographer, we quickly became friends, and I deeply appreciate our conversations and his willingness to share his work with me. I also thank all the students and staff of the Cherokee Language Program for creating such a welcoming and collegial environment for anyone who wants to learn the language. *Wado!*

The Cherokee Elders Council, a small nonprofit organization unrelated to Galvquodi Igatiha and based in Locust Grove, Oklahoma, invited me to present my work on the ethnobotany project during one of their meetings in the summer of 2006. There I met Owen Scott, who had begun work on a similar project on a volunteer contract basis with the Cherokee Nation in the 1990s. Unfortunately, due to the financial demands of a project of this sort and a lack of funding commitment for the project from the tribal government, Mr. Scott was unable to develop his project fully. However, Mr. Scott is still very passionate about this kind of work, and I have benefited greatly from our conversations and his experiential knowledge. His report, titled "Report to the Cherokee Nation on the Cherokee Cultural/Environmental Resources Preservation Project," is an eye-opening assessment of the institutional requirements necessary for maintaining a permanent program of this sort within the Cherokee Nation. Published in 1991, the report was way ahead of its time, and the Cherokee Nation still faces many of the issues Mr. Scott raises therein. When I first read the report in 2006, I was amazed to see that much of the recommendations based on my own work echoed those of Mr. Scott. Since then, I have been an advocate of disseminating his report in hopes that his proposals, along with those that have arisen out of my own work, will find the necessary support (financial and otherwise) in order to develop a lasting tribal program for cultural resources.

Many individuals and groups have helped me in the course of my formal education. At the University of Arizona, Richard Stoffle, Tom Holm (Creek/Cherokee), and Nancy Parezo guided me intellectually and supported me as a young scholar. Sincere thanks to the staff and directors of the University of Arizona Summer Research Institute and the Ronald E. McNair Program for giving me financial and intellectual support for my undergraduate research and for helping me achieve my goal of attending graduate school. At UC Berkeley, I thank my advisor and dissertation chair Nancy Peluso for recognizing my potential and helping this first-generation student successfully navigate the demands of graduate school. Nathan Sayre, Thomas Biolsi, and Lynn Huntsinger made up the rest of a stellar dissertation committee, and this work reflects their careful and committed guidance. Louise Fortmann, Jeff Romm, Isha Ray, Claudia Carr, Kimberly TallBear (Sisseton Wahpeton Dakota), and the late Philip Frickey also deserve special thanks for their advice and encouragement. I also thank my friends and colleagues in the Department of Environmental Science, Policy, and Management, who helped make graduate school a very memorable time: Dan Fahey, Josh Dimon, Kristin Reed, Dorian Fougères, Noer Fouzi Rachman, Logan Hennessey, Chuck Striplen (Ohlone), Beth Rose Middleton, the late Nathaniel Gerhart, and all the members of my 2004 incoming cohort. And thanks to Carmen Foghorn (Isleta Pueblo/ Navajo), director of the American Indian Graduate Program at Berkeley, and the members of the American Indian Graduate Student Association for providing a lively and supportive Native community at Cal.

At the University of Minnesota, I thank the faculty and staff in the Department of American Indian Studies for their support and camaraderie. In particular, M. Bianet Castellanos, David Chang (Kanaka Maoli), Brenda Child (Ojibwe), Katherine Hayes, Angelica Lawson (Northern Arapaho), Jean O'Brien (Ojibwe), and David Wilkins (Lumbee) helped me think through some of the ideas in this book, as well as the members of the UMN American Indian Studies Workshop. Across campus, I have greatly benefitted from the friendship and conversations with Jimmy C. Patiño Jr., David Pellow, David Karjanen, Michael Goldman, and the members of the Faculty of Color Initiative. Thanks to Mark Lindberg in the Geography Department for his help with the map in chapter 2.

Cherokee Nation citizen and sociologist Eva Garroutte at Boston College provided detailed comments on my dissertation project in its early stages and ever since has been very supportive of my work. Albert Wahrhaftig at Sonoma State University and his wife Jane Lukens-Wahrhaftig welcomed me into their home with good coffee, homemade bread, and great conversation. I met UT Austin anthropologist Circe Sturm (Mississippi Choctaw descendant) during the 2008 Cherokee National Holiday, and she readily offered her insights and advice on the challenges of fieldwork. Since that time, Circe has served as a mentor through the First Peoples Manuscript Development Workshop and the Ford Foundation Postdoctoral Fellowship, and her feedback greatly improved the manuscript. I am grateful for her committed mentorship over the years. At the University of Montana, I thank David Moore and Kathryn Shanley (Assiniboine) for their close friendship, mentoring, and stimulating conversations about Native studies generally. Amy Den Ouden and an anonymous reviewer provided much appreciated perceptive comments on the manuscript. Finally, my editor, Jason Weidemann at the University of Minnesota Press, championed the project throughout and graciously invited me to participate in the First Peoples Manuscript Development Workshop in 2012—a venue that significantly strengthened my work. I have been fortunate to know and converse with such a rich intellectual community. Any and all errors or excesses, of course, are entirely mine.

The work herein has been cumulatively supported by a UC Berkeley Graduate Opportunity Program fellowship (2004–5); a U.S. Environmental Protection Agency Science to Achieve Results fellowship (2005–7); a

National Science Foundation Graduate Research fellowship (2007–10); a Morris K. and Stewart L. Udall Foundation Environmental Public Policy and Conflict Resolution PhD Dissertation fellowship (2010–11); a one-year postdoctoral appointment sponsored by UMN's Institute for Diversity, Equity, and Advocacy (IDEA; 2011–12); a First Peoples travel grant (2012); an IDEA Multicultural Research Award (2013); and a Ford Foundation postdoctoral fellowship (2013–14), with additional support from the UC Berkeley Graduate Division. I owe many thanks to these institutions and the members of their respective review committees.

My relatives in Oklahoma transformed my fieldwork into "homework" and enriched my research experience in ways that are difficult to express in words. My cousin, Michael Allan Hunter, who passed over in 2006 at the early age of forty-two, was a dear friend who enthusiastically supported my work, and among many other selfless acts, he gave me a couch to sleep on for an entire summer. His company and lighthearted, humorous disposition were deeply missed when I returned to Oklahoma in 2008 to begin my extended fieldwork. I thank his parents, Nancy and Lester Hunter of Muskogee, for their kindheartedness and for all the dinners and conversations. Barbara McAlister, a distant cousin who I have come to know as "Aunt" Barbara, has been a constant source of encouragement. Her brother John McAlister and his wife Carolyn, although they are no longer with us, always made me feel at home.

Infinite thanks to Mom and Dad and to my stepparents Barry and Larissa for their love, support, and ceaseless faith in my abilities. You've laid the foundation on which I stand, and I'm truly blessed for it. The Lawson family has always been a steady source of encouragement and warmth. My wife, Angelica Lawson, has been my closest colleague, mentor, editor, and friend throughout my work on this book, and I have been privileged to have her encouragement, advice, and love the whole time. She and our daughter, Liliana, cast a beautiful light and bring me inspiration and great happiness. *Stvgeyuhi.*

Appendix

ᏍᏏᏉᏗ ᏔᏎᏗᏈ

Declaration of Divine Equality

June 2012

We, the group hereby called ᏍᏏᏉᏗ ᏔᏎᏗᏈ (*Galvquodi Igatiha;* "all the same, or equal, in a divine way"), stand united in the sight of God, our Creator. We are joined by love and concern for each other and for all people. In our formation as a group, we acknowledge and promote the Original Spirit of Creation that unites us all across the earth. In our actions and deliberations, we seek to ascribe to the original rules and spiritual guidelines that were given in the beginning with the creation of all people, as recounted by our spiritual leaders. It is in this spirit—one of unity and respect for all Creation, and all religions and beliefs—that we put forth a Declaration.

We are a small group of concerned Cherokees, the majority of whom are fluent Cherokee speakers and are considered by the tribal community as well educated on aspects of Cherokee environmental knowledge. One member is a full-time Cherokee healer and spiritual leader. We are partnered with the Cherokee Nation Natural Resources Department to carry out our mission. This department recognizes our role as an advisory council to their activities concerning Cherokee environmental knowledge.

Our mission is to fulfill our responsibility to honor the spirit of the land we inhabit, and to preserve and perpetuate our knowledge of the flora, fauna, and sacred places within the Cherokee Nation. We do this in order to foster the retention of cultural heritage and the spiritual health of future generations of Cherokees, and, furthermore, so that all people may benefit from the knowledge that has been entrusted to us by the Creator. Much of this knowledge pertains to the medicinal properties of wild plants. Whereas we take precautions with regard to those that might harbor selfish or harmful intentions concerning such knowledge, we understand that the medicines were given to us by the Creator for use by the people, regardless of race, creed, or color. Although we Cherokees have been designated the keepers of this knowledge so as to ensure its proper use and perpetuation, we assert that the medicines should be available to anyone who might need them.

We meet in a time when our knowledge of the land is rapidly diminishing, and still is but a fraction of what it once was only one generation ago. We acknowledge that our generation is perhaps the last to hold a significant amount of this knowledge, and we have agreed that now is the time to make a concerted effort to revitalize it. It is our goal to find ways to share this knowledge with other Cherokees with the hope that the practice and transmission of this knowledge be continued for generations to come.

The land is central to our efforts, and our mission and goals will require space. In this spirit, we request that tracts of tribal land be set aside as conservation areas, managed by a partnership between our group and the Natural Resources Department. Such tracts of land will serve as places to teach and practice Cherokee environmental knowledge, and to conserve tribal cultural resources. The ecosystems represented in these tracts should include all those that are home to the many plants used in Cherokee medicine: hills and hollows, fields or prairies, and creeks or streams. Water should be available in the form of springs, as this resource is important in the practice of Cherokee medicine. We recommend that these tracts be designated in conjunction with the locations of Cherokee Nation tribal clinics, so as to encourage the collaboration between practitioners of Western and traditional medicine. If necessary, the group requests that access to these areas be established in the form of dirt roads and/or walking trails.

Our group is made strong by our unity, as well as our autonomy. Although we maintain our loyalty to the Cherokee Nation, its people and government, we require that all decisions regarding the group's activities be made in consensus by the group, and that our course of action be determined internally. To allow otherwise would compromise the participation of many members, and thus dissolve the group.

This declaration is made in the spirit of wellness and spiritual renewal for the Cherokee Nation. We ask these things so as to honor our ancestors and to fulfill our commitment to the future generations through the continuation of our knowledge of, and relationship to, the land.

Notes

Introduction

1. I use this term to describe individuals who have not yet reached the age and status of "elder" but who possess a large amount of traditional knowledge due to their upbringing and continued use of, and interest in, the knowledge.

2. The ridicule and exploitation I speak of were conveyed to me numerous times in the course of my fieldwork, and they both continue to occur today. The ridicule of medicinal knowledge, and traditional knowledge generally (i.e., certain stories and beliefs that Cherokees hold about the nonhuman world around them), can entail seemingly flippant remarks by Cherokees and non-Cherokees alike about the validity of this knowledge when compared to Western-based ways of knowing, as well as simply writing off certain beliefs or stories as superstition. Exploitation of this knowledge has included the marketing of certain plant-based remedies and the publication of medicinal incantations known as *idi:gawésdi*. The latter instance occurred at the hand of Cherokee scholars Jack and Anna Kilpatrick in the 1960s, and although the word *exploitation* may be a little strong here, their publication of these formulas sparked significant controversy, which I will discuss further in chapter 4.

3. Pat Gwin and the other NRD staff member are both Cherokee Nation citizens trained in biology at Northeastern State University. While they have extensive local knowledge of the biota of northeastern Oklahoma, they nevertheless do not consider themselves experts on Cherokee traditional knowledge. As a side note, the humor is not lost on NRD staff that the acronym for the department, when pronounced as a word, comes out as "nerd"—there is, in fact, a lighthearted sense of pride associated with this label.

4. The phrase *out in the communities* is a prominent way to refer to the distance (figurative and literal) of numerous rural traditional Cherokee communities from the tribal governmental offices in Tahlequah. The phrase carries with it the sense that these communities are the source of Cherokee peoplehood, despite the fact that, as Charlie Soap implies, tribal governmental officials often neglect them.

5. After some significant administrative reorganization following the 2011 principal chief election, Pat Gwin relocated from the NRD to become director of the Office of Administrative Support, which deals directly with the Cherokee Nation Secretary of State.

6. I am indebted to Onondaga faith-keeper Oren Lyons, who first articulated the distinction between viewing nonhuman beings as relatives versus resources. For recent works that expound on this in more detail, see LaDuke (1994, 1999), Trosper (1995), Tsosie (1996), Cajete (2000), Robyn (2002), Simpson (2004), McGregor (2005), Turner (2005), Nadasdy (2007), Nelson (2008), Wildcat (2009), and Salmon (2012)—to name a few.

7. For more internal discussion on the field and its development, see Cook-Lynn (1997, 1999), Cook-Lynn et al. (2005), Champagne (1996), Weaver (2007), and Nelson (2011).

8. Admittedly, this definition emphasizes one particular perspective of the field, which could be described as the "poststructural" perspective. This approach to political ecology has received a fair amount of criticism for its lack of attention to biophysical elements and processes, leading some to question the use of the word *ecology* in *political ecology* (as opposed to just *environmental politics*). See Peter Walker's (2005) article "Political Ecology: Where Is the Ecology?" for an excellent review of this debate. Yet, despite this criticism, scholars within the field have asserted that, as a field of inquiry, political ecology's range of approaches (including poststructural ones as well those that pay close attention to biophysical processes) ultimately strengthens its critical edge and utility in understanding environmental issues. Richard Peet and Michael Watts (2004, 15) write, "What political ecology has done obviously is to open up the category of the environment itself and explore its multiform representations."

9. See also the special issues of *Environment and Planning A* (Volume 37, 2005) and *Geoforum* (Volume 37, 2006).

10. An exception to this is Emery and Pierce's (2005) broad survey of subsistence in U.S. forests, which notably includes a discussion of Native Hawaiian harvesting rights and American Indian treaty rights and ultimately urges further study. Powell (2006) has also gestured toward a political-ecological approach to North American indigenous environmental issues in her analysis of environmental justice and renewable energy development in Indian Country. Also notable, while not explicitly engaging political ecology as a field, is other work that analyzes American Indian environmental justice and activism, such as Gedicks (1993), Clark (2002), Krakoff (2002), Ishiyama (2003), Ranco (2008), Willow (2009), Endres (2012), and Holifield (2012).

11. See Ribot and Peluso (2003) for a good review.

12. Smith (2010) provides a useful discussion of this debate. Similar to my argument herein, she later writes, "If one understands oneself as fundamentally constituted through relationship with all of creation and other peoples, then nationhood is not defined as being against other peoples, but through radical relationality. Nationhood is by definition expansive rather than insular" (Smith 2012, 81).

13. Here it is important to distinguish between Alfred's earlier and later work. His earlier work (e.g., Alfred 1995) shows the transformation of Mohawk governance institutions through a concrete and detailed study. Such a focus on tribal specificity and localized struggles is similar to what I advocate herein. Interestingly, this earlier work emphasized "syncretic reformation" and "institutional framework[s] strongly rooted in tradition but adapted to modern political reality" (Alfred 1995, 179). By contrast, his later publications take a more extreme approach to understanding the indigenous use of state structures, give less attention to tribal specificity, and often emphasize the polarization of indigenous versus Western values and political forms. Both *Peace, Power, Righteousness* (1999) and *Wasáse* (2005) appear to struggle with whether to cast off all imposed structures or to renounce tradition altogether. He thus ends up with a zero-sum game of modernity or tradition, indigenous or Western (e.g., 1999, 20–30; 2005, 33–34)—a predicament that I think can be circumvented when indigenous governance institutions are viewed through the lens of indigenous state transformation. While I admire the type of liberating thinking that Alfred's later work represents, my perspective—based on my experiences through fieldwork with my community—differs from his. In other words, I agree with the issues he raises (e.g., pages 36–38 in *Wasáse* display a perspective similar to my assertion that "the political is environmental"), but I disagree with how to get there. My fundamental divergence from Alfred is that we have to acknowledge *vehicles* of resistance (e.g., indigenous states) that appear counterhegemonic but have the ability to contain nonhegemonic principles at their core.

14. Here I invoke Mignolo's (2000) work on transculturation and subaltern studies.

15. While I think Bruyneel's work is applicable to my arguments herein about indigenous states and their significance in settler-state politics, I should be clear that he does not use the term *indigenous state* in his book but rather leaves his discussion much more open—referring instead to indigenous "political identity, agency, and autonomy" (6), "indigenous political expression" (20), and "indigenous political claims" (24). Interestingly, however, he writes that "the third space may also prove of worth as a conceptualization of antistatist autonomy that can be an alternative to the polar imaginaries that either see state sovereignty as the unavoidably exclusive font of legitimate political space or postulate a political world in which we have somehow moved beyond state sovereignty altogether" (222). I think that when viewed in the context of indigenous state transformation, indigenous states inhabit such a space.

16. Anthropologist Anna Tsing (2007, 33) writes, "The global indigenous movement is alive with promising contradictions. Inverting national development standards, it promises unity based on plurality: diversity without assimilation. It endorses authenticity *and* invention, subsistence *and* wealth, traditional

knowledge *and* new technologies, territory *and* diaspora. The excitement of indigenous rights claims draws from the creative possibilities of such juxtapositions."

17. Here I am aligned with Osage scholar Jean Dennison (2012, 7–8), who writes, "It is possible to create new and powerful forms out of an ongoing colonial process. . . . The key is making something out of this structure that does not mirror the oppression of the colonizer."

18. Here I am in conversation with Anna Fleder and Darren Ranco (Penobscot), who present an informative analysis of tribal environmental governance in the context of tribal Treatment as State status in federal environmental law (Fleder and Ranco 2004). They conclude that the indigenous use of so-called Western political structures is necessary for confronting dominant powers, in tandem with the need for critiquing and reforming such structures to account for indigenous values and ideals of governance. This debate, of course, is long standing, both in terms of American Indian governance (e.g., Deloria and Lytle 1984, 242–43, on the conflict between "realism" and "idealism" in the context of the political factionalism that was sparked by the creation of tribal governments through the Indian Reorganization Act of 1934 and reared its head most notably in the Wounded Knee occupation of 1973) and in terms of discussions in postcolonial studies regarding the extent to which drawing from dominant structures both molds and restricts subaltern resistance (see Young 2001, 341). I find Ojibwe/Dakota scholar Scott Lyons's (2010) perspective on this insightful, in which he frames his discussion of Native nationalism in terms of an "x-mark" (20) and the willingness to assent to modernity but on uniquely indigenous terms.

19. Lorenzo Veracini (2011, 7) writes, "The struggle against settler colonialism must aim to keep the settler-Indigenous relationship ongoing. . . . Indigenous peoples routinely demand enduring relations, not their end. . . . Settler colonialism ends with an Indigenous ultimate permanence."

20. Discussions on the ecological Indian stereotype (e.g., Krech 1999) have tended to mask the political issues at stake in indigenous environmental activism and struggle (Willow 2009). Other scholars have admirably addressed this debate, and I do not feel the need to replicate their efforts. The most useful works have been those that decenter European conceptions of ecology when describing indigenous environmental practices and politics (e.g., Nadasdy 2005) and others that emphasize indigenous futures based in both tradition and the generation of new knowledges (e.g., McGregor 2005). This clears the air for talking about indigenous contributions today that should not be held suspect out of fear of cynical use of stereotypes (although Darren Ranco [2007] has shown that the ecological nobility discourse has become one way for Native communities to ensure their seat at the environmental decision-making table) but rather should be seen as sincere efforts to alleviate crises in global environmental governance.

21. Thomas Davis's (2000) work on Menominee forest management shows these foundational values at work and how they guide the Menominee model of sustainability.

22. *Basic Call to Consciousness* (2005 [1978]), edited by the staff of the Mohawk newspaper *Akwesasne Notes*, represents a critical moment in the resurgence of American Indian nationalism that should be acknowledged here. The book recounts and contextualizes the actions of Haudenosaunee (Iroquois) Confederacy representatives in 1977 at the Discrimination against the Indigenous Populations of the Americas conference hosted by the nongovernmental organizations of the United Nations in Geneva, Switzerland. Reprinted in the book are all three position papers presented at this forum by Haudenosaunee Confederacy representatives, which attest to the repeated injustices against American Indian nations by the United States and implore UN leadership to reverse environmentally destructive policies. Notably, one of the representatives, Onondaga Chief Oren Lyons, used a passport issued by the Haudenosaunee Confederacy to enter Switzerland.

23. More broadly, Randel D. Hanson (2004) has shown the devastating effects of U.S. President Ronald Reagan's neoliberal policies on reservation communities through their drastic diminishing of the federal fiduciary relationship with tribal nations. For an informative discussion of neoliberalism and its relation to environmental governance within political ecology, see McCarthy (2005), Heynen et al. (2007), and Himley (2008).

24. Although the official webpage of the Cherokee Nation lists its population as just over 300,000, the most recent *U.S. Bureau of Indian Affairs American Indian Population and Labor Force Report* (2005) lists the Cherokee Nation population as 257,824. In the same report, the Eastern Band numbers 13,562 and the United Keetoowah Band 11,582 (http://www.bia.gov/WhatWeDo/Knowledge/Reports/index.htm). The total number of Cherokee Nation citizens includes at-large citizens living outside Cherokee Nation territory.

25. "Jurisdictional area" refers to the varying levels of civil, criminal, and environmental jurisdictional powers held by the Cherokee Nation within these borders. In 1990, the U.S. Census Bureau created the term "Tribal Jurisdictional *Statistical* Area" as a way for tribes who do not have an established reservation to participate in the decennial census. In 2000, the Census Bureau changed the term to "Oklahoma Tribal Statistical Area" (OTSA) and continued to use this term for the 2010 census. Regardless, most tribal jurisdictions in Oklahoma are still commonly called "Tribal Jurisdictional Service Area."

26. "Tribal trust land" is owned by the Cherokee Nation but held "in trust" by the federal government. Trust status means that certain restrictions apply on what can be done with the land (overseen by the Bureau of Indian Affairs), including resource extraction and development. Property taxes on trust land do not apply, and the federal government holds the actual title to the land.

27. The term *restricted land* refers to individual allotments whose owners or heirs have maintained a blood quantum of one-half or more. The Dawes Commission enacted this policy under the notion that the more biologically Indian a person was, the less economically competent, therefore prohibiting the individual from alienating the land. Restricted land that did not fall out of trust status (via blood quantum) still remains restricted and nontaxable today, as either "restricted fee" or "trust allotted," the difference being who holds the title (the individual or the BIA, respectively). Collectively, these two terms are referred to as *individual trust*. See Anderson and Lueck (1992).

28. According to the 2000 U.S. Census, in Adair County (42.49 percent Native American), 23.2 percent of the population was below the poverty line; in Delaware County (19.64 percent Native American), 19.8 percent of the population was below the poverty line; and in Cherokee County (32.42 percent Native American), 22.9 percent of the population was below the poverty line. These numbers can be compared to Tulsa County (5.2 percent Native American), where 11.6 percent of the population was below the poverty line. See also Sturm (2002, 10).

29. Paul Robbins (2004, 212–16) labels this combined method of approach the "Hybridity Thesis."

1. Before Removal

1. While political ecology is most commonly associated with contemporary cases of environmental struggle in the context of capitalist political economy, I use the term in the title of this chapter as a way to describe how Cherokee responses to profound change were shaped by both ecology and politics. I also hope that this construction further serves to bring the biophysical environment into analyses of state formation, especially in indigenous cases, in which relationships to land and nonhumans are essential variables.

2. See Teuton (2010) for a contemporary account of the *Anikutani* based on his work with Cherokee storytellers.

3. For an in-depth discussion of the landscape and Cherokee environmental practices in the southeast, see Hill (1997).

4. Although Gearing lists four structural poses in his analysis, I focus on the two major poses of "red" and "white" for the sake of a simplified description and argument. Fogelson (1963, 730) points out that the remaining two poses might not necessarily be considered legitimate poses at all.

5. The role of women in Cherokee society during this time was strong, drawing much of its influence from the matrilineal clan system. In this system, when a man and woman married, the man moved to his wife's town and lived with her extended clan family. Any children would be raised as a member of the mother's clan. For male children, the mother's brothers (who were also of the same clan)

served as the primary male figures. Cherokee women also had important leadership roles, mainly in the White government as "Beloved Women." Although the outward face of Cherokee town leadership was male (with the council primarily made up of "Beloved Men" and the "head man" serving as town "chief"), women controlled much of the internal happenings of the village and were the sole owners of village land due to their primary role as the village farmers. Further, the council of Beloved Men often deferred to the Beloved Women, and the Beloved Women also possessed the sole authority over the fate of prisoners of war. "War Women," or younger women who displayed warrior attributes, were also given high status in Cherokee society and most likely transitioned into the role of Beloved Women once they reached elder status. Due to the influence of Euro-American patrilineal values and the fading of the Cherokee clan system, through time the political authority of Cherokee women diminished, although it was certainly not obliterated. See my discussion that follows in this chapter and Perdue (1998) for a thorough treatment of this subject.

6. Echota and Tugalo are old Cherokee villages.

7. For an in-depth account of the relations between the Cherokees and the Colony of South Carolina, see Corkran (1962).

8. Clinton, Goldberg, and Tsosie (2003, 87) note that this quote is most likely apocryphal. For an excellent assessment of the Marshall cases and a sharp critique of the tendency of scholars to valorize Chief Justice Marshall's "dictum" as a compassionate affirmation of indigenous sovereignty (thereby decentering Native oppression), see Wolfe (2012).

9. Dunaway (1997, 190, n. 149) notes that this movement has been erroneously labeled the "Ghost Dance Movement."

10. Scholars of Cherokee history have debated early Cherokee state-building in terms of the purpose and efficacy of resistance movements that sought to curb acculturation and revitalize traditional governance values and practices. Turtle Mountain Chippewa scholar Duane Champagne (1983) has argued that the level of social differentiation within Cherokee society rendered it more amenable to the development of European-based state forms, in contrast to other indigenous nations like the Delaware and Iroquois. While he states that the foundation for Cherokee state-building was to resist U.S. threats to territory and sovereignty, his analysis rests on the assumption that Cherokee political development was driven primarily by agrarian-class formation, which led Cherokee society to "readily accept American economic and political innovations" (759). In response, Cherokee scholar Russell Thornton (1985) centers Cherokee revitalization movements as examples of resistance to state-building, including the 1811–13 movement and White Path's rebellion. Thornton claims that these resistances show how the development of the Cherokee state was a colonial imposition and not something that Cherokees accepted. In a rebuttal essay, Champagne (1985) asserts that such

movements "failed" because they were not sustained over long periods of time nor institutionalized as moral-religious orders. My focus herein on *dialectics* cuts across these two analyses. Cherokee social movements were far from failures. They greatly impacted the nation's political development because the individuals who made them up were deeply invested in the outcomes. Therefore, I contend that Cherokee state transformation was neither a colonial imposition nor solely a product of agrarian-class formation.

2. Shaping New Homelands

1. See also Walker and Fortmann (2003) for a discussion of normative landscapes in the "exurban" Sierra of Nevada County, California.

2. Jones (2000) claims that oral history from the current descendants of Cherokees who remained in Arkansas recounts this date as a *return to* the area, as it is believed that the Cherokees had inhabited the Ozarks in prehistoric times.

3. For instance, Baldwin's Ironweed (*Vernonia baldwinii*) grows in the west but not the east. Another Ironweed species, Broadleaf Ironweed (*Vernonia glauca*) grows in the east but not the west. Both can be used to treat fevers and colds.

4. The Little People (*yvwi tsunsdi* in the Cherokee language) are a mysterious people, standing two to four feet tall, who are prevalent in the Cherokee belief system and oral tradition (similar to many North American tribes and other traditional societies around the world). They often appear in the form of helpers but have also been known to lead people astray in the woods. Regardless, they are always referred to with the utmost respect and caution.

5. I have made some slight modifications to the original record of this story for the sake of clarification.

6. Today, a pound of twenty-five-year-old roots can be sold for up to $1,500 (Taylor 2006, 14).

7. The work of James Clifford (1997, 2) adds to this wordplay in his discussion of *routes* as phenomena of "dwelling-in-travel." Interestingly, Vick (2011, 412–13) highlights—through the work of Cherokee anthropologists Jack and Anna Kilpatrick (1967)—the persistent travel of Cherokees to the homelands even shortly after Removal in order to procure medicinal plant species.

8. The Indian-Pioneer Papers are a collection of interviews conducted by government workers in the 1930s with both Indians and non-Indians regarding life in the Indian Territory and the early days of Oklahoma statehood. The Doris Duke Collection of American Indian Oral History is a collection of interviews with Indians in Oklahoma conducted by personnel of the University of Oklahoma's American Indian Institute (many of whom were American Indian) between 1967 and 1972. Both are housed in the University of Oklahoma's Western History Collection (http://digital.libraries.ou.edu/WHC).

9. Note the mention of "wild pigeons," referring to the existence of the once plentiful (but now extinct) passenger pigeon in the Indian Territory. See Littlefield (1969) for a full discussion.

10. Interview with Mr. E. F. Vann, March 10, 1938, Muskogee, OK (interviewer: L. W. Wilson, journalist), vol. 93, interview ID 13177, Indian-Pioneer Papers, Western History Collections, University of Oklahoma, Norman, OK (hereafter IPP).

11. Mrs. Elinor Boudinot Meigs, informant, March 2–4, 1937, Ft. Gibson, OK (interviewer: Jas. S. Buchanan), vol. 62, IPP.

12. Interview with Mr. Lynch Sixkiller, April 19, 1937 (interviewer: W. J. B. Bigby), vol. 84, interview ID S-149, IPP.

13. Interview with Mrs. Phillis Pettit, February 22, 1937 (interviewer: O. C. Davidson, field worker), vol. 71, IPP.

14. Land leases at this time generally consisted of cattle-grazing leases on the Cherokee Outlet, a large tract of land to the west that was granted to the Cherokee Nation upon Removal.

15. "Jake Whitmire, Cherokee," May 29, 1969 (J. W. Tyner, interviewer), vol. 22, interview ID T-468-3, Doris Duke Collection, Western History Collections, University of Oklahoma, Norman, OK (hereafter DDC).

16. "*As much Land* as Man Tills, Plants, Improves, Cultivates, and can use the Product of, so much is his *Property*. He by his Labour does, as it were, inclose it from the Common" (Locke 1978 [1689], 19; emphasis in original).

17. A non-Cherokee editor of a Fort Smith newspaper is said to have remarked about the Indian Territory, "As to the condition of the poor classes . . . they are much better off in every respect than the poor people of our own state . . . they are happy in the possession of their small farms . . . there are no paupers among them" (Bloom 2002, 513).

18. Stremlau (2011) provides a compelling narrative of Cherokee adaptation, resilience, and cultural persistence in the face of allotment through the maintenance of traditional kinship practices. Her work shows how Cherokees were able to mitigate the impacts of allotment through their adherence to community values and relationship obligations and therefore "did not succumb to powerlessness and victimization" (6). This is important to note because although the Cherokee Nation was forced to allot its lands, the architects of the allotment policy did not fulfill their overarching assimilative goals. In the end, allotment "failed to make Indians indistinguishable from other Americans or to obliterate the sovereignty of Native nations" (Chang 2011, 112).

3. The "Greening" of Oklahoma

1. It is worth noting that in 1905, as a last ditch attempt for autonomy, representatives of the Five Civilized Tribes proposed an Indian "State of Sequoyah" to

be admitted into the Union as the forty-sixth state. This proposal was denied—perhaps fortunately, due to the repercussions it would have had on tribal sovereignty today. See Leeds (2007) for an in-depth discussion.

2. "Ross Bowlin, Cherokee," August 26, 1969 (interviewer: J. W. Tyner), vol. 11, interview ID T-512-2, DDC.

3. Transcript, "The Convention of Duly Enrolled Cherokees by Blood in Oklahoma, July 30, 1948, Tahlequah, Oklahoma" (Oklahoma City: The Stenotype Reporter), p. 35.

4. Here Wahrhaftig is referring to the outmigration of many Cherokees to California during this time.

5. Travelok.com (accessed May 7, 2010). The video has been removed and is no longer accessible, but the tourism regions are still viewable on this site. Note that Arbuckle Country has changed to "Chickasaw Country," the only tourism region that bears the name of an existing tribal nation.

6. The Cherokee Outlet had been granted to the Cherokee Nation after Removal in addition to the lands that make up present-day northeastern Oklahoma. The legendary Oklahoma land run of 1893 had settled the area, granting 160-acre plots to non-Indian homesteaders (McLoughlin 1993, 375).

7. Personal communication, Mr. Pat Gwin, Cherokee Nation Natural Resources Department director, June 16, 2013.

8. Transcript, "The Convention of Duly Enrolled Cherokees by Blood in Oklahoma, July 30, 1948, Tahlequah, Oklahoma" (Oklahoma City: The Stenotype Reporter), p. 60.

9. I also collected many personal accounts of approval for Keeler during my fieldwork, mostly from middle-aged individuals remembering what their parents had said about him.

10. Wahrhaftig (1975b, 68) claims that Keeler's election was not truly a popular election, stating that less than half of the Cherokee people participated in the election. However, this could also be viewed as a consequence of a broken political system that was just beginning to reestablish itself.

11. The name comes from the cohesive rural Cherokee settlements that are predominately located within five contiguous counties in northeastern Oklahoma: Cherokee, Adair, Mayes, Sequoyah, and Delaware. Kenneth Fink's (1979) dissertation provides a full chapter on the OCCO.

12. Presumably, old women would have remembered Cherokee national sovereignty and would have understood life sacredly, too.

13. Presently, the Cherokee Nation hunting and fishing code states that all one needs is a tribal citizenship card to hunt and fish within the fourteen-county jurisdictional area; however, a fact sheet states,

> WARNING—there is not yet any written agreement with the State of Oklahoma on these provisions; therefore, it is possible that you may be

stopped, or even cited, for hunting off of trust or restricted land using only your Cherokee Nation license [i.e., tribal citizenship card]. If you are in full compliance with Cherokee Nation regulations and you receive such a citation, notify the Cherokee Nation Office of the Attorney General or Marshal Service. The Nation may or may not attempt to assert its hunting/ fishing rights in your case as a defense. UNTIL THERE IS A FORMAL AGREEMENT WITH THE STATE, YOU MAY BE SUBJECT TO FINES AND/OR OTHER PENALTIES FOR HUNTING ON STATE LAND WITHOUT A STATE LICENSE. While the Nation believes that such penalties would be improper, there is no guarantee that you will not be subject to them.

Gathering rights are still being codified by the Cherokee Nation and also have not yet been legally tested.

14. Other work during this time (mostly carried out by researchers associated with the University of Chicago's Carnegie Cross-Cultural Education Project directed by Sol Tax) reaches similar conclusions (M. Wax 1971; R. Wax 1971; Wahrhaftig and Thomas 1981; Fink 1979). I should emphasize the value of this work in providing thoughtful and thorough cultural analyses, as well as important snapshots of Cherokee life during this time. It is obvious that I rely on Wahrhaftig throughout this book in that regard. I present my critical assessment of this work in order to provide a fuller picture of Cherokee politics, which I have gleaned from my own fieldwork and political/historical analysis.

15. See also Williams (2005) for an exegesis of the concept of "plenary power" in federal Indian law.

16. Wahrhaftig and Lukens-Wahrhaftig (1979, 226) write, "Elsewhere, factionalism occurs between more and less *acculturated* Indians, whereas in eastern Oklahoma ethnic conflict occurs between a culturally Indian population (within which some individuals and settlements are considerably more acculturated than others) and a long-*assimilated* population identifying with Indian ancestors." To me, this statement is riddled with essentialist understandings of "purity" and "authenticity" that once again speak to the era and time within which Wahrhaftig was writing.

17. The similar issue of the United Keetoowah Band (UKB), however, resulted in the formal and permanent establishment of political factionalism within the Cherokee Nation due to the intervention of the federal government (see Leeds 1996). In 1946, the UKB was formally recognized by Congress under the guidelines of the 1936 Oklahoma Indian General Welfare Act, and in 1950, the UKB was legally recognized by the secretary of the interior. The federal government's legal recognition of the UKB (whose members are descendants of the same people as those represented by the Cherokee Nation) further divided the nation and inhibited possibilities for solidarity.

18. This fiasco involved numerous cases of blatant mismanagement of tribal development programs and funds by BIA personnel and was exposed through a series of articles run by the *Arizona Republic* in 1987 titled "Fraud in Indian Country: A Billion Dollar Betrayal."

19. Personal communication, Dr. Richard Allen, Cherokee Nation policy analyst, March 15, 2005. As a side note, the self-governance agreement only formalized a process that had been gradually developing since the Swimmer administration. Principal Chief Swimmer had been making significant strides with regard to the management of Indian Health Service programs in the Cherokee Nation since the late 1970s.

20. For accounts of this crisis and the controversial Joe Byrd administration, see Heck, Keen, and Wilds (2001), Mouser (1998), Lemont (2006, 293–94), and Sturm (2010, 147–48).

21. Ratification of the new constitution was a lengthy process due to the issue of federal approval. The 1976 constitution required that the assistant secretary for Indian affairs approve any amendments or new constitutions. Lemont (2006, 308) notes that this was a defensive maneuver by Principal Chief Swimmer to ensure its recognition by the U.S. government after a period of federal control of tribal affairs. The BIA's reaction to the 1999 constitution was disapproving and comprised a series of both mandatory and recommended changes. In 2000, the tribal council reacted by proposing a new amendment to delete the federal approval process. In 2002, after a change of guard at the BIA, this amendment was approved, although this act would later be questioned. Regardless, on July 26, 2003, the Cherokee people ratified the 1999 constitution by vote. While many Cherokee politicians have taken the stance that this vote confirms the validity of the 1999 constitution (a sovereign act of self-governance), the reality is that, despite the 2002 approval (and even a subsequent one dated August 9, 2007), to this day this issue has not been formally resolved with the BIA. On September 9, 2011, Assistant Secretary for Indian Affairs Larry Echo Hawk sent a letter to Acting Principal Chief S. Joe Crittenden claiming that the BIA had never approved the 1999 constitution or the amendment that led to its implementation. The issue has been drawn out due to the controversial case of the Cherokee Freedmen, who at the time of the 2003 election were not allowed to vote. For more, see Chavez (2011).

22. Author's field notes, July 20, 2006.

23. Author's field notes, June 27, 2005.

4. Indigenous Ethnobotany

1. I do acknowledge the slippery ground here in referring to elders as wolves and thus potentially conveying cliché (likening Indians to mysterious and majestic creatures) or, even worse, diminutiveness (relegating Indians to a "lesser"

status of animals). However, I will stress that these are the words of an elder himself and, further, that because of the Cherokee reverence of wolves (demonstrated in one of the seven clans—the wolf clan), this reference would be seen as a compliment to many Cherokees.

2. The work of Cherokee physician Richard Foreman (1857) represents an earlier, less-referenced account, although it lacks the academic scrutiny of Mooney. Various sketches of Cherokee plant knowledge from pre-Removal times (before 1838) are included in the writings of John Timberlake, William Bartram, John Haywood, James Adair, John Lawson, and John Howard Payne.

3. Recently, Cozzo (2004) carried out a secondary data analysis of Mooney's extensive unpublished notes on the subject. Cozzo reconstructs an elaborate Cherokee botanical classification system based on this work.

4. The Swimmer Manuscript was revived and completed by anthropologist Franz Olbrechts after Mooney's death. Olbrechts adds his own ethnographic work with the eastern Cherokees and provides supplemental data to Mooney's manuscript.

5. The literal translation is "to be said, they." This is the Cherokee term for medical or magical texts. The singular form is i:gawé:sdi (Kilpatrick and Kilpatrick 1970, 86).

6. To my knowledge, the term man-killer has multiple connotations. Some translate the term as a historical war title like major or captain (in this case, anisgaya:dihi—literally "killer of men"; Mankiller and Wallis 1993, 3). It is also a surname made famous by the late former Principal Chief of the Cherokee Nation, Wilma Mankiller. As it is used by Mooney and Olbrechts (1932, 33; written as didá:hnese:sgi), it is more accurately translated as "putter-in and drawer-out of them, he" (Fogelson 1975, 123). In his description of the term, Olbrechts (in Mooney and Olbrechts 1932, 29) seems to suggest that this belief served as a general cautionary rule to be nice to one's neighbor (for one did not always know the identity of man-killers).

7. Both Jack and Anna Kilpatrick grew up in the Cherokee Nation and spoke the language fluently.

8. The significance of the Cherokee written language (Sequoyah's syllabary, completed in 1821) cannot be overstated. The ability to write in the language revolutionized the practice of Cherokee medicine (Fogelson 1980, 61–62). Using the syllabary, healers could write out healing formulas in order to aid their memory. Altman and Belt (2009, 11) state, "The formula book of any one healer often contained his or her complete repertoire of words and actions designed to care for his or her patients. The notebooks were kept over the span of the healer's practice and some contained dozens of formulas." See also Teuton (2010) for more significance behind Seqouyah, the syllabary, and traditional knowledge in Cherokee society.

9. Alan Kilpatrick (1997, xviii) recounts his father's words, "A few months before my father's death in 1967 he wrote this note: 'Recently I read in the *Encyclopedia Britannica* that no Native American society north of Mexico had produced a literature: yet during the past five years alone I have collected from attics, barns, caves, and jars buried in the ground some ten thousand poetical texts, many of which would excite the envy of a Hafiz or a Li Tai Po.'"

10. As academics, I do not think any substantial "profit" would have been gained from their publications. However, I think the comment expresses the concern that they were benefiting from the formulas by building a career based on their publication.

11. The Cherokee name for the eastern plant is *yú:gwil.* There are actually two original *yú:gwil* plants: Venus's flytrap (*Dionaea muscipula*) and pitcher plant (*Sarracenia purpurea*), neither of which are found in the western Ozarks. Adam-and-Eve plant (*Aplectrum hyemale,* or *Adawi-iwi* in Cherokee), a rare but native plant to the western Ozarks, became the substitute. The roots of these plants possess the ability to be "remade" (prayed over using the proper incantations) in order to bring out special powers that aid the owner in extraordinary ways (Kilpatrick and Kilpatrick 1967, 87–88).

12. For instance, it is still common for a medicine person to be approached by a patient needing a relationship counselor, however reluctantly the healer may take up this responsibility.

13. In English, Cherokees usually refer to the Creator in the masculine form. However, in the Cherokee language, the word for Creator, *Unehlvnvhi,* does not specify masculinity or femininity.

14. Pronounced "doo-YOOK-duh." See Fogelson (1975, 126).

15. Author's field notes, October 16, 2008. I should note that this section is not intended to give an exhaustive description of the Cherokee philosophy of medicine. Elaborate descriptions of Cherokee beliefs regarding disease and medicine are provided by Mooney (1891) and Mooney and Olbrechts (1932), some aspects of which have been retained by contemporary Oklahoma Cherokee healers. This section takes this work for granted, and its purpose is rather to highlight areas of thought and practice received firsthand from fieldwork that broadly demonstrate current attitudes toward medicine and relationships toward the environment.

16. The Cherokee name translates to "old tobacco." It is considered more potent than the commercial variety *Nicotiana tabacum,* and it was the primary species used in earlier times. Because of the scarcity of *Nicotiana rustica* today, many healers employ the *tabacum* variety, although recent cultivation efforts by the Cherokee Nation Natural Resources Department have made available *Nicotiana rustica* for tribal citizens. See Eads (2008) for an interesting study of contemporary tobacco use among Oklahoma Cherokees.

17. See also Fogelson (1980) for an in-depth account on the role of medicine people and the acquisition of medicinal knowledge in eastern Cherokee society. This work, although published in 1980, was carried out in the late 1950s.

18. Author's field notes, July 10, 2008.

19. Again, see Fogelson (1980, esp. 67–69) for accounts of medicine apprenticeships among the Eastern Band in the 1950s.

20. Author's field notes, October 23, 2008.

21. Author's field notes, July 9, 2008.

22. Author's field notes, April 23, 2009.

23. Author's field notes, May 29, 2008.

24. Author's field notes, August 22, 2008.

5. The Spirit of This Land

1. I thank Dr. Albert Wahrhaftig for sharing his thoughts on this with me during a personal visit to his home in 2006.

2. A "hog fry" is a large cookout featuring a variety of prized Cherokee foods like beans, potatoes, squash, corn, and of course, "fried" pork shoulder. (The meat is slow cooked in water and lard to produce a delicious and tender final product.)

3. The corporate style of the document is less surprising when one considers that Smith holds a Master of Business Administration degree and that he served as tribal planner for Principal Chief Swimmer during his administration.

4. Nørreklit (2003, 611) asserts that Kaplan and Norton and the BSC system belong to the genre of "management gurus." She writes, "The authors may succeed in persuading—although without convincing—because the audience associates them with prestigious academia, but the text has little to do with scholarly work. The authors draw on the prestige and not the expertise of academia."

5. Here I define an institution as a group of individuals that have formed out of a reaction to a specific problem or issue and, as such, have united around a set of common goals to address this problem.

6. Yet I should stress that Cherokees, like all people, are flexible and resilient and also have to function within the everyday norms and expectations of mainstream American society (which many would argue does not go through the same lengths to guarantee social harmony). The oft-cited Cherokee "harmony ethic," then, is really only an *ideal* to be aspired to, *not* a rigid rule that, if broken, results in chaos.

Conclusion

1. See also Lemos and Agrawal (2006, 313) on deliberative democracy and environmental governance.

2. See also Dryzek (2002, 6) on the notion of "green democracy" that "seeks effectiveness in communication that transcends the boundary of the human and non-human worlds."

3. For an in-depth treatment of the many potential contributions of indigenous peoples to the world ecological crisis, see also Ridgeway and Jacques (2014).

4. I stress the animal representations of each of the clans for emphasis, based on traditionalist/elder Benny Smith's "A Perspective of the Clans" (n.d.), but Cherokees will more readily recognize the bear, lion, and hawk clans as the blue, long hair, and paint clans, respectively.

5. See, for example, this presentation on the San Carlos Apache Elders Cultural Advisory Council available at the University of Arizona Indigenous Governance Database: http://nnidatabase.org/db/video/honoring-nations-jeanette-clark-cassa -san-carlos-apache-elders-cultural-advisory-council.

Bibliography

Abrams, Phillip. 1988. "Notes on the Difficulty of Studying the State." *Journal of Historical Sociology* 1, no. 1: 58–89.

Agrawal, Arun. 2005. *Environmentality: Technologies of Government and the Making of Subjects.* Durham, N.C.: Duke University Press.

Agrawal, Arun, and Maria Carmen Lemos. 2007. "A Greener Revolution in the Making? Environmental Governance in the 21st Century." *Environment: Science and Policy for Sustainable Development* 49, no. 5: 36–45.

Akwesasne Notes, ed. 2005. *Basic Call to Consciousness.* Summertown, Tenn.: Native Voices.

Alfred, Gerald R. 1995. *Heeding the Voices of Our Ancestors: Kahnawake Mohawk Politics and the Rise of Native Nationalism.* Toronto: Oxford University Press.

Alfred, Taiaiake. 1999. *Peace, Power, Righteousness: An Indigenous Manifesto.* Toronto: Oxford University Press.

———. 2005. *Wasase: Indigenous Pathways of Action and Freedom.* Orchard Park, N.Y.: Broadview.

Alfred, Taiaiake, and Jeff Corntassel. 2005. "Being Indigenous: Resurgences against Contemporary Colonialism." *Government and Opposition* 40, no. 4: 597–614.

Altman, Heidi M., and Thomas N. Belt. 2009. "Tohi: The Cherokee Concept of Well-Being." In *Under the Rattlesnake: Cherokee Health and Resiliency,* edited by Lisa J. Lefler, 9–22. Tuscaloosa: University of Alabama Press.

Anderson, Kay. 2000. "Thinking 'Postnationally': Dialogue across Multicultural, Indigenous, and Settler Spaces." *Annals of the Association of American Geographers* 90, no. 2: 381–91.

Anderson, Terry L., and Dean Lueck. 1992. "Land Tenure and Agricultural Productivity on Indian Reservations." *Journal of Law and Economics* 35, no. 2: 427–54.

Bailey, Robert G. 1995. "Description of the Ecoregions of the United States (with Map)." U.S. Forest Service. http://www.fs.fed.us/land/ecosysmgmt.

Baird, W. David, and Danney Goble. 1994. *The Story of Oklahoma.* Norman: University of Oklahoma Press.

Banks, William H., Jr. 2004. *Plants of the Cherokee.* Gatlinburg, Tenn.: Great Smoky Mountains Association.

Barker, Joanne, ed. 2005. *Sovereignty Matters: Locations of Contestation and Possibility in Indigenous Struggles for Self-Determination*. Lincoln: University of Nebraska Press.

———. 2011. *Native Acts: Law, Recognition, and Cultural Authenticity*. Durham, N.C.: Duke University Press.

Barreiro, Jose. 2010. "John Mohawk's Essential Legacy: 'The Sovereignty Which Is Sought Can Be Real.'" In *Thinking in Indian: A John Mohawk Reader*, edited by Jose Barreiro, xiii–xxvi. Golden, Colo.: Fulcrum.

Barry, John, and Robyn Eckersley, eds. 2005. *The State and the Global Ecological Crisis*. Cambridge, Mass.: MIT Press.

Bays, Brad A. 1998. *Townsite Settlement and Dispossession in the Cherokee Nation, 1866–1907*. New York: Garland.

Berkes, Fikret. 1999. *Sacred Ecology: Traditional Ecological Knowledge and Resource Management*. Philadelphia: Taylor and Francis.

Bhabha, Homi K. 1994. *The Location of Culture*. New York: Routledge.

Biolsi, Thomas. 2005. "Imagined Geographies: Sovereignty, Indigenous Space, and American Indian Struggle." *American Ethnologist* 32, no. 2: 239–59.

Blackburn, Thomas C., and M. Kat Anderson, eds. 1993. *Before the Wilderness: Environmental Management by Native Californians*. Menlo Park, Calif.: Ballena.

Blaikie, Piers. 1985. *The Political Economy of Soil Erosion in Developing Countries*. London: Longman Scientific and Technical.

Blaikie, Piers, and Harold Brookfield, eds. 1987. *Land Degradation and Society*. London: Methuen.

Bloom, Khaled. 2002. "An American Tragedy of the Commons: Land and Labor in the Cherokee Nation, 1870–1900." *Agricultural History* 76, no. 3: 497–523.

Borrows, John. 2002. *Recovering Canada: The Resurgence of Indigenous Law*. Toronto: University of Toronto Press.

Brantley, Christopher G., and Steven G. Platt. 2001. "Canebrake Conservation in the Southeastern United States." *Wildlife Society Bulletin* 29, no. 4: 1175–81.

Braun, Bruce W. 1997. "Buried Epistemologies: The Politics of Nature in (Post)colonial British Columbia." *Annals of the Association of American Geographers* 87, no. 1: 3–31.

———. 2002. *The Intemperate Rainforest: Nature, Culture, and Power on Canada's West Coast*. Minneapolis: University of Minnesota Press.

Bruyneel, Kevin. 2007. *The Third Space of Sovereignty: The Postcolonial Politics of U.S.-Indigenous Relations*. Minneapolis: University of Minnesota Press.

Burton, Lloyd. 2002. *Worship and Wilderness: Culture, Religion, and Law in Public Lands Management*. Madison: University of Wisconsin Press.

Cajete, Gregory. 2000. *Native Science: Natural Laws of Interdependence*. Santa Fe: Clear Light.

Carroll, Clint. 2012. "Articulating Indigenous Statehood: Cherokee State Formation and Implications for the UN Declaration on the Rights of Indigenous Peoples." In *Indigenous Rights in the Age of the UN Declaration,* edited by Elvira Pulitano, 143–71. Cambridge: Cambridge University Press.

Cattelino, Jessica R. 2008. *High Stakes: Florida Seminole Gaming and Sovereignty.* Durham, N.C.: Duke University Press.

Champagne, Duane. 1983. "Social Structure, Revitalization Movements, and State Building: Social Change in Four Native American Societies." *American Sociological Review* 48, no. 6: 754–63.

———. 1985. "Cherokee Social Movements: A Response to Thornton." *American Sociological Review* 50, no. 1: 127–30.

———. 1992. *Social Order and Political Change: Constitutional Governments among the Cherokee, the Choctaw, the Chickasaw, and the Creek.* Palo Alto: Stanford University Press.

———. 1996. "American Indian Studies Is for Everyone." *American Indian Quarterly* 20, no. 1: 77–82.

———. 2004. "Renewing Tribal Governments: Uniting Political Theory and Sacred Communities." *Indigenous Peoples' Journal of Law, Culture and Resistance* 1, no. 1: 24–66.

———. 2006. "Remaking Tribal Constitutions: Meeting the Challenges of Tradition, Colonialism, and Globalization." In *American Indian Constitutional Reform and the Rebuilding of Native Nations,* edited by Eric D. Lemont, 11–34. Austin: University of Texas Press.

Champagne, Duane, and Jay Stauss, eds. 2002. *Native American Studies in Higher Education: Models for Collaboration between Universities and Indigenous Nations.* Walnut Creek, Calif.: AltaMira.

Chang, David A. 2011. "Enclosures of Land and Sovereignty: The Allotment of American Indian Lands." *Radical History Review* 109 (Winter): 108–19.

Chavez, Will. 2011. "Echo Hawk Opinion May Have 'Drastic Consequences.'" *Cherokee Phoenix,* November 22.

Cherokee Executive Committee. 1969 [1852]. *Constitution and Laws of the Cherokee Nation: Passed at Tahlequah, Cherokee Nation, 1839–1851.* Oklahoma City: Oklahoma.

Clark, Brett. 2002. "The Indigenous Environmental Movement in the United States: Transcending Borders in Struggles against Mining, Manufacturing, and the Capitalist State." *Organization and Environment* 15, no. 4: 410–42.

Clifford, James. 1997. *Routes: Travel and Translation in the Late Twentieth Century.* Cambridge, Mass.: Harvard University Press.

———. 2001. "Indigenous Articulations." *The Contemporary Pacific* 13, no. 2: 468–90.

Clinton, Robert N., Carole E. Goldberg, and Rebecca Tsosie. 2003. *American Indian Law: Native Nations and the Federal System*. Fourth edition. Newark, N.J.: LexisNexis.

Clow, Richmond, and Imre Sutton, eds. 2001. *Trusteeship in Change: Toward Tribal Autonomy in Resource Management*. Boulder: University Press of Colorado.

Cochran, Wendell. 1983. *A Guide to Gathering and Using Cherokee Medicinal Herbs*. Welling, Okla.: Cross Cultural Education Center.

Conley, Robert J. 2005a. *Cherokee Medicine Man: The Life and Work of a Modern-Day Healer*. Norman: University of Oklahoma Press.

———. 2005b. *The Cherokee Nation: A History*. Albuquerque: University of New Mexico Press.

Connor, Walker. 1978. "A Nation Is a Nation, Is a State, Is an Ethnic Group, Is a . . ." *Ethnic and Racial Studies* 1, no. 4: 377–400.

Cook-Lynn, Elizabeth. 1997. "Who Stole Native American Studies?" *Wicazo Sa Review* 12, no. 1: 9–28.

———. 1999. "American Indian Studies: An Overview. Keynote Address at the Native Studies Conferences, Yale University, February 5, 1998." *Wicazo Sa Review* 14, no. 2: 14–24.

Cook-Lynn, Elizabeth, Tom Holm, John Red Horse, and James Riding In. 2005. "First Panel: Reclaiming American Indian Studies." *Wicazo Sa Review* 20, no. 1: 169–77.

Cooter, Robert D., and Robert K. Thomas. 1998. "Individuals and Relatives." In *A Good Cherokee, A Good Anthropologist: Papers in Honor of Robert K. Thomas*, edited by Steve Pavlik, 57–92. Los Angeles: American Indian Studies Center.

Corkran, David H. 1962. *The Cherokee Frontier: Conflict and Survival 1740–62*. Norman: University of Oklahoma Press.

Cornell, Stephen, and Joseph P. Kalt. 1998. "Sovereignty and Nation-Building: The Development Challenge in Indian Country Today." *American Indian Culture and Research Journal* 22, no. 3: 187–214.

Corntassel, Jeff. 2008. "Toward Sustainable Self-Determination: Rethinking the Contemporary Indigenous-Rights Discourse." *Alternatives: Global, Local, Political* 33, no. 1: 105–32.

———. 2012. "Re-envisioning Resurgence: Indigenous Pathways to Decolonization and Sustainable Self-Determination." *Decolonization: Indigeneity, Education & Society* 1, no. 1: 86–101.

Corrigan, Philip. 1990. *Social Forms / Human Capacities: Essays in Authority and Difference*. London: Routledge.

Corrigan, Philip, and Derek Sayer. 1985. *The Great Arch: English State Formation as Cultural Revolution*. Oxford: Basil Blackwell.

Coulthard, Glen S. 2007. "Subjects of Empire: Indigenous Peoples and the 'Politics of Recognition' in Canada." *Contemporary Political Theory* 6, no. 4: 437–60.

Cowan, Agnes. 1975. *Cherokee Medicinal Herbs*. Tahlequah, Okla.: Cherokee Bilingual Education Center.

Cozzo, David N. 2004. "Ethnobotanical Classification System and Medical Ethnobotany of the Eastern Band of the Cherokee Indians." PhD diss. (Anthropology), University of Georgia, Athens.

Cronon, William. 1983. *Changes in the Land: Indians, Colonists, and the Ecology of New England*. New York: Hill and Wang.

Crumley, Carole L. 2003. "Historical Ecology: Integrated Thinking at Multiple Temporal and Spatial Scales." Proceedings of the World System History and Global Environmental Change Conference, Lund University, Sweden, September 19–22.

Curley, Andrew, and Roxanne Dunbar-Ortiz. 2012. "The International Indigenous Movement for Self-Determination (Part II)." *New Socialist Webzine*. http://www.newsocialist.org/609-the-international-indigenous-movement-for-self-determination-part-ii.

Davis, Thomas. 2000. *Sustaining the Forest, the People, and the Spirit*. Albany: State University of New York Press.

Dean, Mitchell. 1999. *Governmentality: Power and Rule in Modern Society*. London: Sage.

Debo, Angie. 1940. *And Still the Waters Run: The Betrayal of the Five Civilized Tribes*. Princeton, N.J.: Princeton University Press.

Deloria, Vine, Jr. 2003 [1973]. *God Is Red: A Native View of Religion*. Golden, Colo.: Fulcrum.

———. 2007 [1970]. *We Talk, You Listen: New Tribes, New Turf*. Lincoln: University of Nebraska Press.

Deloria, Vine, Jr., and Clifford M. Lytle. 1984. *The Nations Within: The Past and Future of American Indian Sovereignty*. New York: Pantheon.

Denetdale, Jennifer Nez. 2006. "Chairmen, Presidents, and Princesses: The Navajo Nation, Gender, and the Politics of Tradition." *Wicazo Sa Review* 21, no. 1: 9–28.

Dennison, Jean. 2012. *Colonial Entanglement: Constituting a Twenty-First-Century Osage Nation*. Chapel Hill: University of North Carolina Press.

Denson, Andrew. 2004. *Demanding the Cherokee Nation: Indian Autonomy and American Culture 1830–1900*. Lincoln: University of Nebraska Press.

Donaldson, Laura E. 2010. "'But We Are Your Mothers, You Are Our Sons': Gender, Sovereignty, and the Nation in Early Cherokee Women's Writing." In *Indigenous Women and Feminism: Politics, Activism, Culture*, edited by Cheryl Suzack, Shari M. Huhndorf, Jeanne Perreault, and Jean Barman, 43–55. Vancouver: University of British Columbia Press.

Dove, Michael R. 1994. "The Existential Status of the Pakistani Farmer: Studying Official Constructions of Social Reality." *Ethnology* 33, no. 4: 331–51.

———. 1999. "Writing for, versus about, the Ethnographic Other: Issues of Engagement and Reflexivity in Working with a Tribal NGO in Indonesia." *Identities* 6, no. 2–3: 225–53.

Dryzek, John S. 2000. *Deliberative Democracy and Beyond: Liberals, Critics, Contestations.* Oxford: Oxford University Press.

Dunaway, Wilma. 1997. "Rethinking Cherokee Acculturation: Agrarian Capitalism and Women's Resistance to the Cult of Domesticity, 1800–1838." *American Indian Culture and Research Journal* 12, no. 1: 155–92.

Eads, Jason Allen. 2008. "Cherokee Tobacco Use in Oklahoma." MA thesis (Native American Studies), University of Oklahoma, Norman.

Emery, Marla R., and Alan R. Pierce. 2005. "Interrupting the Telos: Locating Subsistence in Contemporary US Forests." *Environment and Planning A* 37, no. 6: 981–93.

Endres, Danielle. 2012. "Sacred Land or National Sacrifice Zone? The Role of Values in the Yucca Mountain Participation Process." *Environmental Communication: A Journal of Nature and Culture* 6, no. 3: 328–45.

Fairhead, James, and Melissa Leach. 1996. *Misreading the African Landscape: Society and Ecology in a Forest-Savanna Mosaic.* Cambridge: Cambridge University Press.

Feld, Steven, and Keith H. Basso. 1996. "Introduction." In *Senses of Place,* edited by Steven Feld and Keith H. Basso, 3–11. Santa Fe, N.M.: School of American Research Press.

Fink, Kenneth Ernest. 1979. "A Cherokee Notion of Development." PhD diss., Union Graduate School, Cincinnati, Ohio.

Fleder, Anna, and Darren Ranco. 2004. "Tribal Environmental Sovereignty: Culturally Appropriate Protection or Paternalism?" *Journal of Natural Resources and Environmental Law* 19, no. 1: 35–58.

Fogelson, Raymond D. 1963. "[Review of] Priests and Warriors: Social Structures for Cherokee Politics in the 18th Century." *American Anthropologist* 65: 726–30.

———. 1971. "The Cherokee Ballgame Cycle: An Ethnographer's View." *Society for Ethnomusicology* 15, no. 3: 327–38.

———. 1975. "An Analysis of Cherokee Sorcery and Witchcraft." In *Four Centuries of Southern Indians,* edited by Charles M. Hudson, 113–31. Athens: University of Georgia Press.

———. 1980. "The Conjuror in Eastern Cherokee Society." *Journal of Cherokee Studies* 5, no. 2: 60–87.

———. 1984. "Who Were the Ani-Kutani? An Excursion into Cherokee Historical Thought." *Ethnohistory* 31, no. 4: 255–63.

Fogelson, Raymond D., and Paul Kutsche. 1961. "Cherokee Economic Cooperatives: The Gadugi." In *Bureau of American Ethnology Bulletin 180: Symposium on Cherokee and Iroquois Culture,* 87–123. Washington, D.C.: Smithsonian Institution.

Foreman, Richard. 1857. *The Cherokee Physician or Indian Guide to Health*. New York: James M. Edney.

Fortmann, Louise. 1996. "Bonanza! The Unasked Questions: Domestic Land Tenure through International Lenses." *Society and Natural Resources* 9, no. 5: 537–47.

Fowler, Cynthia, and Evelyn Konopik. 2007. "The History of Fire in the Southern United States." *Human Ecology Review* 14, no. 2: 165–76.

Garrett, J. T. 2003. *The Cherokee Herbal: Native Plant Medicine from the Four Directions*. Rochester, Vt.: Bear.

Garroutte, Eva Marie. 2003. *Real Indians: Identity and the Survival of Native America*. Berkeley: University of California Press.

Gearing, Fred O. 1961. "The Rise of the Cherokee State as an Instance in a Class: The 'Mesopotamian' Career to Statehood." In *Bureau of American Ethnology Bulletin 180: Symposium on Cherokee and Iroquois Culture*, 127–34. Washington, D.C.: Smithsonian Institution.

———. 1962. "Priests and Warriors: Social Structures for Cherokee Politics in the 18th Century." *American Anthropological Association Memoir* no. 93.

Gedicks, Al. 1993. *The New Resource Wars: Native and Environmental Struggles against Multinational Corporations*. Cambridge, Mass.: South End Press.

Geniusz, Wendy Makoons. 2009. *Our Knowledge Is Not Primitive: Decolonizing Botanical Anishinaabe Teachings*. Syracuse, N.Y.: Syracuse University Press.

Goeman, Mishuana R. 2009. "Notes toward a Native Feminism's Spatial Practice." *Wicazo Sa Review* 24, no. 2: 169–87.

Goodwin, Gary C. 1977. *Cherokees in Transition: A Study of Changing Culture and Environment Prior to 1775*. University of Chicago Department of Geography Research Paper No. 181.

Graeber, David. 2001. *Toward an Anthropological Theory of Value: The False Coin of Our Own Dreams*. New York: Palgrave.

Gregory, Jack, and Rennard Strickland, eds. 1967. *Starr's History of the Cherokee Indians*. Fayetteville, Ark.: Indian Heritage Association.

Grossman, Zoltán, and Alan Parker, eds. 2012. *Asserting Native Resilience: Pacific Rim Indigenous Nations Face the Climate Crisis*. Corvallis: Oregon State University Press.

Hall, Karen C. 2006. "Ethnobotany of the Eastern Band of Cherokee Indians: A Path to Sustaining Traditional Identity with an Emphasis on Medicinal Plant Use." PhD diss. (Plant Physiology), Clemson University, South Carolina.

Hamel, Paul B., and Mary U. Chiltoskey. 1975. *Cherokee Plants and Their Uses: A 400 Year History*. Sylva, N.C.: Herald.

Hansen, Thomas Blom, and Finn Stepputat. 2001. "Introduction." In *States of Imagination: Ethnographic Explorations of the Postcolonial State*, edited by Thomas Blom Hansen and Finn Stepputat, 1–38. Durham, N.C.: Duke University Press.

Hanson, Randel D. 2004. "Contemporary Globalization and Tribal Sovereignty." In *A Companion to the Anthropology of American Indians*, edited by Thomas Biolsi, 284–303. Malden, Mass.: Blackwell.

Harris, Stuart G., and Barbara L. Harper. 1997. "A Native American Exposure Scenario." *Risk Analysis* 17, no. 6: 789–95.

Hart, Gillian. 2006. "Denaturalizing Dispossession: Critical Ethnography in the Age of Resurgent Imperialism." *Antipode* 38, no. 5: 977–1004.

Heck, William P., Ralph Keen Jr., and Michael R. Wilds. 2001. "Structuring the Cherokee Nation Justice System: The History and Function of the Cherokee Nation Marshal Service." *Criminal Justice Policy Review* 12, no. 1: 26–42.

Hempel, Lamont C. 1996. *Environmental Governance: The Global Challenge*. Washington, D.C.: Island.

Hewes, Leslie. 1978. *Occupying the Cherokee Country of Oklahoma*. Lincoln: University of Nebraska.

Heynen, Nik, James McCarthy, Scott Prudham, and Paul Robbins, eds. 2007. *Neoliberal Environments: False Promises and Unnatural Consequences*. New York: Routledge.

Hill, Sarah H. 1997. *Weaving New Worlds: Southeastern Cherokee Women and Their Basketry*. Chapel Hill: University of North Carolina Press.

Himley, Matthew. 2008. "Geographies of Environmental Governance: The Nexus of Nature and Neoliberalism." *Geography Compass* 2, no. 2: 433–51.

Holifield, Ryan. 2012. "Environmental Justice as Recognition and Participation in Risk Assessment: Negotiating and Translating Health Risk at a Superfund Site in Indian Country." *Annals of the Association of American Geographers* 102, no. 3: 591–613.

Holm, Tom. 2005. *The Great Confusion in Indian Affairs: Native Americans and Whites in the Progressive Era*. Austin: University of Texas Press.

Holm, Tom, J. Diane Pearson, and Ben Chavis. 2003. "Peoplehood: A Model for the Extension of Sovereignty in American Indian Studies." *Wicazo Sa Review* 18, no. 1: 7–24.

Huhndorf, Shari M. 2009a. *Mapping the Americas: The Transnational Politics of Contemporary Native Culture*. Ithaca, N.Y.: Cornell University Press.

———. 2009b. "Picture Revolution: Transnationalism, American Studies, and the Politics of Contemporary Native Culture." *American Quarterly* 61, no. 2: 359–81.

Huntsinger, Lynn, and Sarah McCaffrey. 1995. "A Forest for the Trees: Forest Management and the Yurok Environment 1850 to 1994." *American Indian Culture and Research Journal* 19, no. 4: 155–92.

Ishiyama, Noriko. 2003. "Environmental Justice and American Indian Tribal Sovereignty: Case Study of a Land-Use Conflict in Skull Valley, Utah." *Antipode* 35, no. 1: 119–39.

Johannsen, Kristin. 2006. *Ginseng Dreams: The Secret World of America's Most Valuable Plant.* Lexington: University Press of Kentucky.

Johnson, Jay T. 2008. "Indigeneity's Challenges to the White Settler-State: Creating a Thirdspace for Dynamic Citizenship." *Alternatives* 33, no. 1: 29–52.

Johnson, Kenneth S. 1998. "Mountains, Streams, and Lakes of Oklahoma." *Oklahoma Geological Survey Information Series* no. 1: 1–6.

Johnson, Tadd M., and James Hamilton. 1994. "Self-Governance for Indian Tribes: From Paternalism to Empowerment." *Connecticut Law Review* 27: 1251–79.

Jones, Timothy W. 2000. "Commentary on 'Cultural Conservation of Medicinal Plant Use in the Ozarks.'" *Human Organization* 59, no. 1: 136–40.

Joseph, Gilbert M., and Daniel Nugent, eds. 1994a. *Everyday Forms of State Formation: Revolution and the Negotiation of Rule in Modern Mexico.* Durham, N.C.: Duke University Press.

———. 1994b. "Popular Culture and State Formation in Revolutionary Mexico." In *Everyday Forms of State Formation: Revolution and the Negotiation of Rule in Modern Mexico,* edited by Gilbert M. Joseph and Daniel Nugent, 3–23. Durham, N.C.: Duke University Press.

Justice, Daniel Heath. 2006. *Our Fire Survives the Storm: A Cherokee Literary History.* Minneapolis: University of Minnesota Press.

Kidwell, Clara Sue, and Alan Velie. 2005. *Native American Studies.* Lincoln: University of Nebraska Press.

Kilpatrick, Alan E. 1991. "'Going to the Water': A Structural Analysis of Cherokee Purification Rituals." *American Indian Culture and Research Journal* 15, no. 4: 49–58.

———. 1997. *The Night Has a Naked Soul: Witchcraft and Sorcery among the Western Cherokee.* Syracuse, N.Y.: Syracuse University Press.

Kilpatrick, Jack, and Anna Kilpatrick. 1964. *Friends of Thunder: Folktales of the Oklahoma Cherokees.* Norman: University of Oklahoma Press.

———. 1965a. *The Shadow of Sequoyah.* Norman: University of Oklahoma Press.

———. 1965b. *Walk in Your Soul: Love Incantations of the Oklahoma Cherokees.* Dallas: Southern Methodist University Press.

———. 1967. *Run toward the Nightland: Magic of the Oklahoma Cherokees.* Dallas: Southern Methodist University Press.

———. 1970. "Notebook of a Cherokee Shaman." *Smithsonian Contributions to Anthropology* 2, no. 6: 83–125.

Kimmerer, Robin Wall. 2013. *Braiding Sweetgrass: Indigenous Wisdom, Scientific Knowledge, and the Teachings of Plants.* Minneapolis, Minn.: Milkweed.

Krakoff, Sarah. 2002. "Tribal Sovereignty and Environmental Justice." In *Justice and Natural Resources: Concepts, Strategies, and Applications,* edited by Kathryn M. Mutz, Gary C. Bryner, and Douglas S. Kenney, 161–85. Washington, D.C.: Island.

Krech, Shepard. 1999. *The Ecological Indian: Myth and History.* New York: W. W. Norton.

Kronk, Elizabeth Ann. 2010. "Alternative Energy Development in Indian Country: Lighting the Way for the Seventh Generation." *Idaho Law Review* 46, no. 2: 449–71.

Kuehls, Thom. 1996. *Beyond Sovereign Territory: The Space of Ecopolitics.* Minneapolis: University of Minnesota Press.

———. 2003. "The Environment of Sovereignty." In *A Political Space: Reading the Global through Clayoquot Sound,* edited by Warren Magnusson and Karena Shaw, 179–98. Minneapolis: University of Minnesota Press.

Kuokkanen, Rauna. 2011. "Indigenous Economies, Theories of Subsistence, and Women: Exploring the Social Economy Model for Indigenous Governance." *American Indian Quarterly* 35, no. 2: 215–40.

LaDuke, Winona. 1994. "Traditional Ecological Knowledge and Environmental Futures." *Colorado Journal of International Environmental Law and Policy* 5: 127–48.

———. 1999. *All Our Relations: Native Struggles for Land and Life.* Cambridge, Mass.: South End Press.

Leeds, Georgia Rae. 1996. *The United Keetoowah Band of Cherokee Indians in Oklahoma.* New York: Peter Lang.

Leeds, Stacy L. 2006. "Moving toward Exclusive Tribal Autonomy over Lands and Natural Resources." *Natural Resources Journal* 46, no. 2: 439–61.

———. 2007. "Defeat or Mixed Blessing? Tribal Sovereignty and the State of Sequoyah." *Tulsa Law Review* 43, no. 5: 5–16.

Lemont, Eric D. 2006. "Overcoming the Politics of Reform: The Story of the Cherokee Nation of Oklahoma Constitutional Convention." In *American Indian Constitutional Reform and the Rebuilding of Native Nations,* edited by Eric D. Lemont, 287–322. Austin: University of Texas Press.

Lemos, Maria Carmen, and Arun Agrawal. 2006. "Environmental Governance." *Annual Review of Environment and Resources* 31, no. 1: 297–325.

Leopold, Aldo. 1989 [1949]. *A Sand County Almanac, and Sketches Here and There.* New York: Oxford University Press.

Lewis, Henry T. 1993. "Patterns of Indian Burning in California." In *Before the Wilderness: Environmental Management by Native Californians,* edited by Thomas C. Blackburn and M. Kat Anderson, 55–116. Menlo Park, Calif.: Ballena.

Littlefield, Daniel F., Jr. 1969. "Pigeoners in the Indian Territory." *Chronicles of Oklahoma* 47, no. 2: 154–59.

Locke, John. 1978 [1689]. "Of Property." In *Property: Mainstream and Critical Positions,* edited by C. B. MacPherson, 15–28. Toronto: University of Toronto Press.

Lowe, Marjorie J. 1996. "'Let's Make It Happen': W. W. Keeler and Cherokee Renewal." *Chronicles of Oklahoma* 74, no. 2: 116–29.

Lyons, Scott Richard. 2010. *X-Marks: Native Signatures of Assent.* Minneapolis: University of Minnesota Press.

Maffi, Luisa, ed. 2001. *On Biocultural Diversity: Linking Language, Knowledge, and the Environment.* Washington, D.C.: Smithsonian Institution.

Mails, Thomas E. 1992. *The Cherokee People: The Story of the Cherokees from Earliest Origins to Contemporary Times.* Tulsa, Okla.: Council Oak.

Mankiller, Wilma, and Michael Wallis. 1993. *Mankiller: A Chief and Her People.* New York: St. Martin's Griffin.

McCarthy, James. 2002. "First World Political Ecology: Lessons from the Wise Use Movement." *Environment and Planning A* 34, no. 7: 1281–302.

———. 2005. "Devolution in the Woods: Community Forestry as Hybrid Neoliberalism." *Environment and Planning A* 37, no. 6: 995–1014.

McGregor, Deborah. 2005. "Coming Full Circle: Indigenous Knowledge, Environment, and Our Future." *American Indian Quarterly* 28, no. 3: 385–410.

McLoughlin, William G. 1986. *Cherokee Renascence in the New Republic.* Princeton: Princeton University Press.

———. 1993. *After the Trail of Tears: The Cherokees' Struggle for Sovereignty 1839–1880.* Chapel Hill: University of North Carolina Press.

Medicine, Beatrice. 2001. *Learning to Be an Anthropologist and Remaining "Native": Selected Writings of Dr. Beatrice Medicine.* Urbana: University of Illinois Press.

Merchant, Carolyn. 1989. *Ecological Revolutions: Nature, Gender, and Science in New England.* Chapel Hill: University of North Carolina Press.

Middleton, Beth Rose. 2010. "A Political Ecology of Healing." *Journal of Political Ecology* 17: 1–28.

———. 2011. *Trust in the Land: New Directions in Tribal Conservation.* Tucson: University of Arizona Press.

Mignolo, Walter D. 2000. *Local Histories/Global Designs: Coloniality, Subaltern Knowledges, and Border Thinking.* Princeton: Princeton University Press.

Miles, Tiya. 2005. *Ties That Bind: The Story of an Afro-Cherokee Family in Slavery and Freedom.* Berkeley: University of California Press.

Milligan, Dorothy. 1977. *The Indian Way: Cherokees.* Austin, Tex.: Nortex.

Mitchell, Timothy. 1991. "The Limits of the State: Beyond Statist Approaches and Their Critics." *American Political Science Review* 85, no. 1: 77–96.

Mooney, James. 1891. *Sacred Formulas of the Cherokees.* Cherokee, N.C.: Cherokee (reprinted in 2006).

———. 1900. *Myths of the Cherokees.* Cherokee, N.C.: Cherokee (reprinted in 2006).

Mooney, James, and Frans M. Olbrechts. 1932. "The Swimmer Manuscript: Cherokee Sacred Formulas and Medicinal Prescriptions." *Smithsonian Institution Bureau of American Ethnology Bulletin* no. 99.

Mouffe, Chantal. 1979. "Hegemony and Ideology in Gramsci." In *Gramsci and Marxist Theory,* edited by Chantal Mouffe, 168–204. London: Routledge and Kagan Paul.

Mouser, Denette A. 1998. "A Nation in Crisis: The Government of the Cherokee Nation Struggles to Survive." *American Indian Law Review* 23, no. 2: 359–74.

Nadasdy, Paul. 1999. "The Politics of TEK: Power and the 'Integration' of Knowledge." *Arctic Anthropology* 36, no. 1–2: 1–18.

———. 2003. *Hunters and Bureaucrats: Power, Knowledge, and Aboriginal-State Relations in the Southwest Yukon.* Vancouver: University of British Columbia Press.

———. 2005. "Transcending the Debate over the Ecologically Noble Indian: Indigenous Peoples and Environmentalism." *Ethnohistory* 52, no. 2: 291–331.

———. 2007. "The Gift in the Animal: The Ontology of Hunting and Human-Animal Sociality." *American Ethnologist* 34, no. 1: 25–43.

Natcher, David C., Clifford G. Hickey, and Susan Davis. 2004. "The Political Ecology of Yukon Forestry: Managing the Forest as if People Mattered." *International Journal of Sustainable Development and World Ecology* 11, no. 4: 343–55.

Nelson, Melissa K., ed. 2008. *Original Instructions: Indigenous Teachings for a Sustainable Future.* Rochester, Vt.: Bear.

———. 2011. "The Future of Native Studies: A Modest Manifesto." *American Indian Culture and Research Journal* 35, no. 1: 39–45.

Nesper, Larry. 2007. "Negotiating Jurisprudence in Tribal Court and the Emergence of a Tribal State: The Lac Du Flambeau Ojibwe." *Current Anthropology* 48, no. 5: 675–99.

Nettheim, Garth, Gary D. Meyers, and Donna Craig. 2002. *Indigenous Peoples and Governance Structures: A Comparative Analysis of Land and Resource Management Rights.* Canberra, Australia: Aboriginal Studies.

Neumann, Roderick P. 2004. "Nature-State-Territory: Toward a Critical Theorization of Conservation Enclosures." In *Liberation Ecologies: Environment, Development, Social Movements,* edited by Richard Peet and Michael Watts, 195–217. Second edition. London: Routledge.

Niezen, Ronald. 2003. *The Origins of Indigenism: Human Rights and the Politics of Identity.* Berkeley: University of California Press.

Nørreklit, Hanne. 2003. "The Balanced Scorecard: What Is the Score? A Rhetorical Analysis of the Balanced Scorecard." *Accounting, Organizations, and Society* 28, no. 6: 591–619.

Parker, Alan. 2012. "Recommendations to Native Government Leadership." In *Asserting Native Resilience: Pacific Rim Indigenous Nations Face the Climate Crisis,* edited by Zoltán Grossman and Alan Parker, 189–92. Corvallis: Oregon State University Press.

Parker, Alan, and Zoltán Grossman. 2012. "Introduction." In *Asserting Native Resilience: Pacific Rim Indigenous Nations Face the Climate Crisis*, edited by Zoltán Grossman and Alan Parker, 13–19. Corvallis: Oregon State University Press.

Peet, Richard, and Michael Watts, eds. 2004. *Liberation Ecologies: Environment, Development, Social Movements*. Second edition. London: Routledge.

Peluso, Nancy Lee, and Christian Lund. 2011. "New Frontiers of Land Control: Introduction." *Journal of Peasant Studies* 38, no. 4: 667–81.

Perdue, Theda. 1998. *Cherokee Women*. Lincoln: University of Nebraska Press.

Platt, Steven G., and Christopher G. Brantley. 1997. "Canebrakes: An Ecological and Historical Perspective." *Castanea* 612, no. 1: 8–21.

Powell, Dana. 2006. "Technologies of Existence: The Indigenous Environmental Justice Movement." *Development* 49, no. 3: 125–32.

Powell, Dana E., and Andrew Curley. 2009. "K'e, Hozhó, and Non-Governmental Politics on the Navajo Nation: Ontologies of Difference Manifest in Environmental Activism." *World Anthropologies Network E-Journal* 4 (April): 109–35.

Pyne, Stephen. 1982. *Fire in America: A Cultural History of Wildland and Rural Fire*. Princeton: Princeton University Press.

Ramirez, Renya K. 2007. "Race, Tribal Nation, and Gender: A Native Feminist Approach to Belonging." *Meridians: Feminism, Race, Transnationalism* 7, no. 2: 22–40.

Ranco, Darren J. 2006. "Toward a Native Anthropology: Hermeneutics, Hunting Stories, and Theorizing from Within." *Wicazo Sa Review* 21, no. 2: 61–78.

———. 2007. "The Ecological Indian and the Politics of Representation: Critiquing the Ecological Indian in the Age of Ecocide." In *Native Americans and the Environment: Perspectives on the Ecological Indian*, edited by Michael E. Harkin and David Rich Lewis, 32–51. Lincoln: University of Nebraska Press.

———. 2008. "The Trust Responsibility and Limited Sovereignty: What Can Environmental Justice Groups Learn from Indian Nations?" *Society and Natural Resources* 21, no. 4: 354–62.

Ribot, Jesse, and Nancy Lee Peluso. 2003. "A Theory of Access." *Rural Sociology* 68, no. 2: 153–81.

Richardson, Benjamin J. 2009. "The Ties that Bind: Indigenous Peoples and Environmental Governance." In *Indigenous Peoples and the Law: Comparative and Critical Perspectives*, edited by Benjamin J. Richardson, Shin Imai, and Kent McNeil, 337–70. Oxford: Hart.

Ridgeway, Sharon J., and Peter J. Jacques. 2014. *The Power of the Talking Stick: Indigenous Politics and the World Ecological Crisis*. Boulder, Colo.: Paradigm.

Robbins, Paul. 2000. "The Practical Politics of Knowing: State Environmental Knowledge and Local Political Economy." *Economic Geography* 76, no. 2: 126–44.

―――――. 2002. "Obstacles to a First World Political Ecology? Looking Near without Looking Up (Letter to the Editor)." *Environment and Planning A* 34, no. 8: 1509–13.

―――――. 2004. *Political Ecology: A Critical Introduction.* Malden, Mass.: Blackwell.

Robyn, Linda. 2002. "Indigenous Knowledge and Technology: Creating Environmental Justice in the Twenty-First Century." *American Indian Quarterly* 26, no. 2: 198–220.

Rose, Nikolas. 1996. *Foucault and Political Reason: Liberalism, Neo-Liberalism, and Rationalities of Government.* Chicago: University of Chicago Press.

―――――. 1999. *Powers of Freedom: Reframing Political Thought.* Cambridge: Cambridge University Press.

Royster, Judith V., and Rory SnowArrow Fausett. 1989. "Control of the Reservation Environment: Tribal Primacy, Federal Delegation, and the Limits of State Intrusion." *Washington Law Review* 64: 581–659.

Russell, Steve. 2010. *Seqouyah Rising: Problems in Post-Colonial Tribal Governance.* Durham, N.C.: Carolina Academic.

Salmón, Enrique. 2012. *Eating the Landscape: American Indian Stories of Food, Identity, and Resilience.* Tucson: University of Arizona Press.

Scott, James C. 1998. *Seeing like a State: How Certain Schemes to Improve the Human Condition Have Failed.* New Haven: Yale University Press.

Self-Governance Communication and Education Project (SGCEP). 2006. *Self-Governance: The Red Book.* Bellingham, Wash.: SGCEP.

Silk, John. 1967. *A True Cherokee Story.* Interview by Crosslin Smith (Volume 19, Tape 311, Part 2). University of Oklahoma Western History Collections. http://digital.libraries.ou.edu/WHC/duke.

Silvern, Steven. 1999. "Scales of Justice: Law, American Indian Treaty Rights, and the Political Construction of Scale." *Political Geography* 18, no. 6: 639–68.

―――――. 2000. "Reclaiming the Reservation: The Geopolitics of Wisconsin Anishinaabe Resource Rights." *American Indian Culture and Research Journal* 24, no. 3: 131–53.

―――――. 2002a. "State Centrism, the Equal-Footing Doctrine, and the Historical-Legal Geographies of American Indian Treaty Rights." *Historical Geography* 30: 33–58.

―――――. 2002b. "Tribes, States, the EPA, and the Territorial Politics of Environmental Protection." In *The Tribes and the States: Geographies of Intergovernmental Interaction,* edited by Brad A. Bays and Erin Hogan Fouberg, 119–38. Lanham, Md.: Rowman and Littlefield.

Simpson, Audra. 2000. "Paths toward a Mohawk Nation: Narratives of Citizenship and Nationhood in Kahnawake." In *Political Theory and the Rights of Indigenous Peoples,* edited by Duncan Ivison, Paul Patton, and Will Sanders, 113–36. Cambridge: Cambridge University Press.

————. 2007. "On Ethnographic Refusal: Indigeneity, 'Voice,' and Colonial Citizenship." *Junctures* 9: 67–80.

Simpson, Leanne R. 2004. "Anticolonial Strategies for the Recovery of Indigenous Knowledge." *American Indian Quarterly* 28, no. 3–4: 373–84.

Sivaramakrishnan, K. 1999. *Modern Forests: Statemaking and Environmental Change in Colonial Eastern India.* Oxford: Oxford University Press.

Sivaramakrishnan, K., and Gunnel Cederlöf. 2006. "Introduction: Claiming Nature for Making History." In *Ecological Nationalisms: Nature, Livelihoods, and Identities in South Asia,* edited by Gunnel Cederlöf and K. Sivaramakrishnan, 1–40. Seattle: University of Washington Press.

Smith, Adam. 1901 [1776]. *An Inquiry into the Nature and Causes of the Wealth of Nations.* New York: P. F. Collier.

Smith, Andrea. 2010. "Queer Theory and Native Studies: The Heteronormativity of Settler Colonialism." *GLQ: A Journal of Lesbian and Gay Studies* 16, no. 1–2: 41–68.

————. 2012. "Indigeneity, Settler Colonialism, White Supremacy." In *Racial Formation in the Twentieth Century,* edited by Daniel Martinez HoSang, Oneka LaBennet, and Laura Pulido, 66–90. Berkeley: University of California Press.

Smith, Benny. n.d. "A Perspective of the Clans." Author's collection.

Smith, Linda Tuhiwai. 1999. *Decolonizing Methodologies: Research and Indigenous Peoples.* Dunedin, New Zealand: University of Otago Press.

Smith, Mick. 2011. *Against Ecological Sovereignty: Ethics, Biopolitics, and Saving the Natural World.* Minneapolis: University of Minnesota Press.

Spade, Watt, and Willard Walker. 1966. *Cherokee Stories.* Chicago: Wesleyan University Laboratory of Anthropology and the Carnegie Corporation Cross-Cultural Education Project.

Stauber, Rose. 2007. "Delaware County." *Encyclopedia of Oklahoma History and Culture.* Oklahoma Historical Society. http://digital.library.okstate.edu/encyclopedia/entries/D/DE010.html.

Steiner, Stan. 1968. *The New Indians.* New York: Harper and Row.

Stewart, Omer C. 2002. *Forgotten Fires: Native Americans and the Transient Wilderness,* edited and with introductions by Henry T. Lewis and M. Kat Anderson. Norman: University of Oklahoma Press.

Stoffle, Richard W., David B. Halmo, and Diane E. Austin. 1997. "Cultural Landscapes and Traditional Cultural Properties: A Southern Paiute View of the Grand Canyon and Colorado River." *American Indian Quarterly* 21, no. 2: 229–49.

Stoffle, Richard W., Rebecca Toupal, and Nieves Zedeño. 2003. "Landscape, Nature, and Culture: A Diachronic Model of Human-Nature Adaptations." In *Nature across Cultures: Views of Nature and the Environment in Non-Western Cultures,* edited by Helaine Selin, 97–114. Dordrecht, The Netherlands: Kluwer Academic.

Storey, David. 2012. *Territories: The Claiming of Space.* Third edition. Oxford: Routledge.

Stremlau, Rose. 2011. *Sustaining the Cherokee Family: Kinship and the Allotment of an Indigenous Nation.* Chapel Hill: University of North Carolina Press.

Strickland, Rennard. 1975. *Fire and the Spirits: Cherokee Law from Clan to Court.* Norman: University of Oklahoma Press.

Strickland, Rennard, and William M. Strickland. 1991. "Beyond the Trail of Tears: One Hundred Fifty Years of Cherokee Survival." In *Essays on Cherokee Removal,* edited by William Anderson, 112–38. Athens: University of Georgia Press.

Sturm, Circe. 2002. *Blood Politics: Race, Culture, and Identity in the Cherokee Nation of Oklahoma.* Berkeley: University of California Press.

———. 2010. *Becoming Indian: The Struggle over Cherokee Identity in the Twenty-First Century.* Santa Fe, N.M.: SAR.

Sullivan, Patrick. 2006. "Indigenous Governance: The Harvard Project on Native American Economic Development and Appropriate Principles of Governance for Aboriginal Australia." Australian Institute of Aboriginal and Torres Strait Islander Studies Discussion Paper no. 17.

TallBear, Kim. 2013. *Native American DNA: Tribal Belonging and the False Promise of Genetic Science.* Minneapolis: University of Minnesota Press.

Taylor, David A. 2006. *Ginseng, the Divine Root: The Curious History of the Plant that Captivated the World.* Chapel Hill, N.C.: Algonquin.

Teuton, Christopher B. 2010. *Deep Waters: The Textual Continuum in American Indian Literature.* Lincoln: University of Nebraska Press.

Thomas, Robert K. 1953. "The Origin and Development of the Redbird Smith Movement." MA thesis, University of Arizona, Tucson.

———. 1958. "Cherokee Values and Worldview." SelectedWorks. http://works.bepress.com/robert_thomas/40.

———. 1961. "The Redbird Smith Movement." In *Bureau of American Ethnology Bulletin 180: Symposium on Cherokee and Iroquois Culture,* 161–66. Washington, D.C.: Smithsonian Institution.

Thornton, Russell. 1985. "Nineteenth-Century Cherokee History." *American Sociological Review* 50, no. 1: 124–27.

———. 1990. *The Cherokees: A Population History.* Lincoln: University of Nebraska Press.

Trosper, Ronald L. 1995. "Traditional American Indian Economic Policy." *American Indian Culture and Research Journal* 19, no. 1: 65–95.

Tsing, Anna Lowenhaupt. 2007. "Indigenous Voice." In *Indigenous Experience Today,* edited by Marisol de la Cadena and Orin Starn, 33–67. Oxford: Berg.

Tsosie, Rebecca. 1996. "Tribal Environmental Policy in an Era of Self-Determination: The Role of Ethics, Economics, and Traditional Ecological Knowledge." *Vermont Law Review* 21: 225–333.

Turner, Nancy J. 2005. *The Earth's Blanket: Traditional Teachings for Sustainable Living.* Seattle: University of Washington Press.

United States Department of the Interior (USDOI). 1912. *Reports of the Department of the Interior for the Fiscal Year Ended June 30 1911. Vol. 2, Indian Affairs Territories.* Washington, D.C.: Government Printing Office.

Vanbuskirk, Perry, and Kathy Vanbuskirk. 2000. "Medicine Tales." In *An Oral History of Tahlequah and the Cherokee Nation,* edited by Deborah L. Duvall, 53–54. Chicago: Arcadia.

Vandergeest, Peter, and Nancy Lee Peluso. 1995. "Territorialization and State Power in Thailand." *Theory and Society* 24, no. 3: 385–426.

Veracini, Lorenzo. 2011. "Introducing Settler Colonial Studies." *Settler Colonial Studies* 1, no. 1: 1–12.

Vick, R. Alfred. 2011. "Cherokee Adaptation to the Landscape of the West and Overcoming the Loss of Culturally Significant Plants." *American Indian Quarterly* 35, no. 3: 394–417.

Wahrhaftig, Albert L. 1966a. "Community and the Caretakers." *New University Thought* 4, no. 4: 54–76.

———. 1966b. "[Review of] Walk in Your Soul: Love Incantations of the Oklahoma Cherokee by Jack Frederick Kilpatrick and Anna Gritts Kilpatrick." *American Anthropologist* 68, no. 2: 563–64.

———. 1968. "The Tribal Cherokee Population of Oklahoma." *Current Anthropology* 9, no. 5: 510–18.

———. 1975a. "Institution Building among Oklahoma's Traditional Cherokees." In *Four Centuries of Southern Indians,* edited by Charles M. Hudson, 132–47. Athens: University of Georgia Press.

———. 1975b. "In the Aftermath of Civilization: The Persistence of Cherokee Indians in Oklahoma." PhD diss., University of Chicago.

———. 1975c. "More than Mere Work: The Subsistence System of Oklahoma." *Appalachian Journal* 2, no. 4: 327–31.

———. 1978. "Making Do with the Dark Meat: A Report on the Cherokee Indians of Oklahoma." In *American Indian Economic Development,* edited by Sam Stanley, 409–510. The Hague: Mouton.

———. 1979. "We Who Act Right: The Persistent Identity of Cherokee Indians." In *Currents in Anthropology: Essays in Honor of Sol Tax,* edited by Robert Hinshaw, 255–69. The Hague: Mouton.

Wahrhaftig, Albert L., and Jane Lukens-Wahrhaftig. 1977. "The Thrice Powerless: Cherokee Indians in Oklahoma." In *The Anthropology of Power: Ethnographic Studies from Asia, Oceania, and the New World,* edited by Raymond D. Fogelson and Richard Newbold Adams, 225–36. New York: Academic.

———. 1979. "New Militants or Resurrected State? The Five County Northeastern Oklahoma Cherokee Organization." In *The Cherokee Indian Nation: A*

Troubled History, edited by Duane H. King, 223–46. Knoxville: University of Tennessee Press.

Wahrhaftig, Albert L., and Robert K. Thomas. 1981. "Renaissance and Repression: The Oklahoma Cherokee." In *Anthropological Realities: Readings in the Science of Culture,* edited by Jeanne Guillemin, 168–77. New Brunswick, N.J.: Transaction.

Wainwright, Joel, and Morgan Robertson. 2003. "Territorialization, Science, and the Colonial State: The Case of Highway 55 in Minnesota." *Cultural Geographies* 10, no. 2: 196–217.

Walker, Peter A. 2003. "Reconsidering 'Regional' Political Ecologies: Toward a Political Ecology of the Rural American West." *Progress in Human Geography* 27, no. 1: 7–24.

———. 2005. "Political Ecology: Where Is the Ecology?" *Progress in Human Geography* 29, no. 1: 73–82.

Walker, Peter A., and Louise Fortmann. 2003. "Whose Landscape? A Political Ecology of the 'Exurban' Sierra." *Cultural Geographies* 10, no. 4: 469–91.

Warrior, Robert. 2005. "Native Critics in the World: Edward Said and Nationalism." In *American Indian Literary Nationalism,* edited by Jace Weaver, Craig S. Womack, and Robert Warrior, 179–223. Albuquerque: University of New Mexico Press.

Wax, Murray. 1971. *Indians and Other Americans.* New York: Prentice-Hall.

Wax, Rosalie H. 1971. *Doing Fieldwork: Warnings and Advice.* Chicago: University of Chicago Press.

Weaver, Jace. 2007. "More Light Than Heat: The Current State of Native American Studies." *American Indian Quarterly* 31, no. 2: 233–55.

Weber, Max. 1946a. "Bureaucracy." In *From Max Weber: Essays in Sociology,* edited by H. H. Gerth and C. Wright Mills, 196–244. New York: Oxford University Press.

———. 1946b. "Politics as a Vocation." In *From Max Weber: Essays in Sociology,* edited by H. H. Gerth and C. Wright Mills, 77–128. New York: Oxford University Press.

Wildcat, Daniel R. 2009. *Red Alert: Saving the Planet with Indigenous Knowledge.* Golden, Colo.: Fulcrum.

Wilkins, David E. 1993. "Modernization, Colonialism, Dependency: How Appropriate Are These Models for Providing an Explanation of North American Indian 'Underdevelopment'?" *Ethnic and Racial Studies* 16, no. 3: 390–419.

Wilkins, David E., and K. Tsianina Lomawaima. 2001. *Uneven Ground: American Indian Sovereignty and Federal Law.* Norman: University of Oklahoma Press.

Wilkins, David E., and Heidi Kiiwetinepinesiik Stark. 2011. *American Indian Politics and the American Political System.* Third edition. Lanham, Md.: Rowman and Littlefield.

Wilkinson, Charles F. 1987. *American Indians, Time, and the Law.* New Haven: Yale University Press.

———. 2005. *Blood Struggle: The Rise of Modern Indian Nations.* New York: W. W. Norton.

Williams, Robert A., Jr. 2005. *Like a Loaded Weapon: The Rehnquist Court, Indian Rights, and the Legal History of Racism in America.* Minneapolis: University of Minnesota Press.

Willow, Anna J. 2009. "Clear-Cutting and Colonialism: The Ethnopolitical Dynamics of Indigenous Environmental Activism in Northwestern Ontario." *Ethnohistory* 56, no. 1: 35–67.

Wilson, Shawn. 2008. *Research Is Ceremony: Indigenous Research Methods.* Halifax and Winnipeg: Fernwood.

Witthoft, John. 1947. "An Early Cherokee Ethnobotanical Note." *Journal of the Washington Academy of Sciences* 37, no. 3: 73–75.

———. 1960. "Cherokee Economic Botany from Western North Carolina: Man and Nature in the Southern Appalachians." Philadelphia: American Philosophical Society.

Wolf, Eric R. 1982. *Europe and the People without History.* Berkeley: University of California Press.

Wolfe, Patrick. 1999. *Settler Colonialism and the Transformation of Anthropology: The Politics and Poetics of an Ethnographic Event.* New York: Cassell.

———. 2006. "Settler Colonialism and the Elimination of the Native." *Journal of Genocide Research* 8, no. 4: 387–409.

———. 2011. "After the Frontier: Separation and Absorption in US Indian Policy." *Settler Colonial Studies* 1 no. 1: 13–51.

———. 2012. "Against the Intentional Fallacy: Legocentrism and Continuity in the Rhetoric of Indian Dispossession." *American Indian Culture and Research Journal* 36, no. 1: 3–45.

Wolfley, Jeannette. 1999. "Ecological Risk Assessment and Management: Their Failure to Value Indigenous Traditional Ecological Knowledge and Protect Tribal Homelands." In *Contemporary Native American Cultural Issues,* edited by Duane Champagne, 293–306. Walnut Creek: Alta Mira.

Wood, Mary, and Zachary Welcker. 2008. "Tribes as Trustees Again (Part I): The Emerging Tribal Role in the Conservation Movement." *Harvard Environmental Law Review* 32: 373–432.

Young, Robert J. C. 2001. *Postcolonialism: An Historical Introduction.* Malden, Mass.: Blackwell.

Index

Abrams, Phillip, 17, 19, 126

accountability: issues of, xii–xiii; relational, xii, xiii

Act of March 3, 1909, 85–86

Adair County, 27, 28, 30, 31, 90, 196n28

Adam-and-Eve plant (*Aplectrum hyemale,* or *Adawi-iwi*), 204n11

adaptation, place-making and environmental, 59–62

Agrawal, Arun, 11, 12, 21, 24, 25, 26, 205n1; on "environmentality," 13; on need for challenging "contempocentrism," 180

agriculture: Cherokee class divisions and, 50, 71, 73–78, 81; clearing farm plots, 69–70; communal ethic of early, 69–71; shift to sedentary agrarian lifestyle, 43–44; subsistence, 44, 50, 69, 70, 81; women's call to traditional agricultural practices (1811–13), 50–51

Akwesasne Notes (Mohawk newspaper), 195n22

Albuquerque v. Browner, 178

Alfred, Taiaiake, 16; critique of institutional approach, 17, 173–74, 175, 176, 193n13

Allen, Richard, 202n19

alliance-building, process of, xiv, 165, 168

Allotment (or Dawes) Act, 77–78

Allotment Era (1887–1934), 27, 34, 57, 157

allotment policy: buying back tribal lands lost during, 90; Cherokee relationship to land and, 81–82, 84, 85–89; Cherokee resistances to, 58, 78–81, 199n18; complexities of legacy of, 103; grafters and exploitation of land policy left behind by, 87, 103; pre- and postallotment boundaries to land claims, 81–82; repercussions for generation of Cherokees following it ("too lates"), 87–88; underlying goal of, 79

Altman, Heidi M., 120, 203n8

American ginseng (*Panax quinquefolius*), 62–63, 105, 106–7

American Indian, use of term, ix

American Indian studies, 11; concepts of land and sovereignty in, 15–16, 18, 19; toward integrative political ecology / indigenous studies framework, 177–81; the political as inherently environmental in, 12–19, 178; political ecology and, 11, 12–19

Anderson, Kay, 15

Anderson, M. Kat, 68

Anderson, Terry L., 196n27

anididá:hnese:sgi or *anisgaya:dihi* (man-killers), 118, 203n6

healing incantations (*idi:gawésdi*), 118,
119, 120, 121, 123, 125, 134, 191n2. *See
also* medicine, plant
Heck, William P., 202n20
Hempel, Lamont C., 22, 26; on
deliberative democracy, 179–80
herbalists, 123
herbicides, 31–32, 105
Hewes, Leslie: on changes after Civil
War, 72, 74; on settlement of Indian
Territory, 57, 59, 65, 66, 71
Heynen, Nik, 195n23
Hickey, Clifford G., 14
hickory bark (*wanēi*, or *Carya spp.*), 122
Hicks, Elijah, 51
Hill, Sarah H., 196n3
Himley, Matthew, 195n23
hog-fencing laws, 86
hog fry, 205n2
Hogshooter's Place (Brewer's Bend), xi
Holifield, Ryan, 178, 192n10
Holm, Tom, 15, 46, 80, 174–75, 192n7;
on peoplehood matrix, 80, 174–75
Hopewell, Treaty of (1785), 43
huckleberry gathering, 73, 87, 142
Huhndorf, Shari, 16–17
hunting and gathering, 40; Cherokee
Nation hunting and fishing code,
200n13; compromised Cherokee
land ethics by 1780s and, 43–44;
gathering rights and politics of
resource access on tribal land,
110–11, 112, 156–60; indigenous
fire regimes and, 68; national fire
suppression policy and, 86; natural
economy as modern version of,
169; NRD silvicultural activities
and, 104; restrictions on, 84,
86, 87; restrictions on, OCCO
in reaction to, 92–94; shift to
sedentary agrarian lifestyle from,

43–44; significance of hunting in
Cherokee worldview, 93
Huntsinger, Lynn, 58, 68, 86
Hybridity Thesis, 196n29

ideals of Cherokee governance,
traditional, 160–68
idi:gawésdi (Cherokee healing
incantations), 118, 119, 120, 121, 123,
125, 134, 191n2
Indian blood quantum, 50, 80, 103,
196n27
Indian Claims Commission, 91–92
Indian Health Service, 100, 202n19
Indian-Pioneer Papers, 66, 71, 82,
198n8
Indian Reorganization Act (1934), 95,
194n18
Indian Territory, 57–82, 199n17;
Cherokee resistances to allotment,
58, 78–81, 199n18; differences
between southeastern homelands
and, 59; early Cherokee inhabitation
of, 59–60; early environment as
human-produced, 34; Industrial
Revolution in, 72–73; place-making
and environmental adaptation
to, 59–62; political reunification
in new lands, 63–65; problem of
white intruders in, 79; produced
environment in, 58, 65–72; state–
territorial relationship in, 55; threats
to the public domain, 72–78, 81
indigenous, use of term, ix
Indigenous Nations Treaty, 178
indigenous state, development of,
10–11
indigenous state transformation, 11,
17; alternative forms of governance
presented by, 25; changing
landscapes and move toward

CLINT CARROLL is a citizen of the Cherokee Nation and assistant professor of ethnic studies at the University of Colorado at Boulder.